D1199222

# SOUTH PACIFIC CAULDRON

# SOUTH PACIFIC CAULDRON

**WORLD WAR II'S GREAT FORGOTTEN BATTLEGROUNDS**

⚬⚬⚬

ALAN REMS

Naval Institute Press
Annapolis, Maryland

Naval Institute Press
291 Wood Road
Annapolis, MD 21402

ISBN 978-1-61251-471-0

*To Those Who Were There*

Tech 4 Sergeants Glenn Moore and John Denlinger, A Company, 533rd Engineer Boat and Shore Regiment, 3rd Engineer Special Brigade (Cape Gloucester and Finschhafen); Major Francis E. Kavanaugh, Executive Officer, 517th Field Artillery Battalion (Bougainville); First Lieutenant Mayo S. Stuntz, Alamo Scouts (New Guinea); Colonel Marion Unruh, CO 5th Bomber Group, 13th Air Force (shot down over Rabaul and then a prisoner of war in Japan); Lieutenant John T. Pigott, destroyer USS *Lansdowne* DD486 (Solomon Islands); Lieutenant Colonel Francis Dougherty, Division G4, 1st Cavalry Division (Admiralty Islands); Corporal Charles S. Murch, 182nd Infantry Regiment, Americal Division (Guadalcanal and Bougainville); and Staff Sergeant Samuel Milner, Army Air Forces (Australia and Papua), author of *Victory in Papua*.

*and to*

Herman Gitelson, my father-in-law, engineering sergeant with the 811th Tank Destroyer Battalion, wounded in Lorraine, France.

Private First Class Harold E. "Snuff" Kurvers, medic with the 194th Tank Battalion, survivor of the Bataan death march, imprisonment at Camp O'Donnell and Cabanatuan, "Hell Ship" voyage to Japan, and heavy labor at Fukuoka #17 POW camp.

Private First Class Robert Don Wendroff, medic with the 194th Tank Battalion, survivor of the Bataan death march and imprisonment at Camp O'Donnell; died in Cabanatuan.

# CONTENTS

# ILLUSTRATIONS AND MAPS

## Maps

—∽∽∽—

# PREFACE

N early forty years ago, Guadalcanal veteran and author James Jones lamented how little was remembered about the World War II battle-fields of the South Pacific. He wrote, "Almost all of them names people in the United States never heard of." The same could likely have been said about how much was remembered by Australians and New Zealanders, whose nations fought there alongside America. Since Jones' lament, the situation can only have worsened with the deaths of most who served there.

Even the setting is largely forgotten. The words "South Pacific," for most, evoke only the fictional island paradise on which Rodgers and Hammerstein set their musical adaptation of James Michener's tales. But there were few "enchanted evenings" in the very different South Pacific region—Melanesia—that we speak of here. Encompassing the Solomon Islands, the eastern half of New Guinea, and the waters and lands of the Solomon and Bismarck seas in between, this region contained some of the worst terrain and weather of all World War II combat zones. With towering mountains; treacherous razorback ridges; dense, disease-ridden jungles; great miasmal swamps; infernal heat and humidity; and torrential rainfall, the environment there was challenging enough without the dangers of battle.

From that war zone, one battlefield, Guadalcanal, has remained etched in American memory as a symbol of courage and endurance. Australians and New Zealanders might remember, too, the Battle of the Coral Sea and the Kokoda Trail, fought when their nations were under dire threat of invasion from Japan.

After these 1942 battles, the Allies went on the offensive and the char-acter of the war in the South Pacific changed. Beachheads were obtained on large islands at relatively low cost, and terrain, weather, and supply difficulties often slowed advances more than the Japanese did. It was slow, hardscrabble fighting, hardly material for dazzling war reporting, and what public attention remained was mostly absorbed by the more spectacular Central Pacific offensive that started in November 1943 with Tarawa. Except for those at home with ties to men whose lives were invested there, the war in the South Pacific was eminently forgettable. But for those who were there it was The War. And its result influenced the outcome of World War II no less than El Alamein, Kursk, Anzio, Normandy, and Iwo Jima did.

James Jones commented about the war in the South Pacific in 1943: "They had a year of battles, fought without any great victories to stimulate troop morale. . . . Short, sharp, costly fights, each of them, which got scant publicity at home." His observation about publicity was correct, but Jones' mordant view about what was accomplished was not. In just nine months, the Allies wrested control of the South Pacific from the Japanese, neutralizing their great base of Rabaul and opening the way to the Philippines and the heart of the Japanese Empire.

After these battles, it was generally assumed that nothing that occurred in the South Pacific could materially affect the war's outcome. But the isolated Japanese fought back, mounting great counteroffensives on Bougainville and New Guinea that are among the least-known major battles fought by the American Army in World War II. Still later, Australian forces fought final battles about which historian Eric Bergerud wrote, "The campaign was never pressed with great vigor and casualties were low on both sides. In none of the areas were the Japanese pushed to the point of surrender or suicide." That was indeed true on New Britain, but the still numerous Japanese on Bougainville and New Guinea were in fact aggressively forced back to last-stand positions and would certainly have fought to the death had the general surrender not intervened. How this situation came about despite the disapproval of much of the Australian army, government, and public is a powerful cautionary tale.

Although essentially *terra incognita* for most people, the South Pacific has been visited repeatedly by historians following varying approaches. Official histories in the United States, Australia, and New Zealand have detailed the contributions of their respective armed forces. Other historians have concentrated on individual battles, with Guadalcanal attracting particular interest commensurate with its importance. Writing on a broader scale, some historians have covered the war on New Guinea while others have dealt with the entire Solomon Islands campaign.

Easily forgotten in such separate treatments is that the South Pacific war, in its principal phase, was fought by both the Allies and the Japanese following strategies covering the entire South Pacific. It was all one battle. Also, although fighting continued until the general Japanese surrender, historians have shown little interest in the theater after Rabaul was surrounded in early 1944. A clear and complete understanding of operations, and a full appreciation of the sacrifices made by those who served there, requires consideration of the South Pacific war in its entirety and to its conclusion.

Until now, no single work has attempted to tell the full story of the war in the South Pacific. This account of the important and stirring land, sea, and air actions fought there makes it obvious that the South Pacific was one of the great battlegrounds of World War II. James Jones' rueful observations about national memory should not stand as the final verdict.

ALAN REMS
Centreville, Virginia, 2013

# ACKNOWLEDGMENTS

I n extending thanks to those who made this volume possible, pride of place belongs to Richard Latture, editor-in-chief of *Naval History* magazine. By selecting me as the magazine's 2008 Author of the Year for my first writing effort, he provided all the encouragement an aspiring writer could desire. My friend Carl Smith, a former English teacher and author of several fine works of military history, read the manuscript closely and offered numerous excellent suggestions for improvement. Jim Wise, prolific author of many books published by the Naval Institute Press and a recipient of its Author of the Year award, generously provided advice from his experience. His recent passing is a loss to those who knew Jim and to the historical community. My daughter Emily Rems, a magazine editor, helped me over a troublesome hurdle, and my wife Janet Rems contributed invaluably from her storehouse of editorial art and production skills acquired in her long career as a journalist and managing editor.

# ABBREVIATIONS

**AIRCRAFT** (number of engines in parentheses)

**United States**

*Army*

| | |
|---|---|
| A-20 | Havoc, light attack bomber (2) |
| B-17 | Flying Fortress, heavy bomber (4) |
| B-24 | Liberator, heavy bomber (4) |
| B-25 | Mitchell, medium bomber (2) |
| C-47 | Skytrain, transport (2) |
| DC-3 | See C-47 above |
| P-38 | Lightning, fighter (2) |
| P-39 | Airacobra, fighter (1) |
| P-40 | Warhawk, fighter (1) |

*Navy*

| | |
|---|---|
| F4F | Wildcat, fighter (1) |
| F4U | Corsair, fighter (1) |
| F6F | Hellcat, fighter (1) |
| PBY | Catalina, patrol seaplane (2) |
| PV-1 | Ventura, medium bomber (2) |
| SB2C | Helldiver, dive bomber (1) |
| SBD | Dauntless, dive bomber (1) |
| TBF | Avenger, torpedo bomber (1) |

**Japan**

| | |
|---|---|
| "Betty" | Mitsubishi Zero-1, medium bomber (2) |
| "Val" | Aichi 99–1, dive bomber (1) |
| "Zero" | Mitsubishi Zero-3, fighter (1) (also called "Zeke") |

**Australia**

| | |
|---|---|
| Beaufighter | night/long-range fighter (2) |
| Beaufort | torpedo bomber (2) |
| Boston | See A-20 Havoc above |
| Kittyhawk | See P-40 Warhawk above |

## LANDING CRAFT AND SHIPS, AND AMPHIBIOUS VEHICLES

| | |
|---|---|
| DUKW | 2 1/2-Ton Amphibious Truck |
| LCI | Landing Craft, Infantry |
| LCM | Landing Craft, Mechanized |
| LCP(R) | Landing Craft, Personnel, Ramped |
| LCT | Landing Craft, Tank |
| LCVP | Landing Craft, Vehicle and Personnel |
| LST | Landing Ship, Tank |
| LVT | Landing Vehicle, Tracked (Amphtrac) |

## OTHER

| | |
|---|---|
| AirSols | Aircraft, Solomons Command |
| APD | Destroyer-Transport |
| BAR | Browning Automatic Rifle |
| EBSR | Engineer Boat and Shore Regiment |
| IJN | Imperial Japanese Navy |
| IMAC | 1st Marine Amphibious Corps |
| JCS | Joint Chiefs of Staff |
| MDB | Marine Defense Battalion |
| NCO | Noncommissioned Officer |
| PT | Motor Torpedo Boat |
| RAAF | Royal Australian Air Force |
| RCT | Regimental Combat Team |
| RNZAF | Royal New Zealand Air Force |
| Seabees | Naval Construction Battalions |
| SNLF | Special Naval Landing Forces |
| TF | Task Force |

# CHRONOLOGY

Regular typeface indicates operations under Southwest Pacific Command (including all Australian Army operations).
*Italic typeface indicates Operations under South Pacific Command.*
ALL CAPS INDICATES OTHER OPERATIONS OR EVENTS.
(*) indicates naval battle.

**1942**

| | |
|---|---|
| 23 Jan. | JAPANESE CAPTURE RABAUL |
| 8 March | Japanese capture Lae and Salamaua, New Guinea (NG) |
| 17 | MacArthur arrives in Australia |
| 18 April | MacArthur appointed supreme commander, SW Pacific |
| 3 May | JAPANESE CAPTURE TULAGI |
| 4–8 | BATTLE OF THE CORAL SEA (*) |
| 21 July | Japanese capture Buna, NG |
| 29 | Japanese take Kokoda, NG |
| 7 Aug. | *Marines land on Guadalcanal (Guad)* |
| 9 | *Battle of Savo Island (*)* |
| 24 | *Battle of the Eastern Solomons (*)* |
| 25 | Japanese land at Milne Bay, NG |
| 12–14 Sept. | *Battle of Bloody Ridge, Guad* |
| 23 | Japanese retreat on Kokoda Trail, NG, begins |
| 11–12 Oct. | *Battle of Cape Esperance (*)* |
| 18 | *Halsey relieves Ghormley as commander, South Pacific* |
| 23–26 | *Battle of Henderson Field, Guad* |
| 26 | *Battle of Santa Cruz Islands (*)* |
| 12–15 Nov. | *Naval Battles of Guadalcanal (*)* |
| 30 | *Battle of Tassafaronga (*)* |
| 9 Dec. | *Marines relieved by Army on Guad* |

**1943**

| | |
|---|---|
| 2 Jan. | Buna, NG, captured |
| 14–23 | CASABLANCA CONFERENCE |
| 29–31 | Japanese attack Wau, NG |
| 7–8 Feb. | *Japanese evacuate Guad* |
| 21 | *Russell Islands occupied* |
| 2–5 March | Battle of the Bismarck Sea (*) |
| 12–28 | PACIFIC MILITARY CONFERENCE |
| 1 April | I-GO AIR CAMPAIGN BEGINS |
| 18 | YAMAMOTO SHOT DOWN |
| 26 | CARTWHEEL PLAN ISSUED |
| 30 June | Landings on Woodlark and Kiriwina islands |
| 30 | *Landing on Rendova* |
| 30 | Landing at Nassau Bay, NG |
| 2 July | *Landing on New Georgia (New Geo)* |
| 6 | *Battle of Kula Gulf (*)* |
| 13 | *Battle of Kolombangara (*)* |
| 5 Aug. | *Munda, New Geo, captured* |
| 6 | *Battle of Vella Gulf (*)* |
| 15 | *Landing on Vella Lavella* |
| 5 Sept. | Nadzab, NG, taken by parachute drop |
| 16 | Lae, NG, captured |
| 22 | Finschhafen, NG, landing |
| 2 Oct. | Finschhafen, NG, captured |
| 4 | Dumpu, NG, captured |
| 6 | *Battle of Vella Lavella (*)* |
| 16–20 | Japanese counterattack at Finschhafen, NG |
| 27 | *Landing in the Treasuries* |
| 28 Oct.–3 Nov. | *Choiseul Raid* |
| 1 Nov. | *Landing at Empress Augusta Bay, Bougainville (Boug)* |
| 1–2 | *Battle of Empress Augusta Bay (*)* |
| 5 | *Carrier raid on Rabaul (*)* |
| 8–9 | *Battle of the Piva Trail, Boug* |
| 11 | *Second carrier raids on Rabaul (*)* |
| 13–14 | *Battle of the Coconut Grove, Boug* |
| 17–25 | Battle of Sattelberg, NG |
| 18–25 | *Battle of Piva Forks, Boug* |
| 25 | *Battle of Cape Saint George (*)* |
| 28–29 | *Koiari Raid, Boug* |

| | |
|---|---|
| 8–18 Dec. | *Battle of Hellzapoppin Ridge, Boug* |
| 10 | *Torokina, Boug, airstrip operational* |
| 15 | *Army XIV Corps replaces Marines on Boug* |
| 15 | Landing at Arawe, New Britain (New Brit) |
| 17 | *AirSols begin air campaign against Rabaul* |
| 26 | Landing at Cape Gloucester, New Brit |

**1944**

| | |
|---|---|
| 2 Jan. | Landing at Saidor, NG |
| 15 | Sio, NG, captured |
| 20–31 | Battle of Shaggy Ridge, NG |
| 15 Feb. | *Landing on Green Islands* |
| 17–18 | CARRIER RAID ON TRUK |
| 19 | *Last major AirSols battle over Rabaul* |
| 29 | Landing on Los Negros, Admiralty Islands |
| 8–25 March | *Japanese offensive on Boug* |
| 15 | Landing on Manus, Admiralty Islands |
| 20 | *Emirau occupied* |
| 6 April | *Company K incident, Boug* |
| 22 | Landing at Aitape, NG |
| 28 | Army replaces Marines on New Brit |
| 15 June | *Halsey departs South Pacific* |
| 10 July–25 Aug. | Battle of the Driniumor, NG |
| 22–27 Nov. | Australians take command of Boug, New Brit, and Aitape area of NG |
| 30–31 Dec. | Battle of Pearl Ridge, Boug |

**1945**

| | |
|---|---|
| 17 Jan.–9 Feb. | Battle of Tsimba Ridge, Boug |
| 26 March | Soraken Peninsula, Boug captured |
| 28 March–6 April | Battle of Slater's Knoll, Boug |
| 22 April | Maprik, NG, captured |
| 11 May | Wewak, NG, captured |
| 8–10 June | Battle of Porton Plantation, Boug |
| 6 and 9 Aug. | ATOMIC BOMBINGS |
| 15 | JAPANESE SURRENDER ANNOUNCEMENT |
| 2 Sept. | JAPANESE SURRENDER ON BOARD USS *MISSOURI* |
| 6 | Japanese surrender at Rabaul |

# CHAPTER 1

# "The Hottest Potato"

"Bull" Halsey always provided good newspaper copy. But in January 1943 he outdid himself by predicting, for the coming year, "Complete, absolute defeat for the Axis Powers."[1] Was Admiral William F. Halsey Jr. indulging in a bit of morale-boosting rhetoric or did he truly believe this seemingly preposterous idea? In the heady atmosphere of his approaching victory, that prediction might have just seemed possible.

On 18 October 1942, less than three months earlier, Halsey arrived in Noumea, New Caledonia, after receiving what he would call "the hottest potato they ever handed me!"[2] The "potato" in question, tossed to him by Pacific Fleet commander Admiral Chester W. Nimitz, was command of the South Pacific Area when the outcome at Guadalcanal was seriously in question.

Guadalcanal, a previously insignificant island, assumed great strategic importance when a reconnaissance plane observed that the Japanese were building an airfield from which aircraft could threaten America's lifeline to Australia. Steps had to be taken quickly by the Allies to seize the island. Code named Operation Watchtower, the invasion of Guadalcanal was hastily organized and planned with little knowledge about the target and enemy dispositions.[3] Under the overall command of Vice Admiral Frank J. Fletcher, Expeditionary Force leader, the invasion fleet arrived on 7 August and landings commenced under the direction of Amphibious Force commander Rear Admiral Richmond K. Turner.

The 1st Marine Division with reinforcing units led by Major General Alexander A. Vandegrift landed unopposed on Guadalcanal and easily captured the unfinished Japanese airstrip. Simultaneously, Marine raiders and parachutists seized nearby Tulagi and the twin islets of Gavutu and Tanambogo after overcoming strong resistance. America's first offensive in the Pacific began with deceptive ease, but that would soon change.

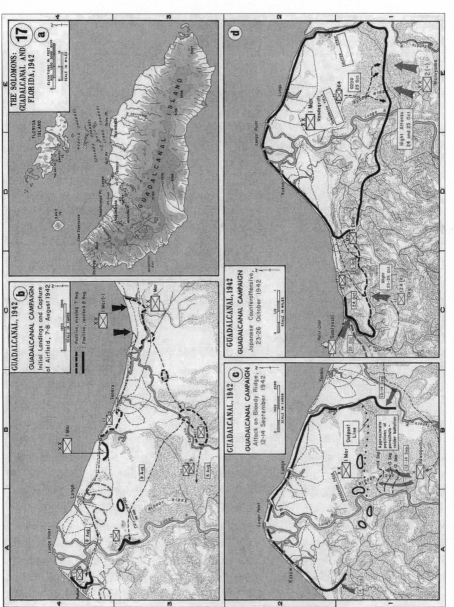

Map 1. Guadalcanal Campaign Area (U.S. Military Academy–Department of History)

Fletcher had agreed during the planning that his carrier task force would remain for three days to protect the beachhead. The day after the invasion, however, Fletcher insisted that he needed to withdraw immediately because of concerns about his fuel situation, aircraft losses, and the risk of air attack. Even before obtaining authorization from South Pacific Area commander Vice Admiral Robert L. Ghormley, Fletcher departed the area.[4]

Deprived of air cover, Turner had no choice except to withdraw his transports and covering vessels as well. Before then, in the early hours of 9 August, Japanese heavy cruisers surprised Turner's warships guarding the waters off Guadalcanal, sinking four heavy cruisers and heavily damaging another, with a loss of more than 1,700 killed and wounded. American cruisers USS *Vincennes*, *Astoria*, and *Quincy* and Australian cruiser HMAS *Canberra* would be the first of many vessels sent to the bottom in waters that sailors would dub Ironbottom Sound.

Only fear of daylight air attack deterred Japanese Eighth Fleet commander Vice Admiral Gunichi Mikawa from proceeding to bombard the vulnerable cargo ships and beachhead. After their battering at the Battle of Savo Island, Turner's ships hastily departed with much of their cargo still unloaded, leaving Vandegrift's 17,000 troops with slender resources, dependent afterwards on an unreliable supply line for provisions and reinforcement.

Clinging to their small beachhead, the Marines withstood attacks from land, sea, and air over the next months. Critical to the American defense of their toehold was the airstrip, rushed to completion within two weeks of the landing. Henderson Field functioned as an unsinkable aircraft carrier, becoming home to the Cactus Air Force, which flexibly used any and all Allied combat aircraft.[5] Under the leadership of Brigadier General Roy S. Geiger (USMC), this polyglot force became a highly energized fighting team that made possible American control of the surrounding waters by day. But after dark, the seas were dominated by the formidable "Tokyo Express," Japanese destroyer-transports and escorts that regularly delivered reinforcements and supplies to their Solomon bases. Efforts to disrupt that flow were sometimes successful, but most runs got through, enabling the Japanese to mount a series of organized land attacks against the lightly held Marine perimeter.

Although they enjoyed a clear view of Marine positions from the commanding height of Mount Austin to the south, the Japanese long failed to appreciate the numbers they were facing.[6] Encouraging their underestimate was the hasty departure of Turner's amphibious ships, suggesting that the operation was no more than a reconnaissance-in-force. Thus, Vandegrift obtained a welcome respite before the Japanese recognized that his Marines were more numerous than they at first believed. Worse yet, the Japanese belatedly realized that the Marines intended to stay. When large-scale Japanese attacks came, the Marines enjoyed the advantage of interior lines, fighting an enemy forced to attack either at the coast with little terrain cover or after long and exhausting marches in dense jungle that made coordination difficult and employment of heavy artillery and tanks impossible.

On 13 August, recognizing the threat if the Americans remained in place and completed the airfield, Imperial General Headquarters ordered the recapture of Tulagi and Guadalcanal. That responsibility belonged to Lieutenant General Haruyoshi Hyakutake, commander of the Rabaul-based 17th Army, whose command then embraced both the Solomons and New Guinea. Already committed to an offensive on New Guinea, and without a realistic appreciation of the size of his opponent, Hyakutake gathered six thousand army and navy troops that he erroneously supposed would be sufficient to overrun the Marine perimeter.

The first echelon sent to Guadalcanal consisted of about half of the two-thousand-man Ichiki Force, a crack combined arms team. The mission of the force, led by Colonel Kiyono Ichiki, was to attempt a quick seizure of the unfinished airfield and, if that failed, to impede construction and await reinforcements. In fact, Henderson Field became operational on 17 August, the day before the Ichiki Force landed to the east of the perimeter.

Possibly motivated by the loss of secrecy after the discovery of his scouting party, Ichiki decided to attack immediately. In the early hours of 21 August, two hundred Japanese charged across the narrow sandbar at the mouth of the Ilu River and met determined Marine resistance. Defeated in hand-to-hand fighting, the survivors withdrew to join the rest of the Ichiki Force on the river's east bank. Taking full advantage of the vulnerable enemy position, a battalion from Vandegrift's reserve crossed the river upstream and attacked their rear. As the Japanese were forced back toward the sea, a platoon of Marine light tanks crossed the sand bar and joined in the attack. Few Japanese escaped, Ichiki dying in battle or by hara-kiri according to different accounts. The virtual annihilation of the Japanese at the Ilu River, misnamed the Battle of the Tenaru, proved that the élan of the Japanese fighting man was insufficient against American tenacity, heavier equipment, and sound tactics.

Before Ichiki's battle, 1,600 more men, including the rest of his command and the 5th Special Naval Landing Force (SNLF)[7] embarked in transports for Guadalcanal, accompanied by a powerful escort that included three aircraft carriers and eight battleships. In employing such a large covering force, the Japanese hoped to provoke a fleet action that might knock out the American carriers. Fletcher also had three carriers but, again concerned about fuel and believing the Japanese were withdrawing, he sent USS Wasp to refuel, leaving him with just two carriers, USS Saratoga and Enterprise, when the fleets engaged on 24 August.

At the Battle of the Eastern Solomons, Enterprise sustained heavy damage, and in exchange the Japanese lost the light carrier Ryujo and were forced to withdraw their troop transports. But the battle only postponed the Japanese landing by a few days, and the American Navy received two severe blows soon after. On 31 August, the carrier Saratoga, Fletcher's flagship, was torpedoed while on patrol and required months to repair. Slightly wounded in the action, Fletcher went on convalescent leave, providing Nimitz the opportunity to replace this commander who had disappointed once too often. Later exiled to the North Pacific, Fletcher would never again command in combat.[8] Just twelve days after *Saratoga* was torpedoed, *Wasp* was torpedoed and sunk. With *Enterprise* under repair, USS *Hornet* remained the only operating American carrier.

USS *Wasp* lists to starboard after being hit by three torpedoes and would later sink, 15 September 1942. (U.S. Navy)

Prompted by Ichiki's failure, the Japanese decided to delay operations on New Guinea and concentrate on retaking Guadalcanal. Hyakutake assembled six thousand troops under Major General Kiyotake Kawaguchi for the task. The plan was for Kawaguchi to launch his principal attack against a ridge immediately south of Henderson Field that presented a natural avenue of approach. Aware that the Japanese were preparing a major attack but uncertain where it would fall, Vandegrift saw the ridge as particularly vulnerable and posted Lieutenant Colonel Merritt A. Edson's (USMC) composite raider-parachutist battalion there.

Outnumbering the defenders two-to-one on what would become known as Bloody Ridge, the Japanese launched twelve successive attacks the night of 13–14 September. Forced back to a last knoll on the ridge, Edson's men held there while 105-mm artillery fire tore into the Japanese. The Battle of Bloody Ridge (or Edson's Ridge) cost Kawaguchi more than 600 killed and hundreds wounded, against 40 Marines killed and 103 wounded. The Japanese survivors then withdrew to the malarial jungle, where many died. Days later, Vandegrift's depleted forces received much-needed supplies along with the welcome arrival from Samoa of the 1st Marine Division's missing regiment, the 7th Marines.

In a renewed bid for victory, Hyakutake sent the Second (Sendai) Division and two 38th Division battalions to Guadalcanal and personally assumed command of the force. Persuaded as well of the need for additional American manpower, Ghormley, South Pacific Area commander, ordered the Americal Division's 164th Regiment to Guadalcanal. On 11–12 October, cruisers and destroyers covering the opposing troop movements came into contact at Cape Esperance. While the Americans came out ahead, sinking heavy cruiser *Furutaka* and a destroyer and killing the Japanese admiral at a cost of one U.S. destroyer, tactical errors prevented the Americans from taking full advantage when their battle line inadvertently crossed the enemy "T." Also, this minor victory failed to slow the Japanese buildup.

An important part of Hyakutake's attack plan was the neutralization of Henderson Field. On 13–15 October, Japanese aircraft heavily bombed the airfield and Japanese artillery bombarded it with 150-mm howitzer fire, against which American artillery lacked the range to respond. Most destructively, Japanese battleships *Haruna* and *Kongo* hurled nine hundred 14-inch shells against the airfield and nearby positions. To those who were there, that terrible night would be remembered as "The Bombardment," with a follow-up performance the next evening by heavy cruisers. Geiger was left with few aircraft and little aviation fuel and, although the Cactus Air Force hastily recovered sufficiently to strike the Japanese beachhead at Cape Esperance, two enemy regiments landed safely. But with the arrival of the Americal Division's 164th Infantry on 13 October, American manpower kept pace with the Japanese. On the eve of the largest ground battle of the campaign, there were approximately 23,000 American troops on Guadalcanal, many sick and undernourished, against 20,000 reasonably fresh Japanese. Believing that he faced only about 7,500 Marines, Hyakutake was confident of success.

With mounting evidence that another major Japanese operation was impending, Ghormley wrote to Nimitz on 15 October: "My forces [are] totally inadequate to meet [the] situation." Nimitz had recently visited Ghormley in Noumea and returned uneasy about his resoluteness. Given this further cause for concern, Nimitz and his staff decided unanimously that Ghormley must be relieved. Using his keen instinct honed as former head of the Navy's personnel bureau, Nimitz selected Halsey as the new South Pacific commander.

A true sea dog whose natural home was on a ship's bridge, Halsey's bold carrier raids against enemy island bases and the Doolittle raid on the Japanese homeland months earlier stood out in a year of Allied defeats elsewhere. Sidelined during Midway because of a skin ailment, Halsey was eager to get back in the fight. At first blush, Halsey seemed wasted behind a desk directing operations far from the fighting front. But it was Halsey's instincts and fighting spirit that were sorely needed at Noumea headquarters. Halsey hated administrative details and left them to his able staff,[9] while he personally controlled naval operations. With Halsey commanding the sea battle, Vandegrift leading the Marines, and Geiger heading the Cactus Air Force, a superb triumvirate was in place as the showdown loomed.

As usual, the Japanese attack plan was complex and relied on deception. Forces under Major General Tadashi Sumiyoshi, the 17th Army artillery commander, would draw the Marines' attention westward to the coast at the Matanikau River. The main thrust, by Lieutenant General Masao Maruyama, commander of the 2nd Division, would again be directed against Bloody Ridge. Their objective was to take Henderson Field. The most powerful Japanese naval force assembled since Midway would stand by, ready to fly in carrier aircraft as soon as the airfield was captured.

But once again, coordination would present a serious problem for the Japanese. Unaware that the principal attack against Bloody Ridge was delayed because of Maruyama's difficulty negotiating the jungle terrain, Sumiyoshi launched his attack against the Marine right on 23 October. Vandegrift had positioned troops far in advance of the perimeter to control a sand bar at the Matanikau River, the only possible approach route for enemy tanks and artillery. His foresight was now rewarded. Following an intensive artillery bombardment to which the Marine artillery roared back, nine Japanese medium tanks lumbered forward and were promptly destroyed by 37-mm antitank gunfire and 75-mm tank destroyer fire. Artillery and mortar fire then killed hundreds of the trailing infantry.

Although it failed completely, Sumiyoshi's diversionary attack induced movement of a Marine battalion from Bloody Ridge to that sector, leaving behind only Marine legend Lieutenant Colonel Lewis B. "Chesty" Puller's 1st Battalion, 7th Marines to cover a 2,500-yard front. At Puller's left flank and in support were two 164th Infantry battalions, Dakota National Guardsmen who would be tested severely in their first action.

On 23 October, while Sumiyoshi was being crushed, Halsey met with Vandegrift, Turner, and other leaders in Noumea. Vandegrift described the low morale of his worn and sick Marines in the face of incessant air and sea attack while undergoing acute shortages of men and supplies. He insisted that to hold he would require air and ground reinforcement. Turner presented a gloomy picture about the difficulty of supplying Guadalcanal given the severe transport and escort shortages. Asked by Halsey whether he could hold, Vandegrift responded that he could, "but I have to have more active support than I have been getting." Halsey responded: "All right. Go on back. I'll promise you everything I've got."[10]

Meanwhile, Maruyama's nine infantry battalions plus artillery and service troops were completing their march from Cape Esperance. Hacking their way over a steeply sloped jungle trail in heavy rains, the exhausted Japanese abandoned their artillery and much of their other equipment. But the dense jungle also served as a screen, enabling the large force to proceed undetected.

Maruyama divided his attack force into two wings of three battalions each that were to attack simultaneously. Had the operation gone as planned, the combined attack could very possibly have achieved a breakthrough against the lightly manned front. But in the dark of night on 24–25 October, the right wing lost its way and mostly missed the fight. In repeated charges against Puller's line immediately east of Bloody Ridge, the Japanese 29th Infantry made some penetrations. The 3rd Battalion, 164th Infantry was quickly summoned from reserve, and the previously untested Guardsmen were immediately thrown into the fight, intermingled with the seasoned Marine battalion. They fought well, and together with Puller's men beat off repeated attacks. For resolutely handling his machine-gun section that wiped out a Japanese company while repeatedly exposing himself to enemy fire, Sergeant John Basilone (USMC) was awarded the Medal of Honor.

Both sides reorganized the next day, with the two 164th Infantry battalions, now veterans, aligned side-by-side to the east of Puller's battalion. That day, 25 October, would afterwards be known as "Dugout Sunday" because of the intensive Japanese shelling and bombing of Henderson Field. Maruyama attacked across the entire front that night using the 29th Infantry Regiment and his reserve, the 16th Infantry. Supported by 37-mm antitank guns firing canister, the defenders once more beat off repeated attacks that continued until daybreak. After every other member of his platoon was killed or wounded, Platoon Sergeant Mitchell Paige of the 7th Marines maintained machine-gun fire, moving from gun to gun until reinforced, then led a bayonet charge that prevented a Japanese breakthrough, actions that earned him the Medal of Honor. Again the Dakota Guardsmen acquitted themselves like seasoned fighters, leading to 3/164 earning a commendation from Vandegrift and the estimable nickname "the 164th Marines."

Hyakutake suffered yet another defeat that night of 25–26 October. Immediately east of the Matanikau River, the Japanese broke through a thinly held position linking the Marines' advance force at the river with the perimeter. An improvised Marine counterattack regained the position and brought Hyakutake's offensive to a close. Three days later, the Japanese pulled out along the whole line to find refuge at both ends of the perimeter.

Meanwhile, off the Santa Cruz Islands, another major naval battle was fought. A powerful Japanese force, including three fleet carriers and a light carrier, put to sea to support the scheduled troop landing once Henderson Field was taken. On 26 October, after the Japanese were spotted, Halsey ordered his new carrier commander, Rear Admiral Thomas C. Kinkaid, to "Attack, Repeat,

Attack."[11] Aircraft from Kinkaid's two carriers, *Hornet* and the newly repaired *Enterprise*, struck the enemy and badly damaged two carriers and a cruiser. But far from vanquished, the Japanese struck back even more forcefully, sinking *Hornet* and two destroyers and damaging other ships including *Enterprise*, the only American carrier then left in the Pacific.

Generally regarded as a Japanese victory, the Battle of Santa Cruz had one important consequence beneficial to the Americans. Aircraft losses were high on both sides, but they were least sustainable by the Japanese, who lost one hundred planes and their even more precious pilots, rendering their carriers incapable of providing sufficient air cover in later operations.

At last recognizing the size of his opponent's forces, Hyakutake attempted to gain supremacy by bringing in his 38th Division. That movement would first require suppression of Henderson Field to prevent air opposition to the landings. The result was a titanic engagement from 12–15 November, the Naval Battle of Guadalcanal, fought according to Halsey's biographer E. B. Potter in the Nelsonian spirit.[12] Outgunned by the Japanese, Halsey's defending cruisers and destroyers held off the enemy in a wild melee.

Although Japanese heavy cruisers succeeded in bombarding Henderson Field and destroyed and damaged many aircraft, the airfield remained operational and played a key part in the fighting. For two days, aircraft from Henderson Field and *Enterprise* pounced on and destroyed the troopships. Although more than 13,000 troops were rescued by Japanese destroyers, only about 2,000 made it to shore. In the end, both sides took heavy losses and both claimed a victory. American losses consisted of the light cruisers USS *Atlanta* and *Juneau*, seven destroyers, and many sailors, including Rear Admirals Daniel J. Callaghan and Norman Scott. They were exceeded on the Japanese side by the loss of battleships *Hiei* and *Kirishima*, heavy cruiser *Kinugasa*, three destroyers, and all eleven troop transports.

The battle at sea had turned into one of attrition, which the Japanese could not afford to wage. Consequently, they improvised reinforcement and supply techniques, but these were inadequate to satisfy Hyakutake's needs. Yet one Tokyo Express supply run by eight destroyers on 30 November provided ample evidence of the continued superiority of Japanese tactics and equipment. Surprised by five radar-equipped American cruisers and six destroyers, the Japanese struck back with their deadly long lance torpedoes,[13] sinking heavy cruiser USS *Northampton* and heavily damaging three other cruisers while losing just one destroyer. The embarrassing American performance at the Battle of Tassafaronga resulted from tying the destroyers too closely to the cruiser column and the failure of the cruisers to effectively maneuver to evade the enemy "fish." Also, as remarked by Samuel E. Morison, "The Navy's marksmanship that night was abominable."[14] Nimitz saw the remedy as "training, *training* and MORE TRAINING,"[15] but it would take some time before that prescription could work.

During December 1942, Lieutenant General Alexander M. Patch's (U.S. Army) XIV Corps relieved Vandegrift's 1st Marine Division. Until then, the American position was little changed from the small lodgment established in August. With fresh forces that included elements from the Army's Americal and 25th Infantry divisions and the 2nd Marine Division, Patch prepared to drive the enemy from Guadalcanal.

The offensive began slowly, as the Japanese fiercely defended hill positions that extended westward to threaten the flank of a force advancing along the coast. After Patch's reduction of these strong points and capture of strategically important Kokumbona, the drive westward began on 26 January and went rapidly. Patch then landed a battalion on the southwest coast hoping to trap the enemy in a pincer movement as the forces converged near Cape Esperance. But his quarry was too nimble to be snared.

Having lost the battle for supply, the Japanese high command reluctantly decided to withdraw from Guadalcanal. Evacuation was accomplished in early February by three destroyer runs during which more than 13,000 troops were brought out. Brilliantly, the Japanese created the impression that another reinforcement effort was being mounted, leaving Halsey unaware of their intentions until the withdrawal was completed on 8 February.[16] When it was discovered that the Japanese were gone, Patch radioed to Halsey: "Tokyo Express no longer has terminus on Guadalcanal."[17] Halsey responded: "When I sent a Patch to act as tailor for Guadalcanal, I did not expect him to remove the enemy's pants and sew it on so quickly."[18] Nine months later, on Bougainville, Hyakutake would again face off against Halsey, Vandegrift, and Geiger.

The Guadalcanal campaign, America's first ground offensive of the war, seized the attention of the public. Of 60,000 Marine and Army troops, 1,592 died in action and 4,245 were wounded. The Japanese committed more than 36,000 men from the 17th Army and SNLF. Of those, 14,800 died in the fighting, 9,000 succumbed to disease, and 1,000 were taken prisoner.[19] Neither side tabulated its losses during the great naval engagements, but it is certain that American naval deaths exceeded ground losses.[20]

Halsey performed exactly as Nimitz had hoped and passed along his winning attitude to all levels of his command. At the height of the battle, three weeks after assuming command at Noumea, he visited Guadalcanal, something Ghormley had never done. According to Vandegrift, Halsey's visit was "like a wonderful breath of fresh air." Exhibiting "interest and enthusiasm," Halsey mingled with the "gaunt, malaria-ridden" Marines, making clear his sympathy and unswerving support.[21] It was a splendid beginning to Halsey's twenty months as area commander in the South Pacific.

Historian Paul S. Dull concluded: "When Japan evacuated Guadalcanal in February 1943, for all practical purposes the war was finally lost."[22] A foremost Japanese naval planner reached the same conclusion, saying after the war: "After

Guadalcanal, in the latter part of 1942, I felt we could not win."[23] And, almost simultaneously with the end at Guadalcanal, across the Solomon Sea on Papua New Guinea, General Douglas MacArthur achieved an equally important, hard-fought victory.

Following a year of defeats and holding actions throughout the Pacific, the initiative in the South Pacific had at last passed to the Allies. If "absolute defeat" of the enemy could not be achieved in 1943, as boldly predicted by Halsey, an unstoppable march now began that would effectively win the South Pacific for the Allies in just over a year and open the way to the heart of the Japanese Empire.

Four recipients of the Medal of Honor for actions on Guadalcanal. From left: Major General Alexander A. Vandegrift, Colonel Merritt Edson, 2nd Lieutenant Mitchell Paige, Platoon Sergeant John Basilone, photographed in Australia, 1943. (USMC)

CHAPTER 2

# "I Want You to Take Buna, or Not Come Back Alive"

O n 17 March 1942, General Douglas MacArthur arrived in Australia after being ordered to leave the Philippines before the islands fell to the Japanese. Without regard to any alternative strategic plans his leaders might have had, MacArthur proclaimed to the waiting journalists, "I came through and I shall return."[1]

MacArthur was then one of America's best-known soldiers, the youngest division general during World War I and a former Army chief of staff whose defense of the Philippines transfixed the nation in the months following Pearl Harbor. Though he was extolled then as a great hero, many would later raise questions about his performance in the Philippines. Historians now shake their heads over some of MacArthur's actions: allowing half his aircraft to be destroyed on the ground twelve hours after Pearl Harbor, his decision to defend the beaches with wholly inadequate forces, and his failure to stockpile adequate food and supplies to sustain his long-planned defense of Bataan.[2] Further, leaving his relatively secure headquarters on Corregidor only once to visit his troops fighting on Bataan, he earned the derisive nickname "Dugout Doug" from the fighting men. MacArthur was actually very brave, but because of his habitual aloofness it would take some time to erase that negative image.

Almost immediately, MacArthur was nominated and quickly accepted by the American and Australian leaderships for the position of supreme commander in the Southwest Pacific Area. At that time, the American high command was considering the thorny question of who would command in the Pacific. Both the Army and Navy favored unity of command but could not agree who the commander should be. With strong support from the War Department, the American president, the Australian government, and the public of both nations, MacArthur was the obvious choice if an Army general was appointed. But the Navy could not accept subordination to an Army commander who might not fully appreciate its methods and doctrines. Expecting that the conflict in the Pacific would principally be a naval war, Admiral Ernest J. King, chief of naval operations and commander in chief of the U.S. fleet, wanted overall command to go to Nimitz.

The compromise that emerged on 30 March divided the Pacific between MacArthur and Nimitz. As supreme commander of the Southwest Pacific Area, MacArthur's command included Australia, the Philippines, New Guinea, the Solomons, the Bismarck Archipelago, and most of the Netherlands Indies. Those boundaries would be slightly altered to assign Guadalcanal and nearby positions to Nimitz, whose Pacific Ocean Area domain essentially embraced the rest of the Pacific. Further, Nimitz retained command of the Pacific Fleet wherever it might operate.[3]

In marked contrast to MacArthur's vast area of responsibility were the slender resources then available to him: fewer than 250 American combat aircraft, a single regular Australian division, and several divisions of partially trained Australian militia. MacArthur later claimed that he immediately scrapped a defense plan established by the Australian chiefs of staff that would have meant retreating well into Australia's frontiers and instead resolved to aggressively confront the enemy on New Guinea. He described this as "one of the most decisive [and] radical and difficult decisions of the war."[4] But the Australian leadership countered that no fundamental changes were in fact made at that time and that the strategy was only revised later with the arrival of reinforcements from the Middle East and the United States.[5] Whatever the truth, it was ultimately decided that New Guinea would be the battleground where Australia would be defended.

Because they were fighting from Australia with primary dependence on Australian troops, command of ground forces logically went to an Australian. General Sir Thomas A. Blamey, who had led Australian forces in the Middle East, was appointed commander in chief of the Australian army and commander of Allied land forces. MacArthur inherited Lieutenant General George H. Brett as his air force commander and Vice Admiral Herbert F. Leary as head of his small naval force. As for the staff positions, American Army chief of staff General George C. Marshall wanted MacArthur to appoint Australian and Dutch officers to some of the higher posts in the interest of Allied cooperation. Intent on maintaining staff loyalty, though, MacArthur would not reach outside his coterie and essentially ignored Marshall's recommendation; his staff remained American.

Nine days before MacArthur's arrival in Australia, Japanese forces landed at Lae and Salamaua on Huon Gulf, placing them in control of the strategically important Dampier and Vitiaz straits connecting the Solomon and Bismarck seas. The principal enemy thrust came in early May with an attempt by sea to take the Australian base at Port Moresby in Papua New Guinea, from which Australia could be directly threatened. At the Battle of the Coral Sea, fought on 4–8 May

1942, Fletcher's carriers achieved a strategic victory in thwarting the invasion. Among the fruits of the battle for the Americans were the sinking of Japanese light carrier *Shoho* and, most consequential, considerable damage to fleet carrier *Shokaku* and heavy aircraft losses to fleet carrier *Zuikaku*. Consequently, both carriers would be absent during Midway, where they might well have changed the outcome. Still, the American forces were seriously hurt in the battle, losing the venerable fleet carrier USS *Lexington* plus two other ships.

The battle was characterized by a lack of coordination between MacArthur's land-based air forces and Fletcher's warships, resulting in the escape of a damaged enemy carrier. Nimitz was concerned about this, a consequence of divided command, and MacArthur used the opportunity to urge that all land-based air and naval forces operating in a theater be controlled by the theater commander. Despite efforts to devise a solution, nothing resulted that could avert a far worse coordination fiasco two years later at the Battle of Leyte Gulf.

After the American victory at Midway in June and the passing of the initiative, MacArthur wanted to take the offensive using the three divisions then available to him, the untested American 32nd and 41st infantry divisions and the battle-hardened 7th Australian Division that had seen much fighting in Libya. In the same unrealistic spirit that may have prompted Halsey's prediction of a quick victory over the Axis, MacArthur proposed a grandiose plan calling for the capture of Rabaul. Without detailing how such a feat could be accomplished, MacArthur proposed that Japanese air power in Papua and the Solomons be first suppressed by intensive bombing. Supposedly, the great Japanese base could then be taken in eighteen days if MacArthur was provided with two aircraft carriers and an amphibious division to deliver the ground attack. This quick stroke would force the Japanese fleet back to Truk, while MacArthur's three divisions would eliminate the Japanese remaining behind.[6]

With a firmer grasp on reality, Admiral King rejected the idea, and in the next days the Army and Navy hammered out a more feasible plan broken into three tasks. Task one called for Nimitz's forces to capture Tulagi in the Solomons, to which Guadalcanal was later added. Under the overall command of MacArthur, task two would involve simultaneous moves by MacArthur along the New Guinea coast with a jump to the Admiralties and by Nimitz's forces up the chain of the Solomons to Buka. Task three would involve convergence upon Rabaul by the two forces under MacArthur's command.

Of key importance to the plan was development of airfields on Papua from which Lae and Salamaua and other positions could be attacked. Airfield construction began in early July at Milne Bay at the strategic eastern tip of Papua and went forward rapidly. Farther west, near Buna, good ground was identified on the Dobodura plain for an airfield. Buna was situated across the Owen Stanley mountain range, where it was difficult to reach by land and accessible only by small craft from the sea. Plans were made for construction workers to converge on the town in August to develop a base. The delay proved fatal, since the Japanese also had designs on Buna.

Although intelligence reports had for some time signaled Japanese interest in the Buna area, MacArthur made no efforts to get there first. When the Japanese invasion convoy was seen gathering at Rabaul, MacArthur's chief of staff, Major General Richard K. Sutherland, declined to rush forces to Buna, maintaining he had no hard evidence that it was their destination. Also, while sufficient warning was received to allow air attacks during the convoy's approach, Brett allowed his airmen two days of rest. Except for some slight Allied bombing success against shipping after the landing on 21 July was well advanced, the Japanese met no opposition. It would take six months of brutal fighting to eject the Japanese from a key position that was available for the taking in July.

The Japanese invasion force was the elite South Seas Detachment, commanded by Major General Tomitaro Horii. His forces had captured Rabaul in January and had massacred many prisoners. With reinforcements that brought his force to eight thousand troops plus three thousand construction workers, Horii set out to take Port Moresby. The advance on the Kokoda Trail involved an arduous march on a barely passable jungle track across the towering Owen Stanley Range. Horii's unexpected advance alarmed MacArthur, whose intelligence chief, Brigadier General Charles Willoughby, had assured him that the Japanese were interested in Buna only as an air base.

Major General George C. Kenney (left), commander of the U.S. Fifth Air Force, with Brigadier General Kenneth N. Walker (right), commander of Kenney's V Bombing Command, Port Moresby, New Guinea, 1942. Walker was killed in January 1943 leading a hazardous, low-level bombing mission against Japanese shipping at Rabaul. (USAAF)

After the small militia and native constabulary force defending the trail lost Kokoda village, two battalions of the Australian 7th Division were rushed to Port Moresby. These elite troops, who had fought in North Africa, belonged "to the celebrated fraternity of the Rats of Tobruk."[7] Command of all forces on New Guinea passed to Lieutenant General Sydney F. Rowell, who himself had fought with distinction in the Middle East. Also, as the Japanese advanced, their lengthy supply lines were interdicted by the galvanized Allied air forces under its dynamic new commander, Major General George C. Kenney.

MacArthur had long been dissatisfied with his air commander, Brett. Much of the problem was that Brett clashed with Sutherland, who disparaged him to MacArthur. MacArthur may also have viewed Brett as a local rival because of political connections Brett established before MacArthur's arrival.[8] Immediately after taking over from Brett, Kenney faced down Sutherland to assert full control over the air forces, something Brett couldn't do.[9] Kenney would quickly win over MacArthur to the full potential of air power with actions like moving an entire American regiment to Port Moresby from Australia, the first major movement of American troops by air in World War II.

During the Kokoda Trail fighting, about 2,000 Japanese marines landed at Milne Bay and attempted to capture the strategically important airfields under construction. Unknown to the Japanese, the defending forces under Major General Cyril A. Clowes, a veteran of the Greek campaign, had grown to nearly 9,500. Clowes was supported by two Royal Australian Air Force (RAAF) fighter squadrons, whose sinking of Japanese barges on the first day limited enemy movements and was a key factor in the battle. Repulsed attempting to win the airstrip and then forced on the defensive, the beleaguered Japanese were evacuated after losing about 700 men in operations lasting under two weeks. The battle was noteworthy because it was the first time in the war that the Japanese had been repulsed after establishing a beachhead. Milne Bay soon became a major supply port for MacArthur's forces and the site of an important airfield from which the enemy on New Guinea, the Bismarcks, and the Solomons could be attacked without flying over the Owen Stanleys.

During the battle, accustomed to receiving more detailed reports than was customary Australian practice, MacArthur was uneasy, writing to Marshall that he was "not yet convinced of the efficiency of the Australian units."[10] Clowes had proceeded cautiously, as it was difficult to determine the enemy's strength and intentions, but MacArthur was dissatisfied with Clowes' delay in eliminating the enemy and allowing some to escape. This precipitated a conflict when Rowell rushed to Clowes' defense. Pressured by MacArthur to go to New Guinea and take personal control of operations, Blamey clashed with Rowell, who accused him of being subservient to MacArthur. Blamey relieved Rowell, telling MacArthur, "He charged me with having failed to safeguard his interest . . . and said he felt he was being made to eat dirt."[11] But Rowell would not go quietly, incensing Blamey to the extent that he later tried to block Rowell's appointment to a position at the British War Office, which went through only by the involvement of the chief of the Imperial Staff.[12]

The official Australian history rightly lays the blame for the episode on MacArthur for his "ill-advised proposal [i.e., that Blamey assume command] and ill informed criticisms whose consequences were unhappy for the army in general, for [Blamey] and for General Rowell."[13] Succeeding Rowell as New Guinea Force commander would be the diplomatic and highly qualified former commander of the 6th Australian Division, Lieutenant General Edmund Herring. It was a good choice, but there would remain much resentment toward Blamey in the Australian officer corps.

And the turmoil went much further. Two weeks before Rowell's relief, on 10 September, Blamey removed Brigadier Arnold Potts, whose 21st Brigade had conducted a brilliant fighting retreat against greatly superior forces on the Kokoda Trail. Blamey, not fully understanding the situation, accused Potts and his officers of poor performance and ordered him to depart without even the elementary courtesy of being allowed to meet with his successor. This action prompted many officers of the brigade to submit their resignations, which were all rejected.

MacArthur also made changes. His naval commander, Leary, had long angered him for persisting in communicating directly with Admirals Nimitz and King instead of funneling all communications through MacArthur's chain of command. Also, Leary was unwilling to risk his small fleet in the reef-strewn and uncharted waters around Buna, where they were vulnerable to Japanese air attack. In the latter respect, MacArthur would find his new commander, Vice Admiral Arthur S. Carpender, equally uncooperative.

On the Kokoda Trail, in the face of a growing supply crisis and increasing ground opposition, Horii's exhausted forces suspended their attack on 17 September. Having advanced within twenty-five miles of Port Moresby, Horii paused several days before making the final push. Hyakutake, however, then made the painful decision to allocate his available resources for a major offensive on Guadalcanal. At the end of a lengthy supply line, Horii had no choice except to fall back on his base at Buna. He conducted a carefully staged withdrawal, slowly pursued by the Australian 7th Division.

In a now familiar scenario, without reliable information about the situation at the front, MacArthur's wrath about the slow movement fell on division commander Major General Arthur S. Allen. Blamey, again succumbing to pressure from MacArthur, relieved Allen on 27 October, claiming "the tactical handling of our troops in my opinion is faulty." For Allen, the relief was particularly bitter, as he was then preparing a full-scale counterattack. Later, in Australia, Allen let MacArthur know how distressed he was over the messages he had been receiving. In feigned or genuine surprise, MacArthur responded, "But, I've nothing but praise for you and your men. I was only urging you on."[14] Allen's successor as

7th Division commander would be Major General George Vasey, a veteran of the fighting in North Africa and Greece.

As the Japanese slowly retreated, Kokoda village fell on 2 November, and with the capture of the airfield there Kenney was able to bring in troops and supplies that accelerated the Australian advance. After gaining the coast and proceeding by native canoe, Horii and two staff officers were swept out to sea and drowned.[15] Had he not died then, Horii would most likely have ended up on the scaffold for atrocities committed against Australian captives after the capture of Rabaul.

On 18 November, just days after the Naval Battle of Guadalcanal, the Japanese established a new command structure for the Southeast Area. Whereas Hyakutake's 17th Army had responsibility until then for both New Guinea and the Solomons, a new 18th Army, commanded by Lieutenant General Hatazo Adachi, former chief of staff of the North China Area Army, was formed for New Guinea. To oversee both armies, Lieutenant General Hitoshi Imamura, previously the commander in Java, was placed in charge of the new Rabaul-based 8th Area Army. To control the air campaign, Imamura established the 6th Air Division at Rabaul. The navy also reorganized with the creation of the Rabaul-based Southeast Area Fleet, consisting of the 8th Fleet and 11th Air Fleet under Vice Admiral Jinishi Kusaka. Kusaka was subordinate to Admiral Isoroku Yamamoto, commander of the Combined Fleet at Truk, Japan's principal strategist and architect of the Pearl Harbor raid.

As the Australians on the Kokoda Trail neared the Papuan coast, two regiments from the American 32nd Division reached the Dobodura area by land, air, and sea, putting them into position to enter the battle. The plan of attack called for the Australian 7th Division to take Gona and Sanananda while the American 32nd Division captured Buna. The battle was important for both sides. The carefully developed Japanese defenses provided a strong shield for their New Guinea and Bismarck Sea bases. Chief of Staff of the Japanese Combined Fleet, Admiral Matome Ugaki, was especially anxious, fearing correctly that if these bases were lost "air raids upon Rabaul would be intensified, ultimately making it impossible for us to hold there."[16] MacArthur, who had not yet adopted the bypass strategy for which he would be noted, decided that clearing the Japanese from the area was necessary before he could get on with task two of his original offensive plan.

Allied intelligence estimated there were only 1,500 to 2,000 Japanese in the area. From his own intelligence estimates, the 32nd Division commander, Major General Edwin F. Harding, expected "easy pickings with only a shell of sacrifice troops left to defend [Buna]."[17] In reality, there were 6,500 fresh Japanese combatants in the area whose elimination would involve some of the most brutal fighting in the South Pacific. Occupying a pleasant eleven-mile coastal strip connected by a good road, the Japanese defense consisted of a line of concealed bunkers with connecting trenches whose fields of fire dominated the few trails leading from the swamps through which the Allied attackers would advance.

Although the Japanese had their backs to the sea, MacArthur lacked warships and landing craft to exploit their weakness. MacArthur asked Halsey for naval assistance but was told that "Until the Jap air in New Britain and northern Solomons has been reduced, risk of valuable naval units . . . can only be justified by major enemy seaborne movement."[18] Halsey's decision, which infuriated MacArthur, was supported by MacArthur's naval commander, Carpender, as well as by Nimitz and King.

So, the infantry had to go it alone. Badly underequipped, the Australian and American troops made little progress in their attacks that began in mid-November. MacArthur ordered Harding to attack "regardless of cost." Harding's half-trained and underequipped Michigan and Wisconsin National Guardsmen had never received jungle combat training and as a result failed in their repeated attempts. Enemy fire inflicted heavy casualties and malaria and dengue fever contracted in the pestilential swampland also took a heavy toll. MacArthur accused the division of a lack of "fight" and considered replacing it with the still untested 41st Division. But, having previously complained about such deficiencies on the part of the Australians, MacArthur was greatly embarrassed when Blamey suggested that they should instead bring in Australian troops since he knew they would fight.

In one of the greatest crises of his military career, MacArthur called upon his I Corps commander, Lieutenant General Robert L. Eichelberger, to take over the battle, telling him, "I want you to take Buna, or not come back alive."[19] Hearing that Eichelberger was risking his life at the front, MacArthur cold-bloodedly remarked, "I want him to die if he doesn't take Buna."[20] Eichelberger would later bitterly observe that "many members of the General Staff were overconfident and . . . ignorant of conditions as they actually existed. Few of them came to the jungle front to learn at first hand."[21] He was of course thinking primarily of MacArthur, who never got closer to the fighting than Port Moresby.

Eichelberger discovered that the 32nd Division was at the point of collapse. He removed Harding, as well as his two task force commanders and five of six battalion commanders, and assumed direct command of the American forces. After pausing several days to give the troops some rest, unscramble units, and bring in supplies, Eichelberger launched his first attack on 5 December. It failed with many casualties, including the wounding of Brigadier General Albert W. Waldron, who had replaced Harding. After heavy fighting over the next week, the Japanese suddenly evacuated Buna Village. Much fighting was still necessary, including an action during which the acting commander of the 32nd was wounded. Employing a newly arrived Australian battalion and four American tanks, Eichelberger attacked the eastern end of the coastal strip on 18 December. After some of the most desperate fighting of the campaign, Buna Mission fell on 2 January, followed by a mop-up of the emaciated Japanese survivors.

Australian general Thomas Blamey, MacArthur's commander of Allied land forces (foreground), on an inspection tour in Papua with Lieutenant General Robert Eichelberger, commander of American ground forces during the Buna campaign (at rear), January 1943. (Dept. of Defense)

By the time Buna fell, the Australian 7th Division had captured Gona, but the Japanese remained heavily entrenched at Sanananda. Requiring reinforcements for his worn-down Australian forces, Herring was promised the 41st Division's 163rd Infantry Regiment. MacArthur, however, tried to divert the regiment to Buna to boost the American attack. For a change, Blamey protested. Recognizing MacArthur's right to make the change, he considered it "contrary to sound principles of command that the Commander-in Chief . . . take over the duties of a portion of the battle."[22] MacArthur backed down in this instance, but he would later devise a means to keep American troops fully under American control.

The Allies gained complete control of the air, causing a Japanese diarist to lament that "they fly above our position as if they owned the skies."[23] Much of the Allied air effort was to interdict Japanese reinforcement and supply convoys, but success was limited as pilots had not yet fully learned how to execute low-level attacks. More successful were Allied bombing attacks in the Japanese rear using parachute bombs. Because of the close-in fighting, relatively few requests for attacks against ground targets were received and executed, and of these six resulted in casualties to friendly forces.

Supply was a major problem throughout the campaign, with both the Americans and Australians dependent on Kenney's transports, which were insufficient. At one point, the American situation became so desperate that Eichelberger's supply officer was warned that the troops might starve to death if the weather prevented air delivery for three or four days. Circumventing the Australian officer responsible for all Allied supplies, the American supply officer "pleaded, blustered, cajoled, threatened, and made a thorny nuisance of himself"[24] to place every transport plane at his disposal for three days. While this eliminated the immediate crisis, his going outside channels created friction with the Australians. Although the situation was satisfactorily resolved when the American officer took responsibility for all Allied supply depots, it was one of many instances in New Guinea where the two forces did not mesh easily.

On 13 January, Herring turned over the fighting to Eichelberger and left for Port Moresby to assume command of New Guinea Force. MacArthur and Blamey also returned to their headquarters in Australia, marked by a remarkably premature communique by MacArthur announcing that "The Papuan campaign is in its final closing phase."[25] But tanks and artillery had failed to seriously dent the Japanese position and much more fighting was expected. Fortunately for the Allies, the Japanese high command decided to evacuate Papua. Some Japanese troops were evacuated by sea and others slipped through the Allied cordon. Horii's successor, Major General Kensaku Oda, committed suicide.

The Papua fighting ended on 22 January, six months to the day after it began. American and Australian battle casualties totaled about 8,500, including 2,400 killed, triple the casualties suffered on Guadalcanal. Considering as well the many disabled by disease, Papua was one of the costliest campaigns of the Pacific war. MacArthur made the absurd claim that "probably no campaign in history against a thoroughly prepared and trained Army produced such complete and decisive results with so low an expenditure of life and resources." No less remarkably, he maintained that "losses were small because there was no hurry," entirely contrary to the experience of Eichelberger, who had been told that "time was of the essence . . . our dangers increased hour by hour."[26] Eichelberger said in his war memoirs: "At Buna, it was siege warfare . . . the bitterest and most punishing kind of warfare. Considering the number of troops in the front lines, the fatalities closely approach, percentage-wise, the heaviest losses in our own Civil War battles."[27]

The obvious question is whether the Japanese might have been encircled and bypassed instead. Eichelberger would claim that such tactics became feasible only later "at a time when we had secure bases from which such operations could be maintained, when we had achieved air superiority and were on our way to supremacy at sea as well."[28] Still, many Australian commanders believed that containing and starving out the enemy was the appropriate strategy, and that it wasn't used because MacArthur was intent on a quick and complete victory to enhance his prestige.[29] In fact, starvation was a principal reason why the Japanese had no choice in the end except to evacuate.

Unlike Halsey, who was nothing more or less than what he projected, MacArthur's image was in large part his own studied creation. Eichelberger wrote to his wife: "A certain great leader not only wants to be a great commander but he also wants to be known as a great front-line fighting leader. . . . He leaves the impression with the people back home that he has been the one who has been doing the frontline fighting. . . . He just wants all [the credit] for himself."[30] Paying the price of being noticed by the press, Eichelberger was sidelined for more than a year after Buna. Also, intent on emphasizing the American contribution, MacArthur's communiques slighted the Australians by describing their hard-fought battles as involving "Allied troops" while the Americans received full credit for their operations.[31]

On the American home front, aided by the publicity machine he carefully controlled, MacArthur enjoyed tremendous public standing. In particular, he obtained enthusiastic support from the important conservative press that looked to him as a potential candidate who might finally unseat the hated president. MacArthur did nothing to discourage their hopes and openly discussed his expectation of winning the Republican nomination in 1944.[32]

MacArthur learned much from the campaign in Papua. Like a stereotypical World War I general seated far to the rear, he disparaged commanders and repeatedly ordered costly frontal attacks without full firsthand knowledge of battlefield conditions and regard for casualties. Recognizing his errors, he promised "No more Bunas."[33] He would later avoid heavy enemy concentrations and protracted static fighting and would not initiate operations before establishing sound logistics. Also, from the experience of the 32nd Division, he gained an appreciation of the need for thorough troop training under realistic jungle conditions.

Kenney had amply demonstrated what could be achieved through the imaginative use of air power, and this was of great importance to the later conduct of the war. Eventually, according to a leading authority, "There was no leader in World War II more air-minded than MacArthur."[34] Soon, MacArthur would obtain an amphibious commander who would similarly expand his conception of how to best take advantage of an enemy vulnerable to assault by sea.

MacArthur could learn from his mistakes. Utilizing the abundant resources that soon became available and a growing awareness how they might best be employed, his later campaigns would be noted for their speed and low casualty rates, obscuring his less-than-stellar performance during the first Philippine and Papuan campaigns. He would shed his "Dugout Doug" image, conducting himself so as to gain the full respect of the American fighting men. Still, someone who knew them both well observed that MacArthur could not inspire men with electrifying leadership the way Halsey could.

Blamey did less well with the Australian troops. As MacArthur's hatchet man in Papua, he earned considerable enmity. In the view of many, Blamey failed to lend capable officers his support and sacrificed able men to appease MacArthur and to protect his own position. And Blamey could be extraordinarily heavy-handed. In one notable instance, he made ill-advised comments addressing seasoned troops who had conducted a fine fighting retreat on the Kokoda Trail against superior numbers. Expecting commendation, they were instead chastised for allowing themselves to be beaten by an inferior enemy and taunted by the observation that "it is the rabbit that runs that gets shot."[35] Despite MacArthur's full support, rising criticism of Blamey's conduct from the public and political spheres would eventually seriously threaten his position.

# CHAPTER 3

# "There Was Indeed Only One Yamamoto"

Whatever their ambitions and status, both MacArthur and Halsey depended on the Allied high command for authority and resources. At Casablanca during January 1943, American and British military leaders, the Combined Chiefs of Staff, met to plan worldwide strategy. The original plan had been—and always would be—victory in Europe first, then the Pacific. As always, the British were opposed to any Pacific operations that might siphon resources from the war against Germany. Still, they appreciated the value of retaining the initiative while Japan was on the defensive. They understood that allowing the enemy time to reorganize and dig in would make the eventual Allied offensive more difficult. In addition, leaving large forces idle while the war raged on other fronts made little sense. Resisting more ambitious ideas presented by the Americans, the British consented to the capture of Rabaul.[1] It was a compromise with a nod to both sides.

The discussions about Rabaul did not go beyond the concept of taking the Japanese bastion, the details of which were worked out at the Pacific Military Conference in Washington in March. The conference attendees looked to MacArthur to present a concrete plan, and when it was presented by his abrasive chief of staff, Sutherland, it landed like a bombshell. To take Rabaul, MacArthur would require nearly six additional divisions and twenty-four more air groups, a much larger slice of the resource pie than what he once claimed would suffice. Such massive allocation of forces to the Pacific would have violated the understandings reached at Casablanca and was particularly unacceptable to the air leaders, who were firmly committed to the concentration of air power against Germany. Under the agreement that was hammered out, MacArthur was allowed two divisions plus some additional air units. At the same time, the conference recognized that Rabaul could not be captured in 1943. The general plan that emerged became the basis for the detailed Cartwheel plan, finalized in late April.[2]

The thorny problem of divided command was also reconsidered.[3] While unity of command made sense, Army and Navy leaders were not prepared to hand over full control to a rival service commander who would not understand and support its established doctrines and methods. Particularly, Admiral King was entirely opposed to assigning portions of the Pacific Fleet to any specific area, which would cause it to relinquish part of its striking power and mobility. Consequently, divided command continued, with Halsey exercising tactical command when operating within MacArthur's domain under MacArthur's strategic direction. This seemingly awkward arrangement worked very well thanks to the considerable trust that Nimitz had in Halsey and the generally congenial relationship established between Halsey and MacArthur. It was not perfect, but it worked. As Halsey later wrote, "On the few occasions when I disagreed with [MacArthur], I told him so, and we discussed the issue until one of us changed his mind."[4]

The loss of Guadalcanal and Buna only strengthened Japanese resolve to hold their other South Pacific positions. In the central Solomons, at Munda, New Georgia, an airfield was secretly completed in December and a smaller field was begun nearby at Vila on Kolombangara. Farther north, major airfields were situated in the Shortlands, on Bougainville and Buka. On New Guinea, particular attention was given to Lae and Salamaua, which stood directly in MacArthur's path. A Japanese regiment from the 51st Division reinforced those bases in January, with the rest of the division following in late February. Prospects for a safe passage were good, as a reinforcement convoy to Wewak went through safely in mid-February. Fighter planes were expected to accompany the convoy most of the way, and the operation would be timed to maximize cloud cover. Cargoes and troops would be separated so that loss of any ship would not have a catastrophic effect.[5]

Allied air reconnaissance of Rabaul observed the gathering vessels. Days later, by means of message interception and decryption termed Ultra,[6] the convoy's probable schedule and destination were determined. On 28 February, 6,900 members of the Japanese 51st Division departed for Lae on board eight transports escorted by eight destroyers with air cover provided by a hundred aircraft flying in twenty to thirty plane relays. Adachi, the 18th Army commander, was on board one destroyer and Lieutenant General Hidemitsu Nakano, the 51st Division commander, was on another destroyer. The Japanese were unduly optimistic, unaware how much Allied air strength had grown,[7] and how Ultra had given away their plans.

Since becoming MacArthur's air commander, Kenney used his seemingly inexhaustible energy to obtain more and better aircraft and replace burned-out airmen with fresh ones who were taught innovative tactics. Some B-25 bombers were modified with eight .50-caliber nose-mounted machine guns for strafing. They were also armed with 500-pound bombs set on five-second delay to allow masthead-level bombing without danger to the aircraft when the bombs detonated. Pilots were also trained in skip bombing, a technique that caused bombs to bounce in the water and strike vessels near their water lines to effect maximum damage. The aircraft crews achieved high proficiency by practicing on a sunken ship off Port Moresby during six weeks of training.

Aided by a storm front, the Japanese convoy remained hidden until mid-afternoon of 1 March. Shadowed for a while, the ships were again shielded by the weather when a flight of B-17s tried unsuccessfully to find them. The same day, RAAF Boston bombers began a sustained attack on the airfield at Lae to prevent fighter interference from that direction. At midmorning on 2 March, the convoy was sighted fifty miles north of Cape Gloucester. Thirty-nine Flying Fortresses from Port Moresby sank at least three transports and badly damaged other vessels. About eight hundred survivors were rescued and spirited away to Lae by escorting destroyers that rejoined the convoy the next morning.

Japanese ship under low-level attack by Allied aircraft during the Battle of the Bismarck Sea, 3 March 1943. (USAAF)

The main action was fought on 3 March when the convoy was fifty miles southeast of Finschhafen. First, RAAF Beauforts attempted torpedo attacks without success. Then, in close coordination, thirteen Australian Beaufighters made a low-level attack followed immediately by thirteen B-25s in a medium-level attack, while thirteen B-17s bombed at eight thousand feet. In the most spectacular action of the battle, as the vessels scattered, twelve of the specially converted B-25s, using their newly installed forward-firing machine guns plus two .50-caliber guns in the top turret, strafed the enemy ships at a height of five hundred feet, destroying their anti-aircraft defenses. Not expecting such a low-level attack, the Japanese fighters were flying at seven thousand feet, too high to intervene. The B-25s then skipped their 500-pound bombs into several targets. Next, twelve A-20 Havocs and six B-25s attacked, inflicting additional damage. These successful air strikes left all the transports ablaze.

During the battle, enemy fighters largely concentrated on the B-17s but succeeded in bringing down only one. In that case, seven of the crew managed to bail out but were strafed and killed on the way down. Of the twenty-eight P-38s providing cover, three were lost.

Many Allied aircraft missed the continuing battle that afternoon because of bad weather over the Owen Stanleys, but much additional damage was still inflicted on the Japanese. After an initial B-17 attack that sank a destroyer, eight specially equipped B-25s conducted a low-level attack, sinking another destroyer and heavily damaging other ships. Five RAAF Bostons, fifteen B-25s, and a flight of B-17s delivered the final attacks, leaving the sea full of sinking and burning vessels and great numbers of survivors in lifeboats and on rafts.

In the following days, aircraft and motor torpedo (PT) boats finished off the burning hulks and hunted down survivors. Destroying the helpless Japanese in the water was considered essential since it was assumed they would not surrender and it was important they not make it to Lae. The memory of the Japanese killing the B-17 parachutists helped to alleviate some of the guilt in taking this action.[8]

The Battle of the Bismarck Sea is a misnomer. Fought primarily in the Vitiaz Strait and Solomon Sea, the battle resulted in the destruction of all eight transports and four of the eight destroyers. At war's end, MacArthur would declare it "the decisive aerial engagement" by his forces.[9]

Japanese submarines and destroyers rescued about 2,800 soldiers and sailors including Adachi and Nakano. However, only about 1,000 men reached Lae and more than 3,600 were lost. In the air, twenty to thirty Japanese planes were downed versus the loss of six American and Australian aircraft.

Kenney's success involved considerable luck: the extent of information obtained through Ultra, Japanese failure to appreciate Allied air strength, a storm front that perversely changed direction to remove the weather shield, and the slow speed of the convoy. But the official Army Air Forces history could say with justification, "The victory had been a triumph of coordinated effort—of an accurate evaluation of intelligence, of daring technical developments, and of meticulous training."[10]

Never again would the Japanese make such a bold attempt to reinforce their South Pacific bases. Thereafter, reinforcements and supplies were sent by barge, small coastal craft, and submarines, the capacities of which were too limited to meet Adachi's needs. But even these more cautious approaches were costly. According to a Japanese estimate, during the war twenty thousand troops were lost at sea crossing from Rabaul to New Guinea.[11]

MacArthur created much controversy after the battle by issuing a communique that wildly overstated results, accepting uncritically the overenthusiastic reports of his aviators. Occurring when there was little activity elsewhere, the victory was eagerly embraced by the press, including the *New York Times,* which announced in its headline: "M'Arthur Fliers Destroy 22 Japanese Ships; Enemy Loses 15,000 Men in Convoy; 55 Planes." A supplementary communique expanded enemy aircraft losses to 102.

Perhaps instigated by the Navy's skepticism about such spectacular results, Army Air Forces headquarters in Washington undertook a detailed study. Making use of captured documents and prisoner interrogation reports, they reached conclusions that entirely deflated MacArthur's claims. In what would be their customary attitude, MacArthur and Kenney refused to admit error and continued to do so even after the war when information from the Japanese side fully corroborated the Air Forces' findings.[12]

Exaggerating the ability of his air forces was useful to MacArthur in his ongoing struggle with the Navy for primacy in the Pacific. When concern was expressed in Australia about a possible renewed Japanese offensive, MacArthur called attention to the Navy's inability to wrest the sea lanes from the Japanese, claiming that Australia's defense essentially relied on his land-based aviation.[13]

Before this time, in expectation of further movement up the Solomons, Halsey's staff recommended occupation of the Russell Islands, thirty miles northwest of Guadalcanal. The islands were wanted to establish airfields and a torpedo boat base and for use as a landing craft staging area. Essentially a shore-to-shore operation launched from Guadalcanal, the landing on 21 February was conducted by elements of the 43rd Infantry Division and the 3rd Marine Raider Battalion, about nine thousand men in total. Such a large force hardly seemed necessary since the islands were deserted, but there was the possibility the Japanese might strongly react if they were planning to retake Guadalcanal. Also, the operation provided useful amphibious training for the inexperienced 43rd Division National Guardsmen. Immediately upon occupation of the Russells, Seabees went to work developing what would become an important base for the coming campaigns. Attempting to disrupt the Allied buildup, the Japanese hit the Russells with heavy air attacks beginning in May.

With both New Guinea and the Solomons now under immediate threat, a tug-of-war ensued in Tokyo during March as to which area should receive principal support. The army, responsible for New Guinea, the retention of which was essential to hold the resource-rich Netherlands Indies and the Philippines, insisted that theirs was the greater need. Navy representatives countered that the

Solomons needed to be held to safeguard Rabaul and the great fleet anchorage at Truk. Through greater political influence, the army won the argument.[14]

The Japanese high command decided that further efforts would be made to strengthen New Guinea and western New Britain. In preparation for MacArthur's certain advance, roads and airfields would be built, supplies stockpiled, and garrisons reinforced. In the Solomons, the Japanese navy was given responsibility for the defense of New Georgia and Santa Isabel, with the more northerly islands assigned to the army. But obtaining full cooperation between the two armed services proved even more difficult and was far less successful than between the American services. Though the Japanese army and navy were directed to "act in concert," little heed was given to that part of the Imperial directive.[15]

The most significant new order called on the navy "to wage aerial annihilation operations in concert with the Army." Translating that directive into specific action, Admiral Yamamoto planned Operation I-GO, the objective of which was to strike Allied bases forcefully enough to delay their advance and gain additional time for the Japanese to strengthen defenses. Supplementing the 185 naval aircraft of the 11th Air Fleet, Yamamoto added 96 Mitsubishi Zero fighters and 65 Aichi 99–1 Val dive bombers from the carrier force. The aircraft were assembled at airfields on and near Bougainville while Yamamoto moved his headquarters from Truk to Rabaul to personally direct operations.

Operation I-GO commenced on 1 April with a preparatory sweep by 58 Zeros that headed for Guadalcanal and Tulagi, where Halsey was accumulating supplies in preparation for attacking New Georgia. Alerted by coast watchers and radar, 41 F4F Wildcats, F4U Corsairs, and P-38 Lightnings intercepted the attackers over the Russell Islands, downing 18 Zeros at a cost of six Allied aircraft. Next, on 7 April, 67 Val dive bombers and 110 Zeros struck Guadalcanal. Although fully alerted by coast watchers and radar, the 76 fighter planes defending the island were kept so busy by the Zeros that the dive bombers got through. The Vals hit shipping off Tulagi, sinking a destroyer, tanker, and corvette. On his first combat mission while leading four Wildcats, First Lieutenant James E. Swett (USMC) brought down seven Vals. He then flew through friendly anti-aircraft fire to land his badly damaged plane in Tulagi harbor. For this action, Swett was awarded the Medal of Honor and inspired fledgling Marine pilots to also "do a Jimmy Swett."[16] Both sides wildly overestimated their kills, which were determined through postwar analysis to have actually been the loss by the Japanese of 12 Vals and nine Zeros at a cost of seven Marine fighters.

Yamamoto next turned to New Guinea. The target was Oro Bay, twelve miles south of Buna. On 11 April, 72 Zeros and 22 Vals struck Allied ships unloading supplies for the Dobodura air base. The Japanese sank one merchantman and damaged two vessels, losing six planes without downing any of the 50 defending fighters. On the following day, 131 Zeros and 43 Betty medium

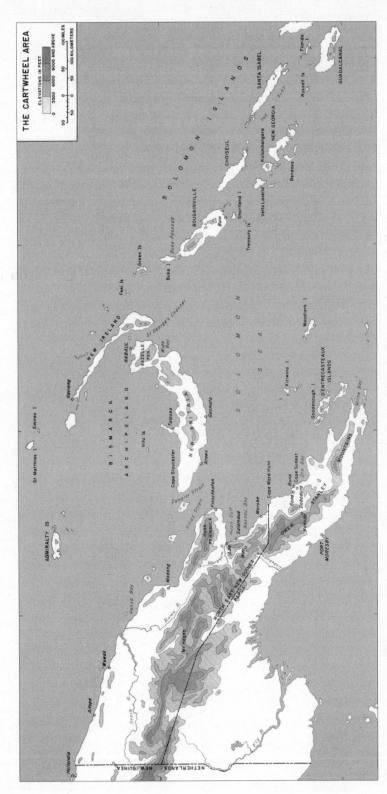

Map 2. Cartwheel Campaign Area (Miller, *The U.S. Army in World War II—The War in the Pacific: Cartwheel*, 23)

bombers crossed the Owen Stanley Range for a high-level bombing attack on Port Moresby. The results were unspectacular. The Japanese damaged some small craft in the harbor and destroyed or damaged some aircraft on the airfield. Five Japanese planes were lost in exchange for two of Kenney's defending fighters. Closing out Operation I-GO, Yamamoto sent 188 aircraft against Milne Bay on 14 April. Penetrating a defensive screen of 24 P-40s, the Japanese damaged three cargo ships. Seven Japanese aircraft and three RAAF planes were lost. Believing he had achieved decisive results, Yamamoto ended the operation on 16 April, ordering the carrier aircraft back to their ships.

Ten days later, on 26 April, MacArthur's detailed plan, code named Cartwheel, was ready. Thirteen separate operations were scheduled over an eight-month period, with MacArthur and Halsey expected to closely coordinate operations to suppress opposition and keep the enemy's attention divided.

In the Southwest Pacific Area, Cartwheel would begin with landings on Woodlark and Kiriwina islands in the Trobriands and at Nassau Bay on New Guinea. Fighters based in the Trobriands would be used to support bomber raids on Rabaul and the northern Solomons, while Nassau Bay would serve as a supply point for the Australian 7th Division advancing overland against Salamaua. Simultaneous with MacArthur's opening moves, Halsey's forces would attack New Georgia, with the airfield at Munda Point their main objective. This would be followed by operations in the Huon Gulf area of New Guinea to capture Lae, Salamaua, and Finschhafen, after which Madang would be attacked. Meanwhile, Halsey was to gain a foothold in the Shortland Islands and at Buin on the south coast of Bougainville. Cartwheel would conclude with a landing by MacArthur's forces on Cape Gloucester, at the western end of New Britain, while Halsey took Kieta on the eastern coast of Bougainville and neutralized Buka. These operations would grip Rabaul in a vise that would be closed later by capture of the base.[17]

Halsey's planners proposed that the New Georgia operation begin on 1 April, but MacArthur's team wanted it deferred to mid-May, when they would have resources to move in lockstep against the Trobriands. MacArthur later imposed a further delay of six weeks because of problems in building up his amphibious forces. Delaying the commencement of Cartwheel to 30 June was unfortunate, as the Trobriands were not important and the Japanese gained valuable additional time to strengthen New Georgia.

Nevertheless, the Allies obtained an enormously important opportunity that profoundly affected the future course of the war. On 18 April, Yamamoto left Rabaul by air for a tour of forward naval air bases. He planned to award medals to his aviators for their supposed great victories during I-GO, with Kahili airfield on Bougainville his first stop. American cryptanalysts intercepted and read the messages relating to Yamamoto's itinerary, including exact departure and arrival times, course, and type and number of aircraft. This was an Allied intelligence coup; perhaps they could intercept Yamamoto.

Admiral Isoroku Yamamoto salutes Japanese pilots at Rabaul in the last known photograph before his death, April 1943. (Govt. of Japan)

Presented with the information by his intelligence officer, Commander Edwin T. Layton, Nimitz asked, "Do we try to get him?" Layton responded: "He's unique among their people. Aside from the Emperor probably no man in Japan is so important to civilian morale. And if he's shot down, it would demoralize the fighting navy." Allaying Nimitz's concerns that the enemy might then produce a more effective fleet commander, Layton told Nimitz: "Yamamoto is head and shoulders above them all. . . . It would be just as if they shot you down. There isn't anybody to replace you."[18]

Recognizing the sensitivity of the situation, Nimitz obtained authorization for Yamamoto's interception from the secretary of the navy and the president. Nimitz then sent an order to Halsey, who passed it to his air commander, Rear Admiral Marc A. Mitscher. Long-range fighter aircraft would be needed, and nothing better for that purpose existed than the Lockheed P-38 Lightning, whose deadly nose packed a 20-mm cannon plus four 0.5-in machine guns and whose twin engines and twin tails gave it power and maneuverability.

Flying a circuitous six-hundred-mile route no higher than fifty feet above the water in the longest fighter interception mission of the war, sixteen Lightnings arrived at Kahili just as the two bombers carrying Yamamoto and his staff were preparing to land. Both bombers were downed, with Yamamoto killed in one aircraft and his chief of staff badly wounded in the other. Three of the escorting Japanese fighters were downed with the loss of only one Lightning.[19]

Halsey was instructed to attribute the interception to the observations of Australian coast watchers near Rabaul. The Japanese, unwilling to accept the possibility that the Allies had broken their five-digit mainline naval operations code, blamed a commander in the Shortlands who had sent a message to army headquarters using an insecure code.

The Japanese leadership withheld the shattering news from the public for as long as possible. When the news finally broke, the nation recoiled from a disaster for which there was no recovery. Layton wrote in his war memoir: "There was indeed only one Yamamoto."[20]

CHAPTER 4

# "The Most Unintelligently Waged Land Campaign"

The delay imposed by MacArthur before Halsey could move against New Georgia gave the Japanese additional time to prepare for invasion.[1] That delay was also useful to Halsey. Scouting expeditions yielded considerable information about the target, plentiful supplies were accumulated, and naval and air forces were expanded. It was a far cry from the hurriedly organized landing on Guadalcanal, when both intelligence and material resources were in short supply. Also, after long expecting an invasion, the Japanese were caught off guard when it finally occurred. Yet as it was fought, Operation Toenails would be called by historian Samuel E. Morison "the most unintelligently waged land campaign of the Pacific war."[2]

Japanese determination to retain control of the central Solomons as long as possible fundamentally shaped the campaign. The defenders were primarily troops from the 6th and 38th divisions, led by Major General Noboru Sasaki, former chief of staff of the 6th Army in China, as resourceful a commander as might have been found. Supporting him under independent command were highly trained forces from the 6th and 7th SNLF. About six thousand army and navy troops were on New Georgia, mostly in the Munda area, with five thousand nearby, primarily on Kolombangara across Kula Gulf. As long as Kusaka's Rabaul-based Eighth Fleet could effectively contest the surrounding waters, Sasaki would be able to draw substantial reinforcements and supplies during the battle. Supported by about four hundred army and navy aircraft based on Rabaul, Bougainville, and the Shortlands, Sasaki was positioned to wage a much longer and harder battle than expected by Halsey's planners.

Halsey's principal target was the airfield at Munda, developed secretly by the Japanese during the Guadalcanal campaign. In the hands of the Allies, fighters

34

operating from Munda could assist the air campaign against Rabaul and help to prepare Bougainville for invasion. Since reefs and other offshore barriers made direct approach to Munda by oceangoing vessels impossible, the initial landing would be on lightly occupied Rendova Island nearby.

The complex invasion plan developed by Halsey's joint staff included three secondary targets southeast of Munda. To obtain a protected line of supply, Wickham Anchorage on nearby Vangunu and Viru Harbor would be occupied to serve as supply points and small craft harbors. Also, to obtain close air support for the ground campaign, Segi Point was wanted for construction of an airstrip. In addition, Allied forces would land at Kula Gulf to capture Japanese barge bases there, preventing enemy troop movements to and from New Georgia.

During the planning, the commander of the 1st Marine Amphibious Corps (IMAC), Major General C. Barney Vogel, recommended that two full divisions be employed in the invasion. Discounting the possibility that the Japanese would make a maximum effort to hold New Georgia, and anxious to withhold troops for later operations, Halsey's planners decided that a single division with supports would suffice.

Of the three Marine divisions then in the Pacific, the 1st and 2nd divisions were recovering from Guadalcanal and the 3rd Division was still being trained, leaving just two battalions from the 1st Marine Raider Regiment available. Thus, by necessity, New Georgia was conducted as an Army campaign.

Four Army infantry XIV Corps divisions were available to Halsey: 25th, 37th, 43rd, and the Americal Division. The 25th and Americal had fought on Guadalcanal while the 37th and 43rd, both National Guard divisions, had no combat experience. Just as MacArthur's expectations at Buna ignored the inexperience of the 32nd Division, the untried 43rd Division was expected to take Munda by itself with the 37th in reserve. Various smaller Marine and Army units would be used for the secondary targets.

A command designated the New Georgia Occupation Force was established to control the widespread land operations. The commander of the 43rd Division, Major General John H. Hester, in his first combat assignment, was to lead both his division and the Occupation Force. This arrangement made it necessary for the assistant division commander, Brigadier General Leonard F. Wing, to act essentially as division commander while Hester gave primary attention to the Occupation Force, with the division staff divided to serve both commands.

A more rational approach would have been placement of the numerous supporting units under the command of the XIV Corps. Responsible for the irrational arrangement was amphibious force commander Admiral Kelly Turner. Known as "Terrible Turner" for his temper and authoritarian ways, Turner was notorious for overstepping his proper boundaries to control land operations. Under the unity-of-command concept, Turner would retain complete command of the invasion force until the ground forces were established on shore.

Worried that Hester was overloaded, the commander of Army forces in the South Pacific, Lieutenant General Millard F. Harmon Jr., recommended early in the campaign that XIV Corps commander Major General Oscar W. Griswold take over the New Georgia Occupation Force after the capture of Munda. Turner vehemently opposed the idea on the grounds that Hester was doing very well, but Harmon convinced Halsey. In fact, a change in command would become necessary long before Munda was taken.

Because the invasion day targets were widely separated, Turner led the principal Rendova landing while Rear Admiral George H. Fort commanded the other landings. Two light cruiser–destroyer groups under Rear Admirals Walden L. "Pug" Ainsworth and A. Stanton "Tip" Merrill provided naval cover. Battleships and carriers were available in case the Japanese fleet intervened from Truk, with seven Brisbane-based submarines keeping watch. After their losses during the Guadalcanal campaign, however, the Japanese chose not to commit heavy fleet units in the central Solomons.

To control Allied air forces in the theater that had grown enormously since Guadalcanal, a separate echelon designated Aircraft, Solomons (AirSols) headed by Mitscher was created within Vice Admiral Aubrey Fitch's Air South Pacific command. AirSols included all land-based U.S. Army, Navy, and Marine, and New Zealand aircraft in the Solomons, of which most of the heavy bombers and a quarter of the fighters belonged to the Army's 13th Air Force.

In the weeks before the landings, Army B-17 Flying Fortresses and B-24 Liberators attacked Japanese airfields heavily on Bougainville and the Shortlands, while Marine dive and torpedo bombers repeatedly struck central Solomons targets on New Georgia, Kolombangara, and Santa Isabel. AirSols would have 533 aircraft including 455 combat planes ready to support the invasion.[3]

Although Cartwheel called for simultaneous attacks by MacArthur and Halsey on 30 June, circumstances required acceleration of the Segi Point landing. Irregular forces led by a coast watcher had occupied Segi Point, but the Japanese were preparing an attack and it was feared the position would be lost. Turner responded by sending elements of the 4th Marine Raider Battalion, who arrived by destroyer-transports in the early hours of 21 June and met no opposition at Segi Point. Another change in plan was at Viru Harbor, where a landing from the sea was canceled when Japanese resistance was encountered. Instead, Marine raiders and 43rd Division forces marched eleven miles from Segi Point to take Viru from the landward side on 30 June.[4]

The Wickham Anchorage operation began on schedule but was beset by continuous problems, starting with a landing so far afield that the troops needed to re-embark. Landing craft became scattered during a second try, with some getting lost on a reef, and the final landing was in the wrong place. Fortunately, no enemy was nearby to take advantage of the disorganization, and by 4 July Wickham Anchorage was taken after light opposition.

Units seizing these positions incurred few casualties. At Segi Point, Seabees quickly completed an airstrip that enjoyed a brief life in supporting operations on New Georgia. Wickham Anchorage would have slight value as a stop-off point for small craft from Guadalcanal and the Russells, while Viru Harbor would be used only for the repair of small craft. In retrospect, the forces absorbed by these operations might have been put to better use.[5]

On the morning of 30 June, the South Pacific came fully to life. While Halsey's forces moved on Viru Harbor and Wickham Anchorage, and MacArthur struck the Trobriands and Nassau Bay, Merrill's cruisers and destroyers bombarded the Shortland Islands, paving the way for the most important landing that day, on Rendova.

A Japanese diary later found on Rendova included the entry, "I can't understand why Headquarters does not reinforce troops on Rendova which is a good landing place. A sad case!"[6] The diarist's sentiments are understandable, as fewer than 150 troops from the 229th Infantry Regiment and the 6th SNLF were posted there—hardly sufficient to oppose the 6,000 American troops that would land.

American 43rd Division troops land on Rendova Island during a heavy rainstorm, 30 June 1943. (National Archives and Records Administration)

To eliminate opposition before the main landing, specially trained jungle fighters from the 43rd called the "Barracudas" landed by destroyer transports in Rendova Harbor. Debarking in the wrong place in the dark, they could not perform their mission by the time the main body arrived. Fortunately, the few Japanese defenders offered only slight resistance and fled after their commander was killed. Japanese shore batteries presented some problem, but were silenced after a damaging hit on the destroyer USS *Gwin*.

The main Japanese effort that day was in the air. Substantial air forces had been built up at Bougainville in anticipation of the invasion but were later withdrawn to Rabaul and were still there. Halsey expected that Kenney's bombers would keep the enemy airfields neutralized, but bad weather kept his planes grounded. At 1100, twenty-seven Zeros arrived, and sixteen of them were shot down by a standing patrol of thirty-two AirSols fighters. Then in the afternoon, twenty-five Betty torpedo planes attacked, covered by twenty-four Zeros. During the action, seventeen Bettys were downed by the patrolling Corsairs and Wildcats and by ship anti-aircraft fire, but ten torpedo planes broke through to deliver their fish. One torpedo found Turner's flagship USS *McCawley*, forcing its evacuation. It was uncertain for some hours whether the ship might be saved, but the matter was settled decisively by a PT boat that mistook *McCawley* for an enemy vessel and sent her to the bottom. A final feeble effort in the early evening by about thirty Japanese aircraft failed, with eighteen of them downed.

Generally, D-day on Rendova was a success in that six thousand men and their supplies were landed with amazing rapidity. But there was chaos on the beaches as the rain-soaked roads made movement to the supply dumps extremely difficult. The next day, while efforts were made to deal with the supply mess, the second echelon of the landing force arrived, and patrols on Roviana Island selected sites from which "Long Tom" 155-mm artillery could bombard Munda. A Japanese air attack was successfully beaten off that morning, but another air strike on the third day of the invasion produced the most ground casualties of any bombing during the entire war in the South Pacific.[7]

At midday on 2 July, signs of a storm prompted AirSols commander Mitscher to order the fighter patrol over the invasion beaches to return to Guadalcanal. By unfortunate coincidence, the only radar set available on Rendova was out of commission for ten minutes for servicing when the Japanese planes arrived. A flight of twenty-four bombers first dropped their loads on the air defenses of the 9th Marine Defense Battalion (MDB), after which dive bombers attacked the beach and fighters strafed at low altitude. Casualties, mostly 43rd Division troops and Marines manning the anti-aircraft guns, amounted to fifty-nine killed and seventy-seven wounded. Heavy raids continued through the first half of July, including a particularly destructive raid on 4 July that destroyed many landing craft. But the Japanese would pay a steep price as air patrols and anti-aircraft fire took a heavy toll of their aircraft stockpile.[8]

For the landing on New Georgia, a good but defended beach at Laiana two miles from Munda was rejected and an undefended beach at Zanana five miles from the target chosen instead. Beginning 2 July and continuing over the next three days, the 43rd Division's 169th and 172nd regiments moved from Rendova to Zanana without opposition.

In coordination with the 43rd Division's movement, the 1st Marine Raider Battalion with two battalions from the 37th Division, 3rd Battalion, 145th Infantry and 3rd Battalion, 148th Infantry, landed at Rice Anchorage on Kula Gulf the night of 4–5 July. The objective of the 2,600-man force, under the command of Colonel Harry B. "The Horse" Liversedge (USMC), was to capture barge bases at Enogai and Bairoko, preventing the movement of enemy troops and supplies to New Georgia and cutting off their line of retreat from Munda.

Seven destroyer transports brought Liversedge's troops to Kula Gulf, escorted by Ainsworth's cruisers and destroyers that prepared the way by bombarding Vila and Bairoko. Coincidentally, three enemy destroyers were then in the gulf bringing the first echelon of a 4,000-man reinforcement force from Rabaul to Vila. Before the ships were within range to engage, USS *Strong* received a lethal blow from a torpedo. Because radar indicated the Japanese destroyers were eleven miles distant, it was then assumed that the torpedo must have come from a coastal defense submarine. Only later would the remarkable range of the Japanese torpedoes be appreciated: 22,000 yards at 49 knots or 44,000 yards at 36 knots.[9]

Japanese 150-mm guns at Enogai Inlet opened up on *Strong* and the destroyers that rushed to rescue her 241 survivors, but they scored no hits and were eventually silenced by two destroyers. Liversedge's force landed while this fighting went on, and by dawn Ainsworth withdrew to Tulagi. The Japanese destroyers withdrew as well with their troops still on board but having accomplished a good night's work.[10]

The next evening, Ainsworth returned to Kula Gulf and obtained an even harsher demonstration of enemy torpedo capabilities in the most significant surface action since Tassafaronga in November. Learning that the Tokyo Express was heading to Vila with reinforcements, Halsey ordered Ainsworth to intercept. Initially, there were seven Japanese destroyer transports escorted by three destroyers, but after three destroyer transports were detached the Japanese went into the action with seven ships. Ainsworth enjoyed far heavier firepower with the guns of light cruisers USS *Honolulu, Helena,* and *Saint Louis.* In addition, his cruisers and four accompanying destroyers were equipped with excellent radar. But the enemy was better trained for such operations. The lead Japanese destroyer had new radar, and all vessels were armed with superb torpedoes.

Arriving at Kula Gulf early on 6 July, Rear Admiral Teruo Akiyama detached three ships to land troops at Vila. Although Ainsworth believed he was first to make radar contact and enjoyed surprise, Akiyama's radar had picked up Ainsworth's ships a half-hour earlier. Both sides held their fire while the range narrowed. The Americans were anxious to close in and deliver medium-range, radar-controlled gunfire; the Japanese were unwilling to give their position away by firing their guns and were waiting for an optimum moment to release their torpedoes. With the range down to only 6,800 yards, Ainsworth's 6-inch guns opened fire, disabling Akiyama's flagship *Niizuki* that was later hit repeatedly before sinking with 300 on board, including Akiyama. But *Helena* gave herself away by using ordinary smokeless powder after using up all her flashless powder the night before, and thus became a perfect target.[11] Three torpedoes found the cruiser, removing *Helena*'s bow and breaking her back.

Later, one of Akiyama's destroyers ran aground and was destroyed in the morning by AirSols planes. The score for the battle was roughly even, the loss of an American light cruiser against two Japanese destroyers. The Japanese succeeded in landing 850 of the 2,600 troops destined for Vila, with the remainder safely withdrawn for a later reinforcement run. Through hesitation and loss of the initiative,[12] Ainsworth forfeited the advantage of greatly superior firepower. But thanks to his spotters who mistook gun flashes for fatal hits on the enemy ships, Kula Gulf became an imagined American victory. A *Helena* survivor described the action in the *Saturday Evening Post* as a resounding triumph during which "our destroyers' gun crews were superb in their marksmanship. The Japs were sunk as they fled."[13] Nothing could have been further from the truth.

The American Navy could not stop the flow of Japanese reinforcements to Vila. And despite a heroic effort, Liversedge was unable to prevent enemy troop movements from there to New Georgia. Through a difficult march in jungle and swampland, overcoming strong resistance with inadequate supplies and weaponry, Liversedge's men took Enogai on 10 July at a cost of fifty-four dead and ninety-one wounded. Meanwhile, 3/148 established a roadblock on the trail leading from Enogai and Bairoko to Munda. But as they were unable to hold it, the battalion withdrew and rejoined the main body. Without sufficient strength to take Bairoko, Liversedge conducted patrols and waited at Enogai for reinforcements.

The two regiments advancing on Munda from Zanana also experienced severe problems reminiscent of Guadalcanal but in reverse. Now it was the Americans who were forced to undertake exhausting jungle marches with unreliable supply lines while fighting a well-prepared opponent. The slow slog through the jungle was punctuated by sniper attacks that slowed the advance to a crawl, including at one point the pinning down of a battalion by an energetic enemy platoon. Nighttime harassment actions took their toll on the nerves of the unseasoned troops, who incurred many friendly fire casualties firing wildly at each other in the dark. The chaotic situation was reflected in a record number of what were then called war neurosis cases.

The slow pace of the advance and lengthening supply line to Zanana created a supply crisis for Hester, which he attempted to remedy by seizing the beach at

Laiana from the inland side. For the 11 July operation, Hester diverted the 172nd Infantry while ordering the 169th Infantry to continue toward Munda. That day, he replaced the commander and other officers of the 169th who had repeatedly failed to take their objectives. Suffering from hunger and thirst, the 172nd made it to Laiana on 13 July, after which supplies and reinforcements were brought to the beach under fire. Taking advantage of this division of Hester's forces, Sasaki cut communications between the regiments and brought both to a halt.

Hours before Laiana was taken, the Battle of Kolombangara was fought in Kula Gulf. Four Japanese destroyer transports with 1,200 troops escorted by light cruiser *Jintsu* and four destroyers sailed from Rabaul for Vila under the command of Rear Admiral Shunji Izaki. Anxious to stop the reinforcement run, Halsey provided Ainsworth with six additional destroyers for a total of eleven ships. Ainsworth would again have the heavier firepower of three cruisers, with New Zealand light cruiser HMNZS *Leander* replacing the lost *Helena*.

In the first minutes of 13 July, a patrol plane spotted the Japanese support group. While Ainsworth expected to catch the enemy unaware, Izaki spotted Ainsworth two hours before action commenced using a new radar detection device. Once radar contact was established, Ainsworth's five leading destroyers released their torpedoes. Then, his cruisers hurled 2,630 shells at the largest target on their radar, cruiser *Jintsu*. After multiple hits including by two torpedoes, Izaki's flagship exploded, killing almost all on board. Thus far, the action was remarkably like Kula Gulf, where in the opening round the enemy admiral and his flagship were eliminated. But, just as happened then, the rest of the action belonged to the Japanese.

While well within range of the enemy destroyers, Ainsworth ordered a turn, during which *Leander* took a torpedo hit that killed twenty-eight and knocked her out of the battle. Afterwards, Ainsworth came upon four destroyers but withheld fire until their identity was established. The delay was costly, as the Japanese commander cleverly waited for Ainsworth to go into a turn. Having swiftly reloaded after an earlier firing, the Japanese destroyers fired a spread of thirty-one torpedoes, one of them striking destroyer USS *Gwin*, which lost sixty-one men and later needed to be scuttled. Then, both American cruisers were knocked out of action, *Saint Louis* by a torpedo hit well forward and *Honolulu* by a hit that blew away her bow. Ainsworth's ships limped back down the Slot, protected by AirSols fighters from the Russells that dealt with Japanese aircraft anxious to finish them off. Meanwhile, 1,200 Japanese soldiers landed safely on Kolombangara.

The Battle of Kolombangara amply confirmed the continued superiority of Japanese tactics and torpedoes. Two of Ainsworth's cruisers would be out of the war for many months and *Leander* would never return to battle. Just as at Kula Gulf, American lookouts misread the nighttime battleground, imagining many hits that never happened. Thus, the citation accompanying Ainsworth's

Distinguished Service Medal, awarded a few weeks later, praised his "two successful night engagements in Kula Gulf."[14]

While Ainsworth could not prevent reinforcements from reaching the Japanese, Kusaka concluded that Kula Gulf had become too dangerous. Thereafter, men and supplies were transported by way of Vella Gulf on the western side of Kolombangara. Despite their victories, the Japanese sustained losses in a war of attrition they could not afford given their inability to replace ships at the rate of their opponent.[15]

Up to this point, there were no special concerns at Halsey's headquarters about the progress of operations other than the delay in capturing Munda. To view the situation in preparation for the agreed change in command of the New Georgia Occupation Force, Harmon ordered Griswold to New Georgia. Appalled by the disarray he found and the dreadful condition of the troops, Griswold sent an alarming message to Harmon on 13 July. The 43rd Division was ready "to fold up" and would "never take Munda."[16]

# CHAPTER 5

# "A Custody Receipt for Munda ... Keep 'Em Dying"

I n Noumea, Halsey conferred immediately with Harmon when they received Griswold's report about conditions on New Georgia. Harmon was told "to take whatever steps were deemed necessary to facilitate the capture of the airfield."[1] This prompt action reflected their close, highly productive relationship in which Harmon essentially functioned as Halsey's deputy commander.

Lieutenant General Millard F. Harmon (behind wheel) with Major General Nathan F. Twining (beside him) and Major General Oscar W. Griswold (in helmet behind Twining), with two members of Harmon's staff, New Georgia, July 1943. (Dept. of Defense)

It was previously arranged with Nimitz that Turner would leave the South Pacific to take command of amphibious forces in the Central Pacific, making his departure just then highly opportune. As Turner had remained a staunch defender of Hester, the next step became easier. Griswold took command of the New Georgia Occupation Force, removing that burden from Hester, who could then give full attention to his division. Turner's replacement was scholarly Rear Admiral Theodore S. "Ping" Wilkinson. The director of naval intelligence at the time of Pearl Harbor, Wilkinson largely avoided blame for the surprise attack because Turner was responsible for interpreting and disseminating intelligence information. In his new position, Wilkinson proved a highly skilled commander and entirely unlike Turner in his ability to work cooperatively.

Turner had agreed to reinforce Liversedge at Enogai, which would enable a fresh attempt against Bairoko. On 18 July, the 4th Raider Battalion arrived on board four destroyer-transports, giving Liversedge just over three thousand men. Surprise would not be possible, and the long delay gave the Japanese ample opportunity to improve their defenses. As Liversedge lacked artillery and heavy mortars, air support on the day of the attack would be critical to soften up the enemy positions. Because the request was submitted late, though, AirSols could not or would not comply, and Liversedge went ahead with the attack without certainty that air support would be provided.[2]

On 20 July, while two raider battalions advanced directly against the port, 3/148 approached on a parallel route to the south with the objective of turning the Japanese right flank. Nearing the harbor, the raiders came up against four heavily fortified lines of mutually supporting bunkers on coral ridges. In the face of intense 90-mm mortar fire and lacking artillery to respond in kind, the raiders managed to penetrate two lines by late afternoon. But with water and ammunition low, casualties heavy, no reserves, and failure by 3/148 to make meaningful progress, Liversedge gave up the assault after losing 51 killed and 200 wounded. He fell back to Enogai the next day with the help of heavy air support that was sorely lacking the day before. Thereafter, activity was confined to patrolling until early August. A roadblock was established on the Munda-Bairoko Trail, but it failed to seriously impede enemy movements. While Liversedge's hard-fought battle failed to close the back door to Munda, he at least drew away Japanese forces that would otherwise have bolstered the defense there.[3]

Harmon and Griswold decided to expand to two divisions for the drive on Munda by committing the 37th Division. The organization and logistics required ten days, and meanwhile Hester's forces were expected to improve their positions and pin down the enemy. At the coast, the 172nd extended the Laiana beachhead west toward Ilangana. M3 Stuart light tanks from the 9th MDB landed and were employed on 16 and 17 July. With three tanks attached to each battalion, elements of the 37th had some successes in destroying the enemy pillboxes. But because the Marine tanks and their supporting Army infantry had never trained together, coordination was poor. In one sector the slope was too steep for the tanks to sufficiently elevate or depress their 37-mm guns. With great skill, and taking advantage of the thick jungle, the Japanese improvised antitank defenses, employing antitank mines, flame throwers, grenades, Molotov cocktails, and TNT charges. By the second day of battle, two of the nine Stuarts were permanently disabled. Still, Griswold was sufficiently encouraged by their limited successes to call in the tanks of the 10th MDB from the Russells.

A gap developed between the two regiments when the 172nd veered toward Laiana, and, taking advantage, the Japanese 13th Infantry penetrated between. With its right flank in the air and an exposed line of communications stretching to Zanana, the 169th was particularly vulnerable. Sasaki saw the opportunity and planned an attack in which the 13th Infantry would get behind the right of the 169th. His troops would then cut the 169th's line of communications on the Munda Trail and hit the Zanana beachhead. Meanwhile, Sasaki's 229th Infantry would attack the 172nd while SNLF forces attacked and occupied the Laiana beachhead.[4]

During the night of 17–18 July, the Japanese 13th Infantry struck the rear of the 169th, reaching as far as the Zanana command post and wrecking the communications center. Artillery on the offshore islands, firing as close as one hundred yards from the American front lines, helped to break up the enemy troop concentrations and prevent banzai attacks. With the beachhead area and its precious supply depot under immediate threat, two members of the 9th MDB, Corporal Maier J. Rothschild and Private John Wantuck, took up forward positions with salvaged 30-caliber machine guns on the enemy's expected path of advance. In the ensuing action, during which Wantuck was killed and Rothschild seriously wounded, about thirty Japanese were killed or wounded and a 90-mm mortar crew was knocked out of action. The Japanese advance then faltered and failed. With the withdrawal of the 13th Infantry, failure of the 229th to win ground in its frontal attack, and the complete inability of the SNLF to participate, Sasaki's attack came to a disappointing end. Recommended for Medals of Honor for their key roles in saving the beachhead, Wantuck and Rothschild were instead each awarded the Navy Cross.[5]

With the 169th greatly in need of relief, the 37th Division's 148th Infantry came forward and attempted to reach it by way of the Munda Trail. Delayed by a series of ambushes, the 148th Infantry relieved the 169th on 20 July, after which the 169th withdrew to Rendova for rest and reorganization and to serve as reserve. Also committed were the 43rd Division's 103rd Infantry and the 37th Division's 145th Infantry. The 145th and 148th regiments were understrength because their 3rd battalions were serving with Liversedge. Consequently, the 161st Infantry was borrowed from the 25th Division and attached to the 37th Division, which reverted to the command of Major General Robert S. Beightler.

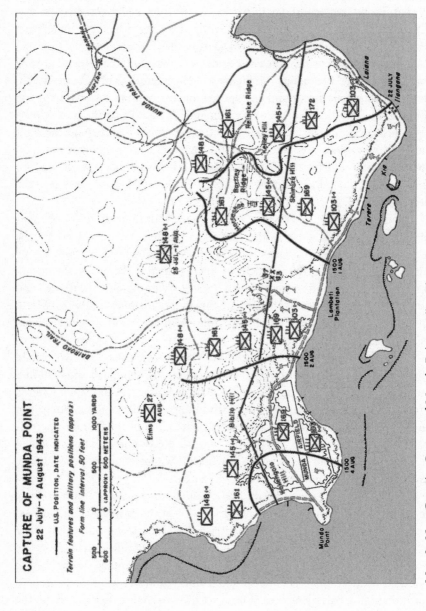

Map 3. New Georgia: Capture of Munda Point (Miller, *The U.S. Army in World War II—The War in the Pacific: Cartwheel*, 145)

By 25 July, Griswold's forces were in position for the drive on Munda along a four-thousand-yard front. The 43rd Division was at left, with its 103rd Infantry at the coast near Ilangana and the 172nd Infantry on the division right. Next in line, in the 37th Division sector, was the 145th Infantry, followed by the 161st Infantry and, at the far right flank and covering the rear, the 148th Infantry.

The plan called for the 37th Division to direct its main attack toward Bibilo Hill that overlooked Munda, while on the left the 43rd aimed for Lambeti Plantation at the coast near the eastern edge of Munda airfield. Opposing them, Sasaki's 229th Regiment occupied a dense line of pillboxes, largely sited on jungle-covered hills, extending from Ilangana on the coast to the front of the 161st. Farther north, the Japanese 13th Infantry prepared to strike Beightler's right flank but was pre-empted when Griswold moved first.[6]

Like Bloody Buna, what followed was a grueling battle of attrition, with daily success measured not in miles but yards. Also like Buna, the fighting was too close to permit close air support.[7] Even along the coastline, where naval gunfire and offshore artillery could conduct massive bombardments of the enemy front and rear, no meaningful gains were made the first day of the offensive. In the 172nd sector, three tanks were disabled attempting to take out pillboxes, while five others could not negotiate the steep slopes. A notable exception to the pace of the offensive occurred the second day, 26 July. With infantry, tanks, heavy weapons, and artillery working effectively together, and with the initial use of flame throwers, seventy-four pillboxes were eliminated. Gaining eight hundred yards, the 103rd Infantry tightened its position by reducing the front by three hundred yards. But from then until month's end, the 43rd scored few gains, and progress by the 37th was little better. As a measure of the severity of the fighting, all three Medals of Honor awarded for New Georgia involved actions during these last days of July.

At the left of the 37th Division's front, the 145th Infantry encountered particularly strong defenses attacking Horseshoe Hill and Bartley Ridge. In this sector, medic Private First Class Frank J. Petrarca administered first aid to casualties from small arms and mortar fire at great risk and was killed by mortar fire in attempting to reach a wounded soldier on 31 July. His Medal of Honor citation notes that this had been the third occasion Petrarca acted above and beyond the call of duty. To the left of the 145th, in the 43rd Division sector, fighting centered on Shimizu Hill, the last significant height before Munda. Using a carbine and grenades, Lieutenant Robert S. Scott with the 172nd held a vital position on 29 July, and although wounded single-handedly repelled a Japanese counterattack.[8]

At the far right, finding no fixed Japanese defenses on their front, the 148th Infantry made substantial advances. Hovering at their northern flank, however, was the Japanese 13th Infantry that attacked their exposed supply line. The regiment also found itself isolated as the rapid advance caused it to lose touch with the 161st at its left rear. While the 148th attempted to re-establish contact with the 161st by withdrawing in that direction, a platoon of B Company was pinned down by fire from a single enemy machine gun. Private Rodger W. Young then chose to crawl toward the gun and eliminate it. Wounded by the first burst of fire and again during his advance, Young destroyed the position using grenades, but he was killed while his unit withdrew to safety.[9]

On the fifth day of the offensive, believing Hester "had lost too much sap," Harmon relieved him. There were no repercussions except that Nimitz later gently reproved Halsey for not having first informed him. Needing a hard-driving leader for the 43rd in the final push to Munda, Harmon borrowed the commander of the uncommitted Americal Division, Major General John R. Hodge, who had performed impressively as assistant commander of the 25th Division on Guadalcanal.

With every expectation that the battle of attrition would continue, evidence was obtained on 1 August that the Japanese might be withdrawing, which was soon confirmed by several patrols. Constant air attacks and artillery bombardment, together with ground attacks by the now seasoned infantry supported by armor, had weakened Sasaki's forces more than the Americans realized. With his 229th Infantry reduced to little more than 1,200 effectives, Sasaki received orders to abandon his defenses and Munda airfield. Although strong Japanese resistance continued at Kokengolo Hill and Bibilo Hill, both were taken by 5 August. A month later than originally expected, Halsey was informed by radio that Munda had fallen, to which he responded with an orally issued "custody receipt for Munda," adding "Keep 'em dying."[10]

Munda airfield, objective of the New Georgia campaign, 8 September 1943, a month after capture and extensive rehabilitation by the Seabees. (Dept. of Defense)

So far, the 43rd and 37th divisions had done most of the fighting and were badly worn. The 25th Division was now fully committed, replacing the 37th Division that then went into reserve. This move was made with great reluctance, since the 25th had been slated for Bougainville. Under Major General J. Lawton "Lightning Joe" Collins, the 25th Division had established a fine record on Guadalcanal.[11] Successively, the division's 27th and 35th infantry regiments arrived, joining the 161st that was already fighting on New Georgia.

Crossing to the north of the peninsula, 1st Battalion, 27th Infantry made contact with Liversedge's forces, while the rest of the regiment fought its way to Zieta on the west coast. Weather conditions and terrain were even worse than already encountered during the campaign, making overland supply extremely difficult and necessitating air supply. Collins, who saw much of the war in both the Pacific and Europe, would say later: "That was the worst physical ordeal I had during the whole period of the war."[12]

The Japanese were not just fleeing. As with all his actions, Sasaki planned his withdrawal well. While the 13th Infantry and the SNLF garrison at Bairoko crossed Kula Gulf to Kolombangara, the 229th Infantry and other forces moved to Baanga Island immediately across from Zieta. Equipped with two 120-mm guns, the Japanese were able to bombard Munda, making it necessary for the Americans to clear Baanga if they were to use the airfield. The 43rd Division, now led by Wing, the former assistant division commander and the division's fourth commander since the campaign began, would require ten days of hard fighting by its 169th and 172nd regiments to clear southern Baanga. At that point, ordered by 8th Fleet commander Mikawa to withdraw, Sasaki moved his troops to adjoining Arundel Island.

Sasaki hoped to build up his forces for a counterinvasion of New Georgia, which seemed possible as all troops brought to Kolombangara had thus far landed safely. The Japanese had no special concerns the night of 6–7 August, when 940 troops from the 6th and 38th divisions sailed for Kolombangara on three destroyers escorted by a fourth destroyer. Anticipating another run of the Tokyo Express, Wilkinson ordered Commander Frederick Moosbrugger at Tulagi to patrol Vella Gulf with six destroyers. Moosbrugger's ships were all equipped with radar, had extensive training in night torpedo attack, and, not tied to a cruiser force, would enjoy complete freedom of maneuver.

First alerted by a patrol aircraft that spotted the Japanese ships north of Bougainville, Moosbrugger's radar picked them up ten miles distant in Vella Gulf. Arranged in two columns, his destroyers closed to 6,300 yards, at which point the column to port launched twenty-four torpedoes. Lacking radar, the Japanese would not sight Moosbrugger for another three minutes, and then it was too late. Torpedoes scored multiple hits on the three troop-carrying destroyers, which were disabled and then sent to the bottom by gunfire and more torpedoes. The

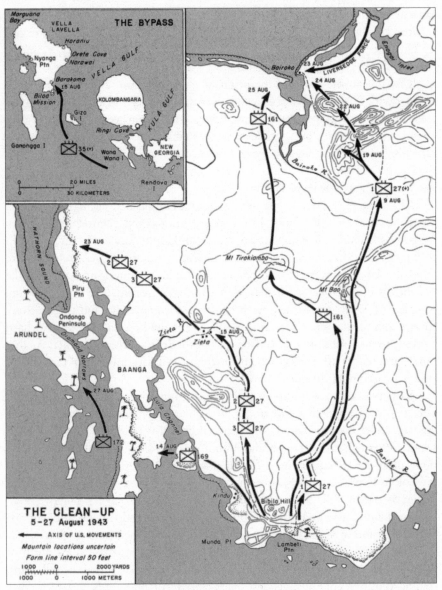

Map 4. New Georgia: Final Phase and Vella Lavella (Miller, *The U.S. Army in World War II—The War in the Pacific: Cartwheel*, 166)

surviving destroyer, which narrowly escaped destruction, made smoke and fled. The waters were full of Japanese soldiers and sailors who all refused rescue,[13] the only survivors being 310 who made it to Vella Lavella. At the Battle of Vella Gulf, the Japanese lost 1,210 soldiers and sailors and learned that they no longer enjoyed clear superiority in destroyer operations.[14] Thereafter, Mikawa would be unwilling to risk additional reinforcement runs to enable Sasaki to recapture New Georgia.

During the final stage of one of the Pacific's worst-fought battles, Halsey scored an outstanding success. The original plan called for the capture of Vila airfield on Kolombangara after Munda was taken. But that idea became highly unattractive when intelligence reports disclosed that Sasaki had 12,000 troops on the island in well-developed defensive positions and that unsuitable soil conditions would limit Vila's usefulness as an Allied air base. When it was suggested that Kolombangara be sidestepped and Vella Lavella, fifteen miles to the northwest, be occupied instead, Halsey leapt at the proposal.[15] Such an operation, known as "leap-frogging," had worked successfully in the Aleutians, where Kiska was bypassed and Attu attacked instead.[16] Without knowing how strongly the Japanese might retaliate, and unable to fully isolate Kolombangara, it was an especially audacious move by Halsey at that point in the war.

Allied reconnaissance in late July had identified Barakoma on the southeast coast as a promising location for an airfield and small naval base. Remarkably, given its strategic position, the Japanese had ignored Vella Lavella, the only enemy there being barely armed survivors from the three destroyers sunk in Vella Gulf. But while ground opposition would not be a concern, Japanese air and naval opposition would present a considerable danger given the proximity of bases in the Shortlands, at Bougainville, and Rabaul. Those airfields were bombed intensively by AirSols in the week before the invasion, including attacks by Marine fighters operating from Munda's rapidly repaired and improved airstrip and from Segi Point.

Before dawn on 15 August, seven destroyer-transports transferred their troops to landing craft, vehicle and personnel (LCVPs) for a run to the beach, followed later by twelve landing craft, infantry (LCIs) and then three landing ship, tanks (LSTs). With the efficiency that became a hallmark of Wilkinson's landings during the war, 4,600 troops and plentiful supplies were brought ashore. Army forces came principally from the 25th Division's 35th Regimental Combat Team (RCT), under the command of assistant division commander Brigadier General Robert B. McClure.

When news of the invasion was received at Rabaul, it was decided that available troops and transports were insufficient for a counterlanding. The Japanese would commit only 390 men to Vella Lavella. They were sent to Horaniu on the northeast coast to establish a staging base for barge movements between the Shortlands and Kolombangara.[17] As expected, the Japanese struck back strongly from the air, first by a flight of fifty-four dive bombers and fighters at midmorning, then a similar force of fifty-nine aircraft after noon, and a final late afternoon strike by eight aircraft. Thanks to good fighter cover provided by Munda-based aircraft and to effective anti-aircraft fire, particularly by LSTs that had tripled their standard armament, the Japanese aircraft failed to hit any shipping. Lieutenant Ken Walsh boldly led five Corsairs against an enemy air formation during which he made his eleventh, twelfth, and thirteenth kills. Fifteen days later, over Kahili on Bougainville, Walsh would take on approximately fifty enemy aircraft by himself, downing four of them before crash landing his badly shot up plane off Vella Lavella, a feat of bravery that earned Walsh the Medal of Honor.[18] At a cost of at least seventeen planes they would admit losing on invasion day, Japanese aircraft returned to base with reports of great success although they only succeeded in downing two AirSols planes and killing twelve and wounding fifty troops on the beach. Much the same happened the next month, during which 319 Japanese aircraft conducted 108 attacks that failed to inflict any significant damage.

While the Barakoma base was being developed, McClure's forces advanced up the island and flushed the Japanese out of Horaniu. On 18 September, his troops were relieved on Vella Lavella by the 3rd New Zealand Division's 14th Brigade Group,[19] commanded by Brigadier Leslie Potter.

Troops of the 3rd New Zealand Division's 14th Brigade Group land on Vella Lavella, 18 September 1943. (U.S. Army)

Setting out along both coasts, Potter's New Zealanders attempted to corner roughly six hundred Japanese who had withdrawn to the northwest shore of the island. The Americans and New Zealanders incurred fewer than two hundred casualties during these operations. Sasaki's forces at Kolombangara were outflanked and Halsey acquired an important base for future operations against Bougainville and Rabaul.

As the Vella Lavella operation proceeded, the 172nd Infantry landed unopposed on Arundel Island on 27 August, expecting an easy mopup, and advanced for five days without encountering the enemy. Sasaki, however, was far from defeated. Still nurturing ambitions to reclaim Munda, he was reinforced from Vila by elements of the 13th Infantry. Japanese resistance was so strong that Griswold was forced to commit a variety of additional units, including the 27th Infantry, two battalions of the 169th, and several Marine tanks. Even this enlarged force had tough going until the night of 20–21 September, when the Japanese abruptly withdrew to Kolombangara.

An Imperial decision to evacuate the central Solomons prompted the evacuation of Arundel. Those forces were needed to strengthen Bougainville, Halsey's obvious next target. To evacuate more than 12,000 men from Kolombangara, the Japanese used 75 daihatsus (landing barges able to hold up to 120 men) plus a variety of other craft, with destroyers providing protective screens. Avoiding detection by clever camouflage during the day, the Japanese vessels dashed away under cover of night, skillfully evading the American radar-equipped destroyers. On three nights between 28 September and 3 October, 9,400 Japanese were spirited away to Choiseul and Bougainville.

A final evacuation run was staged the night of 6–7 October to bring out the 600 Japanese on Vella Lavella. The force assembled by Rear Admiral Matsuji Ijuin consisted of three destroyer-transports and twelve small craft escorted by six destroyers. AirSols planes spotted Ijuin's force headed for the Slot, but Wilkinson only had one group of three destroyers under Captain Frank R. Walker in position to intercept. To support Walker, Wilkinson detached three destroyers under Captain Harold O. Larson from convoy duty south of New Georgia with orders to race north.

Aware of Walker's approach from reconnaissance aircraft reports, Ijuin detached the destroyer-transports and small craft. To confuse his adversary, Ijuin posted two of his six destroyers eight miles from the main body. Expecting to be outnumbered, Walker pressed forward, hoping to push the battle south toward Larson. While the two forces groped in the darkness to fix their opponent's positions, Ijuin executed a series of maneuvers that lost him the opportunity to cap Walker's "T." When the forces were seven thousand yards apart, the battle began, although sources disagree as to which side delivered the first blow.[20]

Walker's three destroyers fired fourteen torpedoes and then commenced firing their 5-inch guns. One torpedo found *Yugumo* and heavily damaged the ship, which took further hits and soon went down. But by then *Yugumo* had launched her own torpedoes, one of them hitting USS *Chevalier*, detonating her magazine and blowing off the bow. USS *O'Bannon*, next in line, collided with *Chevalier* and was put out of the fight, leaving USS *Selfridge* with Walker on board as the only American vessel remaining in the fight. Walker valiantly charged the two destroyers detached by Ijuin, but fell afoul of their long lance torpedoes before getting in range to launch his own torpedoes. A torpedo destroyed the *Selfridge*'s forecastle, caused much flooding, and brought the destroyer to a stop.

Before Ijuin could deliver a coup de grâce, Walker was saved by the approach of Larson's destroyers. Mistaking Larson's ships for cruisers that he felt disinclined to fight, Ijuin promptly retired to Rabaul. While Larson's ships stayed busy assisting Walker's shattered force, saving *Selfridge* and sinking the hopelessly crippled *Chevalier*, the Vella Lavella evacuees were transported safely to Bougainville.

As one authority observed wryly, "Captain Walker should certainly have waited for Larson's destroyers—but he seemed to have a little bit of *banzai* in him, too."[21] Both sides claimed victory based on imagined sinkings, but there was no question that the Japanese had come out on top.[22] The Battle of Vella Lavella, the final substantial naval action of the New Georgia campaign, clearly demonstrated that the Japanese destroyers were still formidable opponents.

Thus ended the campaign. The Japanese had endeavored to hold out as long as possible, providing time to strengthen their defenses elsewhere. They succeeded in meeting that objective, holding off greatly superior forces for more than three months. Much of the credit belonged to the intelligent generalship of Sasaki, who carefully deployed his forces, chose his fights well, and avoided wasting manpower in fruitless attacks. Fortunately for the Allies, they would never again face Sasaki, who gained a star and served out the war as a commander at Rabaul. Important, too, were the skilled Japanese destroyer commanders and crews who adroitly employed their deadly long lance torpedoes. They prevented the isolation of New Georgia, enabling Sasaki to draw supplies and reinforcements throughout the campaign and, at the end, to evacuate his forces to fight again.

Some historians have questioned the necessity of the Munda campaign. Initially, MacArthur believed that after he landed at Cape Gloucester, Halsey could immediately leap from Guadalcanal and the Russells to Bougainville. It was only because Halsey and Harmon insisted that an intermediate base within fighter plane range of Bougainville was needed that the New Georgia operation was included in Cartwheel. Considering the ease with which Segi Point on New Georgia and Barakoma on Vella Lavella were seized for airfields, and the ability of American artillery from captured offshore islands to neutralize Munda airfield, the objectives of the campaign might plausibly have been achieved otherwise.

Still, Halsey's caution was perfectly reasonable at this stage of the war, before Japanese weaknesses were fully apparent and before great leapfrog movements became commonplace.

Much had gone wrong on New Georgia. An inexperienced division was introduced to jungle fighting under the worst possible conditions, while the experienced 25th Division was left out of the fight until desperation forced its use.[23] Further, a division commander was unnecessarily burdened with responsibilities that prevented him and his staff from devoting their full energies to division operations. Among the tactical errors, Morison felt that the worst was not beginning New Georgia by landing at Laiana and, once realizing that Laiana was needed, not taking it from the sea and abandoning Zanana.[24] Another serious error was expecting Liversedge to take Bairoko without heavy weapons, wasting valuable seasoned troops for little benefit. Although tanks were sometimes used to good effect, their availability in greater numbers could have substantially reduced infantry casualties.[25] Also, although Allied aircraft did well against enemy beach defenses, for lack of better ground liaison they were unable to help the infantry advance significantly in the heavy jungle.[26]

More general in its criticism, the official U.S. Army history noted that "ground units were shuffled in a manner that no experienced Army commander would have tolerated."[27] For many reasons, a campaign that was expected to require a single division ultimately required three Army divisions and several Marine battalions, a total of more than 50,000 men, and it would have continued much longer if the Japanese high command had not ordered evacuation.

The official American casualty count for New Georgia was 1,094 killed and 3,873 wounded in action.[28] These numbers exclude the thousands who were evacuated suffering from disease and battle fatigue. No casualty count from the Japanese side exists, although Griswold's troops counted 2,483 enemy dead. Factoring in the many American noncombat casualties, their losses possibly exceeded the Japanese.[29]

Yet there were decided positives on the American side. Although they paid a much higher price than necessary, the Allies gained valuable airfields from which Rabaul and Bougainville could be relentlessly and intensively attacked. More effective tactics using flame throwers were worked out for attacking Japanese pillboxes.[30] Also, despite their uneven performance, the usefulness of tanks in jungle warfare was demonstrated sufficiently so they would become standard elements in later operations.

This difficult campaign also provided invaluable experience for Army generals who would work as a team on Bougainville.[31] Griswold had his first opportunity to lead a corps in combat. Beightler gained valuable field experience as head of the 37th Division, as did Hodge, who returned to the Americal Division after temporarily leading the 43rd Division on New Georgia.

New Georgia would be the last campaign in the South Pacific for the 25th and 43rd divisions, both of which required recuperation and would later see much fighting with MacArthur. For "Lightning Joe" Collins, New Georgia would be his last Pacific campaign, as General Dwight D. Eisenhower needed a corps commander with combat and amphibious experience. Collins would distinguish himself in Europe and rise to become Army chief of staff in the postwar years.

Perhaps most important, Halsey grew as a commander. His readiness to take immediate action as soon as Hester's problems became apparent would be praised in the official Army history as "a mark of the efficiency of the South Pacific command and the close co-operation between the Army and Navy commanders in the area."[32] Taking a calculated risk with his warships and transports to seize virtually undefended Vella Lavella, Halsey's success, in the judgment of one noted historian, "must rank him among the great admirals of history."[33] Thereafter, sidestepping areas of enemy strength would be a hallmark of Halsey's operations as South Pacific Area commander.

Halsey also learned some painful lessons in the art of command. At Guadalcanal, his ground forces had excellent leadership under Vandegrift, whom he would call "my other self,"[34] and later under Patch. In marked contrast, in the initial phase of New Georgia, an untried general was entrusted to execute a complex plan beyond his capacity. While new leadership under Griswold finally brought success, the entire battle would clearly have gone differently with better ground leadership from the start. This goes far in explaining Halsey's conduct later in a crisis of command leading up to the invasion of Bougainville.

Learning from his experiences, Halsey would conduct his next South Pacific campaign in a manner that would prompt the authors of an authoritative study to write, "[Bougainville] stands as an example of the manner in which the entire Solomons fighting should have been waged."[35]

# CHAPTER 6

---oℝo---

# "Lae and Salamaua Must Be Defended to the Death"

After the Japanese occupied Salamaua and Lae in March 1942, several irregular Australian companies waged guerrilla war against them from Wau, an isolated gold mining settlement. Known as Kanga Force, the Australians depended entirely on air supply. In January 1943, as the Buna campaign drew to a close, the Japanese decided to wipe out the Wau base to prevent an Allied advance from there into the Huon Peninsula. Also, one trail in the Wau area led to Port Moresby and could be used by the Japanese for a renewed overland offensive.

On 28 January, using a hidden jungle track, a three-thousand-man detachment from the Japanese 51st Division advanced within six miles of Wau before it was detected. The five hundred defenders desperately held off the Japanese while reinforcements were flown in from the Australian 3rd Division's 17th Brigade. Possession of the airstrip then became the key to the battle. According to one account, with the Japanese at the edge of the strip, "some of the Australians literally came out of the planes with their guns firing . . . troop carriers circled the field until the Aussies below hand grenaded the Japanese far enough back into the jungle to permit a landing."[1] The Australians held, and numerical superiority was achieved with the arrival of the rest of the 17th Brigade. The Japanese, unable to take Wau and short of supplies, fell back on Salamaua with the Australians in hot pursuit. This Australian success prompted Imamura to reinforce Lae and Salamaua, setting the stage for the disastrous Battle of the Bismarck Sea.[2]

For the next months the 17th Brigade, under the command of Brigadier Murray J. Moten, doggedly patrolled, raided, and conducted limited offensive actions in the ridges around the village of Mubo southwest of Salamaua. Even by New Guinea standards, conditions were dreadful. A 3rd Division report said, "Such conditions of rain, mud, rottenness, stench, gloom, and, above all, the feeling of being shut in by everlasting jungle and ever ascending mountains, are sufficient to fray the strongest nerves. But add to them the tension of the constant expectancy of death from behind the impenetrable screen of green."[3] With insufficient numbers to achieve a major breakthrough and with substantial reinforcements unavailable while the Australians recovered from the fierce fighting at Gona and Sanananda, a stalemate developed.

Kanga Force was dissolved in April when 3rd Division commander Major General Stanley G. Savige arrived and established his headquarters at Bulolo, northwest of Wau. Savige was ordered to safeguard the Wau airfield and to develop the Wau-Bulolo area as a base for future operations. The Bulolo and other river valleys radiating into the Huon Peninsula and northwest toward Madang would become major avenues for Allied movements.

To lead the growing American ground forces in Australia, the American Sixth Army was established in February 1943 under the command of Prussianborn Lieutenant General Walter Krueger. A former commander of the Third Army, Krueger and his chief of staff, Colonel Dwight D. Eisenhower, won much attention by scoring a decisive victory in the 1941 Louisiana maneuvers.[4] MacArthur expressly asked Marshall for Krueger but would later become highly critical of Krueger's methodical style. While deeply concerned about the welfare of his fighting men, Krueger angered many subordinates for his sour disposition and lack of support, none more so than Eichelberger, his corps commander.

Disliking the idea of having American troops report to a foreign commander, MacArthur devised a means of keeping them out of Blamey's hands. For Cartwheel, an independent tactical organization called Alamo Force was formed with essentially the same components as the Sixth Army to conduct operations directly under MacArthur. Through this device, Blamey's New Guinea Force was left in control of only Australian troops and those American units attached for particular operations, while the Americans otherwise operated independently.[5]

In creating Alamo Force, MacArthur was high-handed in not clearing his action with the Australian and American governments[6] or even consulting with Blamey, who was understandably displeased about his diminished authority. Nevertheless, the official Australian history recognized the logic behind Alamo, observing that "if separate roles could be found for the Australian and the American Armies, difficulties inseparable from the coordination of forces possessing differing organisation and doctrines could be avoided."[7]

MacArthur's navy also underwent change. In accordance with the fleet numbering system instituted by Admiral King in March 1943, Carpender's still very small force, which included Australian, American, and Netherlands vessels, was designated the Seventh Fleet. Before then, Rear Admiral Daniel E. Barbey arrived to transform MacArthur's seaborne operations, much as Kenney had done for his air operations.

Euphoniously dubbed "Uncle Dan the Amphibious Man," Barbey had organized an amphibious warfare section on King's staff in 1942. Immersed in the
testing and development of landing craft, shallow-water vessels, and amphibious
vehicles, he developed an in-depth knowledge of their capabilities and understood how best to employ them. Arriving in the South Pacific in January 1943,
Barbey took command of what would later be designated the VII Amphibious
Force and commenced training using the limited number of attack transports,
LCTs, and LCIs available.

Barbey's first opportunity to test his ideas was in the Trobriand Island landings. Located between New Guinea and the Solomons, the Trobriands were
MacArthur's initial Cartwheel targets. They were wanted principally for use as
fighter plane bases from which escorts could support long-range bombers in their
attacks on Rabaul.

Finding no Japanese present, advance parties laid out markers to guide
the main landings, conducted on 30 June by the reinforced 158th Infantry
and 112th Cavalry regiments. With more threatening Allied movements under
way at Rendova and Nassau Bay that day, Alamo Force's inaugural operation,
code named Chronicle, drew no immediate interest from the Japanese. Later
the invasion force attracted only two small bomber raids. Over the next weeks
a total of 16,000 troops occupied the islands, and airstrip construction began.
Beginning in July, American and Australian fighter squadrons, based respectively
on Woodlark and Kiriwina islands, flew bomber escort missions against Rabaul,
Kavieng on New Ireland, and the northern Solomons.

Frozen out of the operation, Blamey withheld his anger for his memoirs,
where he derisively commented, "It was hailed as a fine operation of war by the
news hungry. It was in fact one of the jokes of the war. . . . It had the effect of
holding up material and vessels urgently required for the following operations
against Lae."[8] Also critical but more objective, Morison concluded that pouring
substantial resources into the Trobriands was unjustified considering the limited
useful lives of the bases once the war moved westward. But otherwise, "as an
amphibious experiment, the bloodless occupation was a thumping success. Good
theories were proved, bad ones discarded, confidence imparted to Uncle Dan's
webfeet. Before the war was over, VII 'Phib would have over fifty amphibious
landings to its credit."[9]

Ultimately more useful was the simultaneous landing at Nassau Bay, New
Guinea, which had multiple objectives. Australian forces in the Wau area had
until then been supplied by aircraft and native carriers. A coastal base would ease
the supply situation and enable the maintenance of larger forces for conquest of
the Huon Gulf region. With few Japanese in the area, Nassau Bay was attractive
for its proximity to Australian-held areas in the interior and to Salamaua, twenty
miles to the north. Also, looking toward a later amphibious attack, Nassau Bay
was within sixty miles of Lae, the maximum distance considered feasible for a

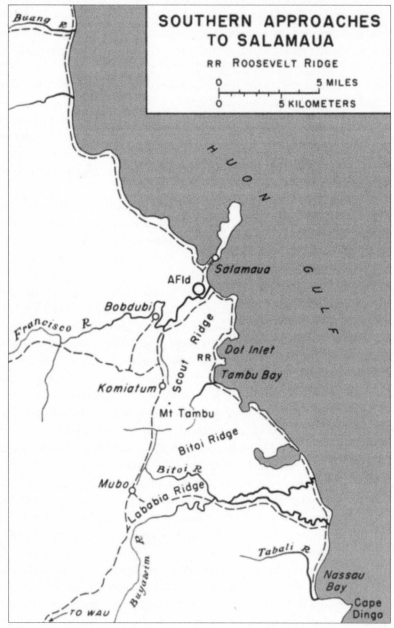

**Map 5. Southern Approaches to Salamaua** (Miller, *The U.S. Army in World War II—The War in the Pacific: Cartwheel*, 62)

shore-to-shore operation. After the landing, the invasion troops were expected to move inland and with Australian forces clear the Japanese from the Mubo area nearby.[10]

No immediate attempt would be made to capture Salamaua. Blamey hoped to lure the Japanese into reinforcing Salamaua, then trap them there by striking their weakened rear at Lae.[11] Kenney believed that Blamey's strategy was motivated by self-interest, theorizing that it was adopted so Australian troops would be left in charge of land operations on New Guinea. An early move against Salamaua, as Kenney saw it, would force Blamey to commit the Australian 7th and 9th Divisions, leaving him insufficient strength to capture Lae and providing an opening for Krueger to bring in the Americans.[12]

Ten days before the scheduled Nassau Bay landings, the Japanese threatened a key height near Mubo, placing the invasion follow-up plan in jeopardy. Lababia Ridge, occupied by a single company of the 17th Brigade's 2/6 Battalion, was surrounded by an estimated 750 Japanese. Rather than trying to stay well-hidden, the defenders removed the ground cover to obtain clear fields of fire. Every weapon at hand, including the bayonet, was used to beat off repeated attacks. When rifle ammunition ran low, the company commander forbade lengthy bursts of fire, ordering "keep your bloody fingers off the trigger." Recognizing the threat, Moten signaled on 21 June, "Postern (code name for the planned capture of Lae) prejudiced by enemy occupation of Lababia Ridge" and called for immediate action. Inexplicably, the Japanese left a hole in the ring, enabling a second company to slip into the perimeter. Finally, on 23 June, pounded by RAAF Beaufighters, the Japanese broke off the action. After the war, Adachi revealed that the 150 Australian defenders faced not 750 Japanese, as had been estimated, but the entire 1,500-man 66th Regiment. At a cost of 11 killed and 12 wounded, the Australians inflicted 172 casualties. Savige lauded the Lababia Ridge defense as "one of the classic engagements of the war."[13]

The Nassau Bay invasion was conducted by the 1st Battalion, 162nd Infantry of the American 41st Division. In command of the battalion was Lieutenant Colonel Harold Taylor, with regimental commander Colonel Archibald R. MacKechnie in overall command of what became known as MacKechnie Force. Nassau Bay was unique as the only Cartwheel operation in which major American forces served under Australian command.[14] Once established ashore, 17th Brigade commander Moten and 3rd Division commander Savige expected that the 162nd would come under their leadership.

For the landings, 210 men were brought in on PT boats and 770 arrived on LCVPs provided by the 532nd Engineer Boat and Shore Regiment (EBSR). Army personnel with nautical experience manned the EBSR landing craft. These soldiers were trained to deliver men and equipment to invasion beaches and then organize the beachheads as unified operations. Three Engineer Special Brigades served in the theater during the war, performing an essential role in MacArthur's amphibious campaigns.

The approximately 150 Japanese in the area offered no resistance and promptly fled. This was fortunate because the landings did not go smoothly. In the dark, rainy night, guidance signals set up by advance parties went unseen, causing the PT boats to lose their way and leave the slower LCVPs in the lurch. The ten- to twelve-foot surf tossed the landing craft so violently they broached or were thrust too far ashore to back off the beach. Radios were soaked and rendered unusable, severing MacKechnie from communication with his head-quarters and air support. No PTs were able to land and only 770 men waded ashore that night.

Australian forces assisted the arriving Americans, including native troops from the Papuan Infantry Battalion and Australian troops from Lababia Ridge, who prepared a path from the inland battlefield to the beach. The Aussies would wryly refer to the second night on shore as "Guy Fawkes night," during which the green Americans fired wildly at every real or imagined form in the pitch dark-ness. The battalion lost eighteen killed and twenty-seven wounded, many (per-haps most) from friendly fire.[15] The following day, 2 July, the rest of the battalion including battalion commander Taylor arrived, and contact was established with the Australian 17th Brigade.

The disorganized landings made for a chaotic supply situation. Savige and Moten assumed that MacKechnie Force would come under Australian tacti-cal control once on shore. MacKechnie, though, believed that he was subject to orders of his division commander, Major General Horace Fuller, as well as Moten. Shocked on hearing about beachhead conditions, Fuller insisted that MacKechnie not advance until he had a reliable line of supply. Backed by Fuller, MacKechnie told Moten that he would be unable to move into the interior for three weeks until a supply road was finished, which would have upended Savige's offensive plan.[16] Fortunately, before the crisis came to a head, the supply situa-tion was sufficiently relieved to induce MacKechnie to advance to Bitoi Ridge, north of Lababia Ridge, to participate with the 17th Brigade in a planned attack.

On 7 July, preceded by intensive bombing by 159 Allied bombers and fight-ers and shelling by American artillery, the offensive opened with an attack on the high ground north of Mubo. The 17th Brigade moved against Observation Hill while the Americans attacked Bitoi Ridge to the east. Mubo village and airfield fell within the week, after which the few surviving Japanese retreated to the southwest.[17] But farther north and nearer Salamaua, the 58th/59th Battalion[18] of the 15th Brigade, in its introduction to combat, failed to penetrate the strong Japanese defenses on Bobdubi Ridge.

During this time, an inter-Allied imbroglio even more serious than the earlier one arose, caused again by unclear command relationships. Nassau Bay was too distant for artillery there to bombard Salamaua and support 3rd Division operations in the Bobdubi Ridge area. Another of MacKechnie's battalions, 3/162, was therefore ordered to advance up the coast to Tambu Bay and establish artillery positions there. While Herring diplomatically allowed Fuller to command this operation, Savige misunderstood Herring's intent, believing he was to exercise command as with MacKechnie Force.

Matters came to a head after Fuller appointed his division artillery commander, Brigadier General Ralph W. Coane, to lead what became known as Coane Force. MacKechnie and Savige were entirely surprised when Fuller advised MacKechnie that 3/162, now known as Coane Force, would hereafter report to Fuller. Unfortunately, when Savige asked Herring for clarification, he received an ambiguous response that left Savige with the impression that he exercised full control of both the Coane and MacKechnie forces.

The situation grew more inflamed after the 3/162 battalion commander, Major Archibald B. Roosevelt, son of President Theodore Roosevelt, received an order from Moten and waspishly responded, "I have no such orders from my commanding officer. As a piece of friendly advice your plans show improper reconnaissance and lack of logistical understanding. Suggest you send competent liaison officer . . . to study situation." After this remarkably undiplomatic missive, Roosevelt wrote an equally inflammatory message to Fuller, concluding, "In my opinion the orders show lamentable lack of intelligence and knowledge of situation and it is possible that disgrace or disaster may be the result of their actions."[19]

Embarrassed by his subordinate, MacKechnie apologized to Moten. Fuller's ire fell fully on MacKechnie, who was relieved for a variety of transgressions, including going inland without clearing the beaches, reporting that there was command confusion while in fact there was none [!!], and taking orders from the Australians without consulting his superior.[20] The ugly dispute was finally resolved when the tactical situation changed, making it practical to place Coane Force under the operational control of the Australian 3rd Division. Also, Fuller relented a bit and permitted MacKechnie to join Coane Force as executive commander. The official Australian history observed that "it was surprising that there should have been such a sorry period of doubt about who was commanding what."[21] Two such mix-ups in rapid succession support the wisdom of MacArthur's efforts to keep the Australian and American forces apart.

After the 17th Brigade's Mubo area success, fighting by the Australian 3rd Division during July and early August produced few gains against Japanese hill positions. Considering it vital to hold the Bobdubi Ridge area, Lieutenant General Hidemitsu Nakano, commanding at Salamaua, went forward to personally direct operations in July. At the coast, after reaching Tambu Bay and establishing American and Australian artillery positions, Coane failed to take the high ground to the north dubbed Roosevelt Ridge, leaving the coastal base in jeopardy. Coane's protestations that he lacked sufficient forces to take the ridge drew a critical response from Savige, who pointed out that Coane had greater strength than Australian units involved in no less difficult missions elsewhere.[22]

By mid-August, the Allies' situation had improved considerably. By strenuous effort, the 17th Brigade cleared the Japanese from Salamaua's outer defense line along Bobdubi and Komiatum ridges and at Mount Tambu. Savige, a veteran of warfare on four continents, called the fighting there "the toughest operational problem" he ever faced. Exhausted, the 3rd Division was withdrawn on 24 August, replaced by Major General Edward J. Milford's 5th Division.

At Tambu Bay, Roosevelt Ridge was finally taken on 13 August. Then, having outlived its usefulness as an independent command, Coane Force was dissolved. Coane returned to the 41st Division base in Australia and MacKechnie resumed command of his entire regiment, including 2/162 and 3/162 at Tambu Bay and 1/162 that reunited with them after the Mount Tambu fighting. Since landing at Nassau Bay, the 162nd Regiment's casualties were 102 killed and 447 wounded.

In the air, in coordination with the commencement of Cartwheel, B-17s and B-24s heavily bombed Rabaul in the first days of July, and at Nassau Bay A-20s helped the beachhead defense with bombing and strafing attacks. Virtually every day during July, heavy and medium bombers targeted Japanese troop concentrations, supply lines, and airfields in the Lae-Salamaua area. On 13 July, Mubo was softened up by a force of more than forty B-25s and a dozen heavy bombers "in an exhibition of faultless bombing which permitted the capture to be made without casualty."[23]

Meanwhile, the Japanese had developed Wewak as their principal air base on New Guinea. During June and July, two hundred aircraft were moved there from Rabaul as Wewak became headquarters for the Japanese 4th Air Army. Thanks to Ultra intelligence, Kenney was kept apprised of the aircraft buildup and planned its destruction.[24]

Fighter coverage was necessary for bombers to mount a sustained attack on such a heavily defended target. As the distance to Wewak from Kenney's New Guinea bases exceeded fighter plane range, a strip nearer the target than Wau was needed for refueling. A search turned up a derelict airstrip fifty miles from Lae that met the requirements but would become unusable in the rainy season. A better-situated abandoned airstrip was then discovered nearby at Tsili Tsili. Improved by native workers and defended by a thousand-man Australian infantry battalion and an American anti-aircraft battery, the strip had C-47s landing there beginning in early July. As a diversion while Tsili Tsili was being developed, a dummy field was created that the Japanese attacked, as hoped. The Japanese did not discover Tsili Tsili until mid-August, and they then conducted just two bombing raids.

Once Tsili Tsili was ready, Kenney unleashed his heaviest air attacks since the Battle of the Bismarck Sea. The initial attack began before dawn on 17

August with the bombing of the four Wewak-area airfields by forty-one B-24s and twelve B-17s. Three fields were struck again two hours later by thirty-three B-25s covered by eighty-three P-38s. Employing machine guns and parafrag bombs, the B-25s caught a large force of Japanese fighters and bombers preparing to take off on a raid. The air strike was spectacular, setting off explosions as guns and bombs hit the gassed-up and bomb-laden aircraft. The Japanese would call that day "the Black Day of August 17th."[25]

According to postwar analysis, the estimated score for attacks through the end of August was 175 Japanese aircraft destroyed at a cost of 22 Allied planes lost in operations and accidentally. One Allied casualty, incurred on the second day of the battle, was the aircraft of Major Ralph Cheli. Leading the principal B-25 formation, Cheli's plane was attacked and set afire while still two miles from the target. Rejecting the option of climbing to a higher altitude and bailing out, which would have disrupted the operation, Cheli continued to lead the low-level attack that destroyed every enemy aircraft on the field. Finally able to break formation and gain altitude, Cheli's aircraft exploded and fell into the sea. For his selfless conduct, Cheli was awarded the Medal of Honor.[26]

Whatever the merit of Kenney's suspicions about Blamey's objectives in delaying the capture of Salamaua, the arduous campaign, borne primarily by the Australians, succeeded brilliantly. At the start of the Allied offensive that began in early September, approximately 5,000 Japanese were committed to the defense of Salamaua, leaving only about 2,500 to protect Lae.[27]

While fighting raged outside Salamaua, Japanese forces were exhorted from the Imperial throne, "The strongholds of Lae and Salamaua must be defended to the Death."[28] In September 1943 the emperor's troops would be put to the test.

# CHAPTER 7

# "Prevent Your Troops Engaging My Troops"

F or the attack on Lae, Blamey took over New Guinea Force in early September, with Herring reverting to command of I Corps.[1] Two battle-toughened Australian divisions were available for the offensive. Well-schooled in jungle fighting, Vasey's 7th Division had already seen heavy combat in Papua. They would be joined by the 9th Division "Desert Rats of Tobruk," whose magnificent service in North Africa had been crowned with victory at El Alamein. After a triumphal return to Australia in February 1943, the division underwent extensive jungle and amphibious training to prepare for warfare under very different conditions. The division also acquired a new commander, Major General George Wootten, commander of the 18th Brigade at Milne Bay and the Buna-Sanananda battles.

Blamey planned to capture Lae through a pincer movement. While the 9th Division landed in Huon Gulf and advanced from the east, the 7th Division would be flown in to the Markham Valley and move against Lae from the west. Once Lae had fallen, the 7th Division would proceed up the Markham and Ramu valleys while the 9th Division took Finschhafen. Encircling the Huon Peninsula, the two divisions would bag the Japanese there, including those lured south to defend Salamaua, clearing the way for an advance westward to Madang and Wewak.

The 5th Air Force was crucial to the plan. Kenney's aircraft would support amphibious assaults near Lae and Finschhafen, drop American paratroopers in the Markham Valley, ferry 7th Division forces to airstrips in the Markham and Ramu valleys, supply the 7th Division during its advance on Lae, and support ground operations of the two divisions.[2]

Estimating there were in excess of seven thousand Japanese in or near Lae, Wootten insisted that the full 9th Division be brought up immediately. This greatly exceeded the carrying capacity of the EBSR landing craft; moreover,

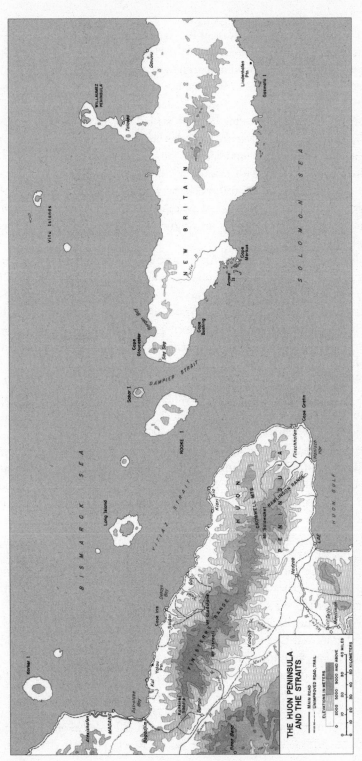

Map 6. Huon Peninsula, the Straits, and Western New Britain (Miller, *The U.S. Army in World War II—The War in the Pacific: Cartwheel*, 189)

there was fear that the chaotic Nassau Bay landing situation might be repeated. Therefore, Wootten turned to Barbey's "VII Phib," which had more and larger vessels, with EBSR forces subordinate to Barbey for this operation only.

Before operations began, a fresh dispute arose between the Americans and Australians. Major General Stephen J. Chamberlin, MacArthur's operations officer, ignited the situation after meeting with Lieutenant General Frank H. Berryman, Blamey's chief of staff. Chamberlin tore the plan of attack apart, claiming it was "elementary and incomplete . . . lacking in vision . . . [and] decentralizes control along with execution." Berryman responded that "the difference is we work on a decentralized basis whilst GHQ [MacArthur's office] have a highly centralized one." When MacArthur took Chamberlin's side, the Australians backed down, but tensions continued until the operations of the two armies fully diverged.[3]

Conflict also existed within the American camp between Barbey and Kenney, stemming from differences in Navy and Army doctrines and exacerbated by their strong personalities. While Barbey insisted on a standing air patrol over the convoy and landing beaches, Kenney advocated intense bombing and then keeping the aircraft on the ground on alert during the landings. In addition, Barbey wanted to surprise the enemy with a dawn attack while Kenney wanted to attack later to enable aircraft to take off in daylight to bomb beach positions. With neither willing to back down and Blamey without authority to settle the matter, the issue was appealed to MacArthur. Possibly to maintain interservice harmony, MacArthur decided in favor of Barbey. Kenney, however, had a deep-seated distrust of the Navy, which would continue throughout the war.[4]

Barbey's fleet that departed Milne Bay on 2 September included eight destroyers, four destroyer-transports, and numerous landing ships and craft, the largest amphibious force up to then in the Southwest Pacific theater.[5] Kenney timed the operation for a period when fog from the Vitiaz Straits to Rabaul would hide the fleet from Japanese observation. The idea worked; the only opposition encountered en route was from nine Betty bombers that scored no hits.

The morning of 4 September, after a preliminary destroyer bombardment and aircraft strafing, the 9th Division's 20th Brigade followed by the 26th Brigade landed at Bulu Plantation fifteen to eighteen miles east of Lae. The beachhead, about twenty yards wide and backed by swamps, lay just beyond range of Lae's coastal defense guns. Because of insufficient information about the waters and beach conditions and Barbey's fear of landing in the wrong place, the landings commenced twenty minutes after sunrise over the objections of Wootten.

Another limitation imposed by Barbey was that his ships would remain only until 1100, as air cover was unavailable after then because of Kenney's commitments to Vasey. Fortunately, there was no ground opposition, and by midmorning 7,800 men and their heavy equipment had landed. Before the end of the day, the 26th Brigade was across the Bungu River, one of five river barriers between the invasion force and Lae. The next evening, the division reserve, the 24th Brigade, arrived and joined the advance.

All invasion day casualties occurred offshore. During the morning, twenty were killed and many wounded by Japanese air attack on an LCI.

Later a more intense attack on two LSTs by torpedo and dive bombers from Rabaul killed and wounded many. On one LST, mortally wounded by a bomb blast, Seaman First Class Johnnie D. Hutchins grasped the wheel and steered the ship out of the path of two torpedoes before dying still clinging to the helm. Hutchins was awarded the Medal of Honor and a destroyer was named for him.

Under cover of a smokescreen, paratroopers from the American 503rd Parachute Regiment jump from C-47 transport planes at Nadzab, New Guinea, 5 September 1943. (USAAF)

The morning after the 9th Division's landing, in a massive show of air power, ninety-six C-47s from Port Moresby dropped 1,700 paratroopers of the American 503rd Parachute Infantry Regiment on an overgrown airstrip at Nadzab. Circling above in one of three "brass hat" B-17 bombers was MacArthur, jubilant over the spectacle, accompanied by a moving picture cameraman to publicize his presence. No Japanese were there, but three died and thirty-three were wounded in accidents during the jump.

Joining the Americans were Australian artillerists who insisted on jumping with their disassembled 25-pounder guns to defend the position, although as it turned out there was no need for such immediate artillery support. Marching overland with a company of Papuan infantry, an Australian pioneer battalion arrived during the afternoon. Together with the paratroopers, they labored through the night to prepare the airstrip for the arrival of the first aircraft.

The next morning, C-47s arrived with elements and equipment of an American engineer battalion that improved the strip, enabling two 7th Division brigades to be flown in by 7 September. Three days later, with Vasey's troops firmly in control of the area, the American paratroopers returned to base.

As Vasey's forces were brought forward by air, a disaster occurred at Jackson's, a rear area base. A fully loaded Lancaster bomber, flying low on takeoff, clipped a tree limb and crashed, spewing burning oil and touching off explosions. The conflagration engulfed troops on five trucks, killing fifty-nine and wounding ninety-two. All eleven on board the Lancaster died. But even a disaster of this magnitude was not allowed to impede the airlift.

Vasey and Wootten then raced each other for Lae. Torrential rains slowed both, hindering air supply for Vasey and swelling the rivers in Wootten's path. EBSR units then provided invaluable support to Wootten by transporting reinforcements and supplies through the flooded areas, a notable instance of American-Australian cooperation.[6]

Vasey's forces moved by way of the Markham Valley. At a place called Heath's Plantation, a hidden Japanese machine gun stopped a platoon. On his own initiative, Private Richard Kelliher of the 2/25 Battalion charged the machine gun

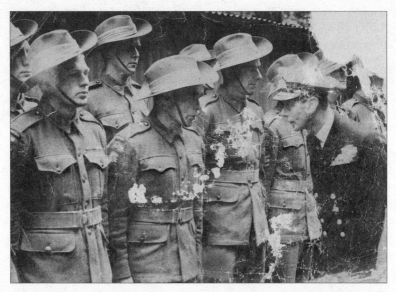

At ceremonies during the 8 June 1946 Victory Parade in London, King George VI stops to talk to Victoria Cross holder Private Richard Kelliher. Flanking Kelliher are Private Frank Partridge (at left of photo) and Sergeant Reginald Rattey (at Kelliher's left), who were awarded their Victoria Crosses for action on Bougainville. See chapter 27. (By authorization of the Australian War Memorial: P08489.001)

hurling two grenades. Obtaining a Bren gun, he charged twice and eliminated the position, then braved heavy fire to rescue his wounded section leader. Kelliher had previously been court-martialed for cowardice, which he had denied and vowed to prove untrue. More than vindicated, Kelliher was awarded the Victoria Cross and would participate in the great victory parade in London at war's end.

The Australian advance went quickly because the approximately two thousand Japanese at Lae were principally base units, with Nakano's combat forces mostly defending Salamaua. Nakano was ready to withdraw troops from Salamaua and put up a hard fight at Lae, but Imamura and Adachi decided against that. Expecting that continued defense would end in the loss of the towns as well as the 51st Division, they decided to evacuate both Salamaua and Lae. Adachi considered Finschhafen the position that needed to be held, as it commanded the Dampier Strait and blocked an Allied advance into the Bismarck Sea.[7]

As with other planned withdrawals, the Japanese were skilled in concealing their intentions. At Salamaua, beginning 6 September, 5,000 men were evacuated by barge to Lae, another 250 marched there, and 600 naval troops were evacuated to Rabaul by submarine. On 11 September, as Milford's 5th Division neared the Francisco River outside Salamaua, Allied intelligence reports at last indicated that the Japanese were pulling out. Salamaua fell the next day.

By 15 September, the 7th Division was seven miles west of Lae while the 9th Division was only one and a quarter miles to the east, seemingly assured of winning the race. But one last water barrier, the Bumbu River, remained before Wootten. While the 9th Division prepared to cross, a 7th Division patrol made it into the town. As 9th Division artillery continued to shell Lae, Vasey sent Wootten a message: "Have occupied Lae. Prevent your troops engaging my troops."[8]

With his customary exaggeration, MacArthur issued a communique proclaiming the encirclement of 20,000 Japanese, although Nakano began with only about 11,000 men, of whom approximately 2,200 were killed or wounded and the rest escaped. Blamey, too, claimed that "only battered remnant likely to have escaped,"[9] whereas about 9,000 Japanese evaded capture and withdrew into the Huon Peninsula. Most of the Japanese crossed the rugged Finisterre Mountains to reach Sio on the northern coast, terrain worse than the Kokoda Trail. Half rations were issued for an expected ten-day march that stretched into twenty-six days, the troops surviving on "potatoes and grass."[10] An estimated 600 died from wounds, disease, and starvation.[11]

Casualties in the two elite, battle-hardened Australian divisions were remarkably low given the scale of operations. Wootten's 9th Division incurred only 547 casualties, of which 77 were killed in action. Even more remarkable were the 142 casualties in Vasey's 7th Division, nine fewer than at the Jackson's airfield disaster, including only 38 deaths in combat.[12]

Australian forces had won a splendid victory but could not rest on their laurels. It was imperative to swiftly exploit their success.

# CHAPTER 8

# "The Weakness of Trying to Fight Battles from a Distance"

With Lae taken, Allied attention quickly shifted to Finschhafen, at the tip of the Huon Peninsula, commanding the Vitiaz Strait passage between the Solomon and Bismarck seas. The original plan called for an attack on Finschhafen six weeks after the fall of Lae. But with the Japanese in disarray and with reports that enemy reinforcements were headed there and to the Ramu Valley, operations were accelerated.[1]

Intelligence estimates varied widely as to the number of Japanese in and near Finschhafen. MacArthur's intelligence staff arrived at a total of only 350 and others believed it was about 1,800. In fact, by the time of the landings, 5,000 Japanese occupied the area.[2]

Since the Japanese were largely deployed to oppose an attack from the direction of Lae, the landing area selected was north of Finschhafen. Possession of that area would threaten the Japanese supply line and avenue of retreat to Sio. The landing place selected, code named Scarlet Beach, was about six hundred yards long and thirty to forty feet wide, in a well-defined bay immediately south of the Song River and backed by the Kreutberg Mountains. It lay in a coastal corridor, up to a half-mile wide, leading to Finschhafen.

For the operation, Wootten selected Brigadier Victor Windeyer's 20th Brigade, which had gained amphibious experience in the Lae landings and was in relatively fresh condition. Wootten wanted to use a larger force but was limited by the number of landing craft available. Initially, two battalions would land, 2/17 Battalion on the right and 2/13 Battalion on the left, with 2/15 Battalion arriving later to lead the advance on Finschhafen.

There was disagreement about the timing of the attack. Wootten wanted the landing at first light, as he feared the troops would be landed in the wrong place

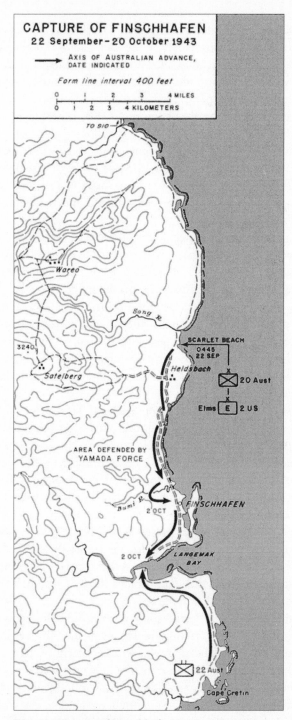

**CAPTURE OF FINSCHHAFEN**
22 September–20 October 1943

→ AXIS OF AUSTRALIAN ADVANCE,
DATE INDICATED

Form line interval 400 feet

0   1   2   3   4 MILES
0   1   2   3   4 KILOMETERS

TO SIO

Wareo

Song R.

SCARLET BEACH
0445
22 SEP

3240

Satelberg                Heldsbach

⊠ 20 Aust

Elms [E] 2 US

AREA DEFENDED BY
YAMADA FORCE

Bumi R.        2 OCT        FINSCHHAFEN

2 OCT        LANGEMAK
BAY

⊠ 22 Aust

Cape Cretin

Map 7. Capture of Finschhafen (Miller, *The U.S. Army
in World War II—The War in the Pacific: Cartwheel*, 217)

and have problems operating in the jungle in darkness. Kenney, too, favored daylight for the same reasons as before the Lae landings. Barbey pushed for a midnight landing that would allow time for his ships to depart before daybreak, when they would likely come under air attack.[3] After Wootten agreed to a shortened unloading period, accepting a reduction of supplies in return for a promise of replenishment in five days, they compromised by scheduling the landings to commence at 0445 on 22 September.

Once again, Barbey and Kenney argued over air cover. Kenney wanted his fighters on stand-by during the landings, while Barbey insisted on strong and continuous air cover. In the aftermath of Lae, when two LSTs had been bombed, Barbey had solid grounds for his view and gained Kenney's reluctant agreement "after a bit of nudging by MacArthur."[4]

Provided only five days' notice, Barbey assembled eight LSTs, sixteen LCIs, four high-speed destroyer-transports (APDs), and ten destroyers. While the LSTs loaded and departed from Buna, the 20th Brigade troops embarked from Lae, sailing under an American and Australian air umbrella.

Expecting an overland attack from the west, Major General Eizo Yamada, commanding at Finschhafen, stationed three thousand troops west of the town and fewer than a thousand in and near Finschhafen, leaving just three to four hundred north of the town in the invasion area. It was fortunate that so few Japanese were there, as Wootten's fears about Barbey's ability to land troops in darkness proved justified.

Kenney's aircraft continuously pounded Japanese airfields on New Guinea and New Britain to minimize intervention, but no air attack was conducted against the invasion beaches to maintain the element of surprise. Instead, the invasion opened with an eleven-minute bombardment by five destroyers that caused few casualties but may have prompted many Japanese to flee.

Although Barbey expressed confidence that the distinctive coast with well-defined headlands could be identified in the dark, the landing craft went badly astray. The first two assault waves missed Scarlet Beach entirely, landing well to the south. Some LCIs struck a sandbar, forcing troops to wade ashore in chest-deep water. Thus, when the third wave arrived in the right place but a half-hour behind schedule, they found they had become the lead troops. Throughout the front, units became hopelessly intermixed.

Despite the chaos, order was soon restored. According to the official Australian history, "In their training the troops of the 9th Division had learnt what they were to do if landed on the wrong beach, as had been done at Gallipoli."[5] Once the troops were ashore, the only opposition they encountered was from a single Japanese machine gun that was soon silenced. The rest of the defenders withdrew toward Sattelberg, a town six miles to the west dominated by a 3,400-foot peak, whose importance would only later be fully appreciated.

After delivering 5,300 troops, the APDs and LCIs departed for Buna at 0600. Of the three LSTs that arrived that morning, all but one was fully unloaded by 0930 when they also departed. In the course of the day, units disentangled themselves and all objectives were taken as planned. Australian and Papuan casualties were twenty killed, sixty-five wounded, and nine missing.

The only substantial opposition occurred after midday, when a flight of twenty to thirty Japanese bombers and thirty to forty fighters went after Barbey's withdrawing flotilla. Inopportunely for the Japanese, they arrived as the standing air patrol was being relieved and found one hundred Allied planes waiting for them. In less than an hour, forty Japanese aircraft were downed by the air cover at a cost of three P-38s. In addition, nine out of ten Japanese torpedo planes were brought down by destroyer anti-aircraft fire. Although no hits were scored on the ships, with remarkable imagination the Japanese pilots claimed to have sunk two cruisers, two destroyers, and two transports. Feeling vindicated, Barbey noted, "There is nothing like an air cover of friendly planes to save a convoy from possible disaster."[6]

The march on Finschhafen began the next day, led by 2/15 Battalion, which set out for the Bumi River, at the northern outskirts of the town, followed by 2/13 Battalion. Encountering opposition at the river, the Australians probed to the west and established a bridgehead across the Bumi. In the following days, the bridgehead was consolidated and enlarged, and supplies were accumulated. During that time, 2/15 Battalion clashed with 100 to 150 Japanese marines. Armed with lightly constructed and erratically fused grenades, they fled in the face of an Aussie bayonet charge.

To create a reserve for the attack on Finschhafen, Windeyer stripped forces from the Scarlet Beach area. This initially caused little concern, as westward probes found no substantial enemy concentrations. Then, on 26 September, the Japanese delivered a sharp attack from the direction of Sattelberg, and documents found on the body of a company commander in the 80th Regiment indicated that elements of at least three battalions were concentrating toward Scarlet Beach. To protect his denuded flank, Windeyer asked for an additional battalion. Wootten agreed and asked Barbey to bring up the troops.

MacArthur's headquarters, remote from the battlefield and believing that the Japanese forces were small, ordered Barbey not to bring additional troops to the area, and Barbey followed MacArthur's orders. An appeal to Carpender produced a remarkable response. Entirely missing the point, Carpender answered that he could not bring ships in until Finschhafen harbor was available. Complicating the situation, the only two men with full authority to take action, MacArthur and Blamey, had just left New Guinea and no one was willing to act in their stead. Meanwhile, strengthened enemy resistance was encountered at the Bumi River and Sattelberg Road, making reinforcement imperative.

When it was finally possible to gain Blamey's ear, he urged MacArthur to send an entire brigade. MacArthur's answer indicated that he had not yet fully progressed from his mindset during Buna. He responded that the requested reinforcement "would cause discouragement of amended program upon which we are engaged. . . . I am sure . . . that Finschhafen within a reasonable time will be in our hands without serious loss."[7] In the end, three days after the crisis emerged, MacArthur agreed to send a single battalion. In the early hours of 30 September, 838 troops from 2/43 arrived on three APDs to relieve 2/17, which then departed to join the attack on Finschhafen.

In the face of strong opposition, the Australians fighting in the Bumi River area slowly advanced against Finschhafen from the west. They held high hopes for a breakthrough on 1 October using heavy bombing as a prelude to a ground attack. But for unexplained reasons, the air attack was conducted too early and provided little help. With every prospect of a protracted battle for Finschhafen, it was found the next day that the Japanese had evacuated the entire area and retreated to Sattelberg. The victorious 20th Brigade troops then met the 4th Brigade's 22nd Battalion, which had meanwhile advanced from Lae along the coast, encountering little resistance and supplied entirely by EBSR craft.

Finschhafen was captured eleven days after the Scarlet Beach landings. The Australians incurred 358 casualties, including 73 killed in action; the supporting American EBSR force suffered 50 casualties including eight dead. Making excellent use of his small force, Windeyer achieved his primary objective of taking Finschhafen. But he now had to deal with the Japanese who had slipped through his net and, uniting at Sattelberg with reinforcements from the 20th Division, were intent on reclaiming Finschhafen.

At the same time Wootten was ordered to take Finschhafen, Vasey was directed to seize positions in the Markham and Ramu valleys. Taking the valleys would deny them to the enemy, preventing the Japanese from fleeing Lae by those routes and providing airfield sites for Kenney's air offensive. The first target was Kaiapit in the Markham Valley.

With considerable improvisation, 2/6 Independent Company was airlifted to a level area eight miles from Kaiapit.[8] Joined there by two platoons of Papuan infantry, the 250-man force moved against the three villages that made up the settlement. With fixed bayonets, the Australians charged the first village and routed the Japanese. The next morning the second village was cleared and the surviving Japanese fled the area. At a cost of 14 killed and 23 wounded, the Australians and Papuans killed more than 250 Japanese and gained an important airfield site and strategic position.[9] In Australian hands, Kaiapit closed off the Markham Valley to Japanese retreating from Lae, leaving them no choice except to withdraw into the rugged Finisterre Mountains.

The day after Kaiapit's capture, the vanguard of Brigadier Ivan N. Dougherty's 21st Brigade was flown in.[10] Kaiapit's capture had been a close-run thing, as would be learned from captured Japanese documents. The two companies the Australians encountered were the vanguard of Major General Masutaro Nakai's 3,500-man 78th Regiment from the 20th Division. Nakai had expected to move his regiment to Kaiapit and continue on to Nadzab, but he lost valuable time occupying key points as he proceeded and forfeited the race. Vasey would probably not have acted so boldly if he had known exactly what he faced. The official Australian history observed: "It is not often that it is well not to know the enemy's intentions, but Kaiapit was an example."[11]

Adachi originally planned that the previously uncommitted 20th Division would thrust through the Ramu and Markham valleys to recover Nadzab. Once Finschhafen was threatened, however, it became Adachi's main concern, and no more than the 78th Regiment could be spared to oppose Vasey and support the 51st Division withdrawing northward from Lae. Any hopes Nakai entertained of seriously impeding the Australian advance were soon dashed.

After capture of Kaiapit on 19 September, Vasey's principal target was Dumpu in the Ramu Valley, the last important stop before Bogadjim at the coast. But he could not move ahead with the 21st Brigade until the 25th Brigade was flown in to hold Kaiapit. With major air operations in progress around Finschhafen, Kenney had insufficient fighters to protect the transports. Vasey protested to Herring that the delay would give the Japanese an opportunity to take control of the river valleys. Not entirely appreciating the strain on air resources presented by Wootten's concurrent operations, Vasey vented to Dougherty: "I am terribly sorry about the delay in getting 25 Brigade up to your area, but this bloody Air Force is too tiresome."[12]

Eight days after the fall of Kaiapit, only the advanced headquarters of the 25th Brigade had arrived. Vasey could delay no longer. Feeling confident that his position was sufficiently secure, he ordered Dougherty to take Marawasa in the Ramu Valley. That village, situated halfway to Dumpu, was thought to be occupied by Japanese 51st Division troops from Lae. During the advance, the daring actions of one Australian patrol at the village of Kasawi would have far-reaching consequences.

Approaching the village, a platoon set an ambush that ensnared sixty members of the 78th Regiment, killing most of them. This action in the Ramu Valley, coupled with the loss of Kaiapit in the Markham Valley, convinced Nakai that his forces could not seriously oppose the Australians in the open river valleys. Believing his troops could be of most use by remaining intact in the Finisterre Mountains, he withdrew to the Kankiryo Saddle, leaving behind only light forces to delay the 7th Division. Dougherty's forces found Marawasa deserted when they arrived.

With little in the way, Vasey now advanced so rapidly his troops regularly outran their supplies and needed to be supplied by air. It then seemed that Bogadjim might be taken, sealing off the Huon Peninsula. But while it had long been supposed that the enemy's 20th Division was headed toward Vasey, it was discovered that most of the division was marching toward Finschhafen to oppose Wootten. Now concerned primarily about the situation on the 9th Division's front, Herring and Blamey did not want Vasey to become more heavily engaged.

Still, there was clear evidence that the Japanese were withdrawing from the Markham and Ramu valleys, so Vasey was authorized to continue as far as Dumpu. On 2 October, the day Finschhafen fell to the 9th Division, the advance began. Wary of a trap, 2/16 Battalion and the 25th Brigade advanced cautiously against little opposition. On 4 October, 2/16 took Dumpu. The key element in the advance was the perfect symbiosis between ground and air forces, the troops capturing and protecting airfield sites and the air forces providing them transportation, supplies, and air cover.[13]

At this time, Blamey decided that Herring needed a rest and replaced him as head of I Corps by II Corps commander Lieutenant General Leslie Morshead. A veteran of Gallipoli and leader of the "Desert Rats" during the epic siege

Australian commanders in the Ramu Valley. From left: Lieutenant General Edmund Herring, 1st Australian Corps; Lieutenant Colonel J. A. Bishop, 2/27th Infantry Battalion; Major General George A. Vasey, 7th Australian Division; Lieutenant General Leslie Morshead, 2nd Australian Corps, 1 October 1943. At this time, command of 1st Corps passed from Herring to Morshead. (By authorization of the Australian War Memorial: 057633)

of Tobruk, Morshead's demanding command style earned him the nickname "Ming the Merciless."[14]

Wootten's forces were then aligned with the 24th Brigade on the right covering the Scarlet Beach area, the 20th Brigade in the center facing the Sattelberg Road, and the 22nd Battalion in the Finschhafen area at left. He had hoped to take Sattelberg and the Wareo supply base and then move against Sio. With growing signs, however, that the Japanese were preparing to attack, and insufficient forces for a pre-emptive strike, Wootten went on the defensive.

When the storm broke, New Guinea Force commander Lieutenant General Iven Mackay wrote to Blamey: "Through not being able to reinforce quickly the enemy has been given time to recover and we have not been able to exploit our original success. Through the piecemeal arrival of reinforcements the momentum of the attack has not been maintained. As was proved in the Lae operations the provision of adequate forces at the right place and time is both the quickest and most economical course."[15]

The Japanese 20th Division under Lieutenant General Shigeru Katagiri had finally arrived after its long march to join the battle. Although his 78th Regiment had been detached to oppose Vasey in the Ramu Valley, the equivalent of another regiment was available to Katagiri, so that his forces were essentially at division strength. In typical Japanese style, Katagiri planned a multipronged attack. After mounting a diversion, 79th Regiment troops would land in the Scarlet Beach area, attacking Australian ammunition dumps, artillery positions, and headquarters in the rear. The main attacks would then be launched astride the Sattelberg Road by the 79th and 80th regiments toward Scarlet Beach. As happened repeatedly, the Japanese plan was discovered from captured documents and the Australians were ready and waiting.

Katagiri's offensive began 16 October with a heavy attack in the 20th Brigade sector and extensive infiltration on the 24th Brigade front. Late that night, seven barges with Japanese troops set out for Scarlet Beach. While en route, PT boats attacked the barges, sinking four. The beach defenders in concealed positions, a mixed force of Australian infantry and American EBSR troops manning 37-mm guns and .50-caliber machine guns, allowed the surviving three barges to come within twenty-five yards before opening fire.

The Japanese who reached shore were pinned down while two of their barges were rendered unusable by the 37-mm guns. But they still resisted strongly with grenades, including one that shattered the leg of EBSR machine gunner Private Nathan Van Noy Jr. and wounded his loader. Van Noy continued to pour out effective fire and died with his finger on the trigger, the first EBSR soldier to be awarded the Medal of Honor. About half of the approximately eighty Japanese who made it to land fled, but almost all were found and killed in the next days.

Much of the fighting swirled around the village of Katika immediately below Scarlet Beach on Siki Creek, which formed the boundary between the

24th and 20th Brigade. On 19 October, Katagiri succeeded in breaking through to the coast, threatening to isolate Windeyer's troops fighting well inland on the Sattelberg Road.

Because of Japanese infiltration between his units, Brigadier Bernard Evans decided to abandon his strong position at Katika and reform on a solid front. This ran contrary to Wootten's philosophy that "in holding defended localities the Japanese might be behind the Australians but the Australians were also behind the Japanese."[16] As the man on the spot, Evans' decision had to stand. But once the front stabilized and Katika was won back, Evans was removed.

During the night of 19–20 October, the 26th Brigade plus a tank squadron arrived from Lae. The official Australian history observed, "The initiative and cooperation of the senior Allied commanders in New Guinea had ensured that there would be no nonsense about reinforcement this time."[17]

It soon became apparent that the Japanese attack was spent. Katagiri lost 1,500 men, while the Australians and the EBSR troops incurred 228 casualties, including 49 dead. With the arrival of the reinforcements, Wootten would finally have sufficient strength to regain the initiative. To gain overwhelming superiority, Morshead authorized him to bring up the rest of the 4th Brigade.

Sattelberg might have been easily secured at the outset if necessary troops were provided and the Navy was willing and able to bring them forward. With obvious reference to MacArthur's headquarters, Mackay later commented to Blamey, "With all due respect to our friends I think this incident shows the weakness of trying to fight battles from a distance with fixed assumptions that the enemy is bent on withdrawal and that he is incapable of increasing the number of his forces."

After the capture of Finschhafen, MacArthur announced that enemy forces between Finschhafen and Madang had been "outflanked and contained."[18] Katagiri's October offensive thoroughly disproved that, and even after his attack was suspended, Adachi and Imamura need not have despaired. While Lae and Finschhafen and important positions in the Markham and Ramu valleys had been lost, they retained Sattelberg and other strong points in the Huon Peninsula. Even if the peninsula was lost, Adachi could expect to wage a protracted battle on the great landmass of New Guinea that would long delay an Allied thrust west. They could not know that MacArthur would soon adopt tactics that would confound such assumptions.

Imamura's principal attention would now be diverted toward his other responsibility, the 17th Army, as Halsey readied his climb to the top of the Solomons ladder—Bougainville.

CHAPTER 9

# "It's Torokina.
# Now Get on Your Horses!"

U nder Cartwheel, Bougainville was to be a two-stage operation starting with landings in the Shortland Islands and the Buin area. In the second stage, timed to coincide with MacArthur's invasion of Cape Gloucester, Halsey was to capture Kieta on Bougainville's eastern coast and neutralize Buka Island immediately north of Bougainville. These operations were to lead to a later invasion of Rabaul.[1]

When MacArthur asked him for a detailed invasion plan during July 1943, Halsey lacked sufficient resources to adhere to the earlier agreement. The unexpected employment of the 25th Division on New Georgia before it had fully recovered from Guadalcanal prevented its being used so soon. Halsey also lost the 2nd Marine Division, which had been permanently assigned to the Central Pacific. Essentially, the forces available for Bougainville were reduced to the fresh 3rd Marine Division, supported by the Army's 37th Division, which came out of New Georgia in better shape than the 25th.

Bougainville was heavily defended, raising the specter of another slow and bloody campaign. Building on his experience during New Georgia, Halsey first proposed invading the Shortlands, where air bases and an anchorage could be established and from which the enemy's Kahili air base on Bougainville could be neutralized by artillery fire. This modified plan was acceptable to MacArthur but discarded when good airstrip sites could not be found. Also, it was discovered that Japanese strength in the Shortlands would require two divisions, which would leave Halsey insufficient forces for a leap to Bougainville in time to meet MacArthur's Cape Gloucester schedule.[2]

The next idea, inspired by Vella Lavella, involved seizing the lightly held Treasury Islands and Choiseul Bay, from which aircraft could strangle the

Shortlands and southern Bougainville, after which a landing would be made on Bougainville if necessary. When the plan was presented to MacArthur, it was rejected. Anxious to accelerate operations, MacArthur decided to invade Cape Gloucester before year's end. In advance of that, he wanted Rabaul brought under heavy air attack with fighter protection from Bougainville. It was left up to Halsey to select a specific invasion point on Bougainville within fighter plane range of Rabaul.[3]

Measuring 130 miles long and 30 miles wide, Bougainville's salient physical features are two central mountain ranges. The Emperor Range in the north is higher and includes two volcanoes: Mount Balbi, measuring more than 10,000 feet, and Mount Bagana. Less rugged and lower to the south is the Crown Prince range. Except for some roads in the south that could accommodate wheeled transport, overland movement was limited to primitive trails through the dense interior jungle. Most important of the island routes was the Numa Numa Trail, which extended southwest from Numa Numa on the northeast coast to Empress Augusta Bay, and the East-West Trail running northwest from Buin on the south coast to Gazelle Harbor below Empress Augusta Bay. Although several possible invasion beaches existed on the eastern coast, there were few on the western coast, and those were backed by extensive swamps. The mostly Melanesian population, numbering 43,000, was clustered in small villages at the north and south ends of the island and on the eastern coastal plain. As a legacy of German rule from 1890 until World War I and the influence of German missionaries, many islanders welcomed the Japanese.[4]

If Halsey could not move against a lightly defended island, as at Vella Lavella, he could obtain much the same result by seeking out a lightly defended area on Bougainville. Unlike the New Georgia campaign, which continued until the enemy was fully ousted, all that was needed was enough territory for an airfield. Because continuous carrier-based air cover would not be available, the invasion area needed to be within range of the nearest fighter bases at Munda and Vella Lavella. This limited the possible invasion beaches to those on the south central coasts, which were studied in detail.

The Kieta area on the eastern coast possessed broad flatlands well suited for landing large bodies of troops and good harbors. But Japanese-occupied Choiseul lay immediately in the path and would need to be secured in advance. Also detrimental, the area was relatively accessible by enemy troops concentrated in the Buin area, and soil conditions were unfavorable for an airfield.

The best alternative found was the Cape Torokina area of Empress Augusta Bay on Bougainville's western coast. Closer to Rabaul than Kieta, the area was approachable without immediate threat from Choiseul or other Japanese-held islands. A five-mile strip of beach considered suitable for a landing was identified, with nearby soil conditions favorable for airfield construction. In addition, given the primitive jungle trails, it would take months before the enemy could assemble there in strength. On the negative side, the inshore waters were poorly charted and treacherous, with beaches unprotected from the monsoon. Also, although few Japanese were deployed there, it was largely because inland conditions made Empress Augusta Bay an unlikely choice for invasion, as the invasion troops would soon discover.

After protracted staff debates about the alternatives, Halsey lost patience, peremptorily announcing at the end of a conference on 22 September: "It's Torokina. Now get on your horses!"[5] Not everyone was enthusiastic over the choice, but events proved it could hardly have been better.

By this point, the Joint Chiefs of Staff (JCS) wisely decided not to capture Rabaul. MacArthur had long insisted that an invasion of Rabaul was essential to safeguard his flank on New Guinea, but after receiving approval for an advance toward his cherished goal, the Philippines, he quietly dropped the idea. As observed by Morison, "Tarawa, Iwo Jima and Okinawa would have faded to pale pink in comparison with the blood that would have flowed if the Allies had attempted an assault on Fortress Rabaul."[6]

By invading the nearby, lightly held Treasury Islands a few days before hitting Bougainville and setting up an advanced base on Vella Lavella, supplies to support the invasion and construct and maintain the airfield could be continuously shuttled forward. This would avert a supply crisis like that experienced at Guadalcanal. As this preliminary operation would create the impression that the next move would be to the western coast of Bougainville, an additional operation was needed to draw Japanese attention to the east. Thus, a hit-and-run raid by the Marines on northern Choiseul was added to give the impression of a coming attack in that direction.[7]

Once the targets were established, Halsey issued the operations plan that would be implemented by five task forces.[8] Task force (TF), 31, led by Wilkinson as Commander III Amphibious Force, included the transports, covering ships, and assault troops. Until the troops were fully established on shore and authority formally transferred, full control would reside with Wilkinson.

Although naval resources far outstripped what was available during Guadalcanal a year earlier, Bougainville was in competition with the Gilberts campaign that marked the start of Nimitz's Central Pacific offensive. Only twelve attack transports and cargo ships commanded by Commodore Lawrence F. Reifsnider were available to transport the assault force to Empress Augusta Bay. Even this modest force was only obtained over the objections of some on Nimitz's staff, who argued that beaching craft would suffice. Wilkinson obtained the vessels by pointing out the need for speed, anticipating correctly a violent enemy air response. The rest of the amphibious force consisted of eleven destroyers, fifteen minesweepers and minelayers, plus two salvage tugboats. A more modest force of beaching craft, staged from Guadalcanal under the command of Rear Admiral George Fort, would conduct the landings in the Treasuries.

Ground forces for the Bougainville, Treasuries, and Choiseul operations were organized in the 1st Marine Amphibious Corps (IMAC). The principal component was the 3rd Marine Division making its battle debut. Organized by Major General Charles D. Barrett in September 1942, the regiments had trained separately and then were brought together in New Zealand. They included the 3rd, 9th, and 21st Marines, the 12th Marines (artillery) and 19th Marines (engineers, pioneers) plus supporting battalions. In successive waves during July and August, the division moved forward to Guadalcanal where training continued under jungle conditions.

Two Marine raider battalions, the 2nd and 3rd that made up the 2nd Provisional Raider Regiment under Colonel Alan Shapley, were assigned to IMAC. The concept of an elite raider force adept at quick strikes was an outgrowth of British success using commandos in Europe. Created in February 1942, raiders made their debut in the August 1942 Makin raid, then went on to fight on Tulagi, Guadalcanal, and New Georgia. On Bougainville they would fight as regular riflemen.

Also assigned to IMAC outside their specialty was the 1st Marine Parachute Regiment under Lieutenant Colonel Robert H. Williams. Trained to fight as a lightly armed, swiftly moving force, the paramarines were particularly well-suited for the raid on Choiseul.

The 3rd MDB, led by Lieutenant Colonel Edward H. Forney, was another IMAC unit. Armed with 90-mm anti-aircraft and 155-mm guns and other weaponry, defense battalions were formed to protect advanced bases from air and naval attack while fighting from relatively static positions, with personnel prepared to fight as infantry in emergencies. These weapons would also prove highly effective against enemy ground forces on Bougainville.

For the Treasuries, IMAC was assigned the 8th New Zealand Brigade Group of the 3rd New Zealand Division under Brigadier Robert A. Row.

In immediate and area reserve, respectively, IMAC had the Army's 37th Infantry and Americal divisions available. Lacking permanently assigned warships, Halsey looked to Nimitz for covering forces. With the Central Pacific offensive about to commence and believing Admiral Mineichi Koga, Yamamoto's successor, would not risk the Combined Fleet in a major naval action in the Solomons, Nimitz gave Halsey the bare minimum. For carrier air protection, Halsey was provided only one carrier task group, TF 33, commanded by Rear Admiral Frederick C. "Ted" Sherman in fleet carrier *Saratoga*, with light carrier USS *Princeton*, light cruisers USS *San Juan* and *San Diego*, and ten destroyers. Described by historian Clark G. Reynolds in *The Fast Carriers* as "headstrong, outspoken and a taskmaster," Sherman had commanded the *Lexington* until its loss at Coral Sea. A favorite of Halsey, he would be entrusted to execute the single most hazardous operation of the campaign. For surface firepower, TF 39, under Rear Admiral A. Stanton "Tip" Merrill, included light cruisers

USS *Montpelier, Columbia, Denver,* and *Cleveland.* Merrill's screen consisted of eight destroyers organized in two divisions, under the command of Captain Arleigh A. Burke. Sherman, Merrill, and Burke, in separate actions, would write some of the Navy's most glorious pages of history during November 1943.

**New Zealand Brigadier Robert A. Row (right) with Admiral Halsey on Guadalcanal during planning for the invasion of the Treasury Islands, October 1943.** (Dept. of Defense)

With seven enemy airfields on Bougainville and the Shortlands, backed by even more formidable air power at Rabaul, seizing and retaining command of the air was essential for the invasion to succeed. That would be the responsibility of AirSols using aircraft operating from Munda, Vella Lavella, Guadalcanal, and elsewhere in the Solomons. AirSols was commanded then by Major General Nathan F. Twining, who would soon depart to lead the 15th Air Force in Europe.

The fifth task force consisted of Brisbane-based submarines organized as TF 72 under Captain James Fife. They would be employed principally as scouts to observe and report on Japanese naval movements.

A week after Halsey's Cape Torokina decision, a new Japanese strategy was announced at an Imperial conference. Acknowledging that Allied air and sea power had grown too powerful to meet on equal terms, time would be needed to rebuild Japan's forces. An inner defense zone was designated bounded by a line extending from the Kurils to the Bonins, Marianas, Carolines, and western New Guinea, then westward to the Netherlands Indies and beyond. This area, deemed essential for Japan to achieve its war aims, was to be heavily fortified and held at all costs. The outer defense zone, including the Solomons and most of New Guinea, would be held as long as possible to buy time.[9]

In his study of the air war in the South Pacific, Eric Bergerud observed that an alternative strategy was then still available to the Japanese. They might have abandoned Rabaul and other advanced positions in the South and Southwest Pacific and sent those forces where they might have avoided encirclement and been employed more usefully against Nimitz's Central Pacific offensive. With the decision to stand fast, the Japanese became, according to Bergerud, "like a rabbit caught in a snare. Movement was impossible, and there was little to do but await the executioner."[10]

Responsibility for carrying out the Imperial orders in the South Pacific was shared at Rabaul by General Imamura, commander of the 8th Area Army, and Admiral Kusaka, commander of the Southeast Area Fleet. Although Japanese leadership believed correctly that Bougainville would be attacked, they could not know the Allies had decided to bypass Rabaul, and so they prepared for invasion there as well.

As part of the strategy of maintaining a hold on the outer defenses, Admiral Koga conceived a plan that unknowingly collided with Halsey's invasion plans. Not expecting a major fleet action, Koga ran a calculated risk and denuded his carriers by sending 173 fighters, dive and torpedo bombers, and patrol aircraft to Rabaul. Joining the 200 aircraft of Kusaka's 11th Air Fleet, they were expected to strengthen Rabaul and slow the Allied advance in the Solomons and New Guinea.

Defending Bougainville and its offshore islands were 40,000 soldiers and 20,000 naval personnel. Not knowing where the Americans would strike, Hyakutake, Halsey's old Guadalcanal opponent, concentrated about 25,000 troops in the Buin and Shortlands areas to defend the principal airfields. The next largest concentration was 6,000 troops in the north at Buka and Bonis. Only light forces were allocated to the Empress Augusta Bay area.[11]

The Japanese hoped their air and sea forces would destroy the invasion at sea. If the invaders did make it ashore they would face Hyakutake's 17th Army, consisting principally of the 6th Division, notorious for its depredations during the Rape of Nanking in 1937. With sufficient support, Hyakutake might yet gain the victory that eluded him at Guadalcanal.

CHAPTER 10

—⊶∞⊷—

# "Halsey Knows the Straight Story"

T he 1st Marine Amphibious Corps (IMAC) was activated in the South Pacific in November 1942 as an administrative command. Its immediate responsibilities included the training, supply and equipment, coordination, and amphibious operations planning of all Marine forces in the Pacific. Eventually, IMAC was expected to undertake combat operations built around one or more Marine divisions. The organization existed by that name for nearly a year and a half until April 1944, when it was redesignated the III Amphibious Corps.[1]

Marine commandant Lieutenant General Thomas Holcomb chose Major General C. Barney Vogel as IMAC's first commander. Before his appointment, Vogel jointly trained Army and Marine troops, during which time he became interested in and promoted the Navajo code-talking concept. In selecting Vogel, Holcomb considered him one of only four Marines then qualified for corps command.[2]

With a bluff personality much like Halsey's and headquartered with him in Noumea, Vogel and Halsey became "great personal friends,"[3] a relationship that caused difficulties for Halsey after he recognized that Vogel wasn't performing effectively.

Reluctant to fire a close friend, Halsey tried to obtain Vogel's removal without revealing his role. First he attempted to work through Vandegrift, then involved in the refit of his division in Australia, by having him act as an intermediary to persuade Holcomb to take action.[4] Nominally subordinate to Vogel, Vandegrift refused.

At Vandegrift's suggestion, a member of Halsey's staff, Brigadier General DeWitt Peck (USMC), wrote Holcomb a letter that harshly criticized Vogel's handling of IMAC, claiming that the corps "has since its inception been characterized by an almost total lack of initiative and punch. It seems to lack that old spirit of up and at 'em."[5] Remarkably, in view of that criticism, Peck proposed "promoting General Vogel to some worthy job in the States if practicable." It was also proposed that Vandegrift be given command of IMAC "with three stars if that can be done," and, to conceal Halsey's hand, "It should not appear that the change originated here." Making Peck's vague complaints all the more unacceptable as a basis for action, Holcomb received soon afterward Vogel's fitness report in which Halsey gave his supposedly failed commander glowing marks.

Since Halsey had full authority as area commander to relieve Vogel, Holcomb refused to act and instead aired the situation with Nimitz in a highly forthright letter.[6] After summarizing the situation, Holcomb told Nimitz that "if Vogel has in fact failed, no one will be more anxious to relieve him and detail someone else than I. But, I cannot act on the basis of a personal letter from a staff officer." A postscript to Holcomb's letter mentioned Vogel's "outstanding" fitness report and Halsey's notation that, in time of war, he "would especially desire to have him." Holcomb concluded by asking, "Can you blame me if I find the situation rather confused?"

After meeting with Halsey in Noumea, Nimitz gave Halsey his full support, laying out the case in a letter to Holcomb.[7] While no specific "acts of omission or commission" were cited, Halsey had developed a "definite lack of confidence . . . in Vogel's military ability and professional competence." Cited as especially problematic was Vogel's conduct during the New Georgia planning. Vogel had prepared an invasion plan calling for the use of two divisions that was rejected by Halsey as unrealistic in its excessive requirements. A new plan was then developed in conjunction with Army planners and amphibious commander Turner. The final result, according to Nimitz, was a loss of time and the handing over of the operation to an Army division without opposition from Vogel. With the Army and Marines in stiff competition for primacy, Nimitz hated to surrender an operation he considered "primarily the dish of Marine amphibious troops."

While it would later be demonstrated that Vogel's performance was indeed wanting, the specific criticisms leveled against him were debatable. With respect to the manpower requirements for New Georgia, Vogel would be fully vindicated when the campaign absorbed the greater part of three Army divisions and various Marine units. As much as Nimitz may have preferred a Marine-run operation, none of the three Marine divisions then in the Pacific were available.[8] Had the 3rd Marine Division been rushed into combat on New Georgia before it was fully trained, as Nimitz seems to have expected, the division might easily have become bogged down in a lengthy campaign, leaving no Marine division available for the Bougainville campaign a few months later.

Further, Nimitz unconvincingly called attention to the date of Vogel's fitness report that he noted had been "long on the way," implying that performance might have spectacularly deteriorated in a relatively short time. Nimitz was on firmer ground in noting that "lack of confidence may come from a gradually growing conviction rather than from specific acts. Certainly no leader should be kept in his position when there is lack of confidence in his professional competence."

Nimitz then turned to the matter of Vogel's successor, urging that if he was to be replaced, "it should be done as early as possible, as planning has already started for the next move which will be in the Bougainville area. As to who should relieve him—Vandegrift or Barrett—I think this should be settled between you and Halsey. I know and admire both and consider both are capable, but would prefer Vandegrift because of his combat experience." In view of later events, Nimitz's regard for Barrett is revealing, as Nimitz had headed the Navy's personnel bureau where he developed a highly practiced eye in evaluating men.

Even with support from Nimitz, Halsey declined to replace Vogel. Ending the impasse, Holcomb acted himself,[9] then ordered Vandegrift to take over IMAC.[10] Vogel returned home to resume training troops, his opportunity as the ranking Marine in the Pacific ended. Vandegrift told Holcomb about Vogel's exit meeting with Halsey: "Halsey told Vogel he was relieved because the people in Washington were dissatisfied with progress and the fact [that] Army and not Marines were doing the present [New Georgia] job. Nothing about how he himself felt. The longer I live the more I think your remarks about the enemies in uniform are correct."[11]

Despite his reluctance to fire a friend, it is to Halsey's credit that he was unwilling to continue with a commander who did not enjoy his full confidence. Such convictions could only have been reinforced later by his unhappy experiences with an inexperienced ground commander on New Georgia.

Halsey had formed a close bond with Vandegrift during the Guadalcanal campaign, about which he wrote, "Archie Vandegrift was my other self."[12] Recognizing that IMAC had been badly mishandled and needed swift correction, Halsey wanted to use Vandegrift again. As Vandegrift had by then been selected to become Marine commandant when Holcomb retired at the end of the year, Vandegrift was installed as IMAC commander on an interim basis.[13]

Vandegrift uncovered problems everywhere.[14] Shaking up IMAC, he improved the Marines' ability to perform their mission. A large-scale overhaul of IMAC's staff brought in a new team of officers with proven abilities from the 1st Marine Division and elsewhere. A visit to New Zealand found that command problems extended to the 2nd Marine Division, resulting in major personnel changes. Other manpower actions included new procedures for the handling of senior appointments and replacements. Equipment supply received particularly close attention and was much improved by new command and procedures.[15]

After just six weeks in command, Vandegrift's replacement was announced. Before Vandegrift took command of IMAC, Holcomb, Vandegrift, Nimitz, and Halsey had agreed on his successor.[16] It was to be fifty-eight-year-old Barrett, descendant of a distinguished Virginia family.[17] A graduate of the prestigious Ecole Superieure de Guerre, Barrett had played a leading part in formulating amphibious operation doctrine and once served as Holcomb's assistant. Particularly fitting, he had formed and trained the 3rd Marine Division slated to lead the Bougainville invasion. Except for his lack of combat experience, Holcomb regarded Barrett as even more qualified than Vandegrift for corps command.[18]

Admiral Halsey (second from left) holding the order appointing Major General Charles D. Barrett (USMC) (far right) to the command of I Marine Amphibious Corps (IMAC); outgoing IMAC commander Vandegrift is at left, with Harmon between Halsey and Barrett, 15 August 1943. (National Archives and Records Administration)

But there was also unease. Holcomb wrote to Vandegrift:[19] "I am particularly sorry that things have worked out so that Barrett will not have the opportunity of commanding his division in battle before getting the Corps; and I am sorry that you are not to have the opportunity of commanding your Corps in battle." Holcomb's concern would prove well-justified with regard to Barrett, but fate would provide Vandegrift an unexpected opportunity to participate in the coming battle.

Barrett had one known failing that would become of great importance, a tendency to overanalyze problems. As Vandegrift later commented to Holcomb,[20] "even when a regimental commander [Barrett] felt it was his duty to constantly step out of character and endeavor to run . . . whatever higher echelon to which he was assigned." He also noted that Barrett "could draw up all kinds of imponderables that would prevent him solving the problem given him." Such tendencies would make for difficulties, especially dealing with a leader like Halsey, whose inclination was for rapid decision and decisive action. In addition to their professional incompatibility, soft-spoken and intellectual Barrett would not easily bond with Halsey, as Vogel had done.

Vandegrift's choice as Barrett's replacement was the 3rd Division's assistant commander, Brigadier General Allen H. Turnage. In recommending him, Vandegrift expressed the reservation that "he should have a spark plug as an Assistant Division Commander for Turnage is definitely not that." Turnage would prove to be an excellent commander who would eventually rise to command the Fleet Marine Force.

Vandegrift and Barrett worked together for a month until 15 September 1943, when Vandegrift departed for an extended tour of Pacific bases in preparation for his duties as Marine commandant. One week afterwards, tired of the endless staff discussions about possible targets, Halsey abruptly announced his decision: "It's Torokina."

In 1996, a memoir titled *No Bended Knee* was published by General Merrill Twining that told what occurred during the Bougainville planning after Vandegrift's departure.[21] As Twining, then an IMAC operations officer tells it, "[Barrett] did not adhere to General Vandegrift's philosophy of doing what you are ordered to do and doing it to the best of your ability with the forces placed at your disposal." After rejecting other landing sites, "even Empress Augusta Bay seemed too fraught with uncertainty for General Barrett to consider. . . . Despite all of his brilliance, personality, and leadership, he increasingly allowed his humanitarian instincts to prevail over every dictate of a dire military necessity . . . he had forgotten why he and his Marines were there."[22] During repeated trips to Noumea to present alternative plans, "Admiral Halsey . . . seemed to be growing impatient at our indecision and lack of progress."

As Twining was sidelined by malaria during the planning, his knowledge of what ensued was most likely learned from Vandegrift and others. As he tells it, "Again confronted with a command problem in IMAC, Admiral Halsey for the second time sent for his old friend Vandegrift to straighten out matters in IMAC. . . . It was too late to save General Barrett. When informed of Halsey's intentions, he returned to his quarters in Noumea, where a few hours later he was found lying in the courtyard, dead of injuries suffered in a fall from a second story window."[23]

A court of inquiry into the cause of Barrett's death was immediately convened by Halsey. After hearing testimony over three days, the court concluded that the general died "in an accidental fall . . . his death was in the line of duty and not the result of his own misconduct."[24]

The complete facts did not emerge until 2007, with the discovery of two letters among the papers of Thomas Holcomb. One was from Barrett's administrative deputy and relative by marriage, Brigadier General David Brewster. The other was from Vandegrift, who was at Pearl Harbor and hurried back to Noumea when word was received of Barrett's death.

Brewster observed, "He did everybody's job and did most of the worrying for everybody and it is a wonder to me that he did not crack before he did."[25] Echoing Brewster and providing Holcomb further details, Vandegrift wondered "why some men crack and others don't" and mused "there save by the grace of God goes any one of us."[26] The two letters, in different words, told the same story. Barrett had drawn up a chair to the porch window, whose sill was nearly four feet from the floor. Footprints on the windowsill and fingerprints high on the window frame clearly told what occurred. A story was given out that a small brain tumor found during the autopsy had caused Barrett to lose his balance. As Vandegrift told Holcomb, however, "Halsey knows the straight story."

Brewster's letter included the line: "There is no person other than those who were there that night who know these details." Without a widespread conspiracy of silence, though, it would have been impossible to hide the truth.[27] During the court of inquiry proceedings, the questions asked by the judge advocate were so superficial, and the three other officers of the court were so incurious in their few innocuous questions, that it is impossible to believe they were not instructed what conclusion to reach. Never did they ask why Barrett was summoned to Noumea nor did they ask about his specific movements that might have affected his state of mind. Most tellingly, the court officers visited the porch from which Barrett fell and saw no problem in the windowsill being nearly four feet from the floor, making an accidental fall virtually impossible. In their testimony, the officer who must have first seen the chair at the window testified that the place was "in excellent police," and Brewster withheld the decisive facts he disclosed to Holcomb. As for Halsey, he hastily departed to visit MacArthur while the court sat but returned to Noumea in time for Barrett's burial.

Apparently unaware of the arrangements to rig the court, Holcomb wrote to Vandegrift: "Poor Charlie; what an utterly tragic death. I shall tell no one; but I suppose the inquest will tell the facts; if so, it will probably leak out."[28] Halsey wrote of the situation in his book: "This was a double blow, since we had no one to replace him."[29] This was pure fabrication, as Halsey was in process of removing Barrett and had already arranged for Vandegrift's return.

According to Vandegrift, Nimitz was not pleased to have him return temporarily to IMAC but had to yield to Halsey's wishes.[30] Meanwhile, a permanent IMAC commander was selected. It would be Roy Geiger, who had done a superlative job leading the air effort during the Guadalcanal campaign. So impressed was Halsey with Geiger's abilities and energy extracting a maximum effort from his airmen that he was not concerned that Geiger had served most of his career in Marine aviation. A born fighter, Geiger happily made ready to leave his position in Washington as chief of Marine aviation for a combat command. Vandegrift was pleased too, as was Holcomb, who breathed a sigh of relief.[31] There was fear that Halsey would instead choose Major General Charles Price, commander of the garrison on Samoa, something Halsey had considered until dissuaded by Vandegrift.

Given the consequences if the truth was revealed, the risk Halsey ran in authorizing the cover-up was enormous. In a career replete with crises, the death of Barrett was as dangerous for Halsey as any one of them. While Halsey's quickness of action and pugnacity was greatly admired when directed against the enemy, the firing of a highly respected officer before a shot was fired, followed by the officer's suicide, was another matter. Holcomb said as much to Vandegrift:[32] "It would have been terrible if H[alsey] had relieved him; and few people would have believed that H[alsey] was right."

Doubtless Halsey recalled the bad start made on New Georgia leading off with the wrong commander and wanted no repetition. Barrett's indecisiveness, perhaps indicating mental breakdown, presented a risk that Halsey could not accept. Given the thousands of lives that would be at stake on Bougainville, Halsey's actions in this hitherto unknown episode must be counted among his most audacious—and correct.

CHAPTER 11

# "Make Sure They Think the Invasion Has Commenced"

Japanese air power radiating from Rabaul constituted the principal threat to the Bougainville invasion. Suppression of Rabaul's air bases fell to Kenney, while AirSols dealt with Japanese air power in the Solomons.

Beginning 12 October, Kenney mounted large-scale attacks using B-24 Liberator and B-25 Mitchell bombers based at Dobodura, escorted by P-38 Lightnings and RAAF Beaufighters staged through Kiriwina Island in the Coral Sea. The initial attack was a maximum effort during which Kenney used "everything that I owned that was in commission and could fly that far."[1] For that daylight raid, Kenney sent 87 heavy bombers, 114 B-25s, 125 P-38s, and 12 Beaufighters, plus weather and reconnaissance aircraft. This was the largest air attack up to that point in the Pacific and came as a complete surprise to the Japanese. The highly trained B-25 fliers used their machine guns against Japanese airfield defenses, then hit the parked aircraft at low level with parafrag bombs. Meanwhile, the Liberators worked over Rabaul's Simpson Harbor, sinking three merchantmen and hitting numerous other vessels. The relatively few Japanese fighters that managed to get airborne were dealt with easily by the P-38s.[2]

Had such attacks been sustained throughout October, Rabaul might have been seriously injured. But bad weather prevented flying on many days, the narrow harbor limited the use of Kenney's favored skip-bombing tactic, and a now alert foe would make better use of the most formidable air defenses in the Pacific. Also, attrition is a two-edged sword. The campaign over Rabaul and New Guinea took its toll on Kenney's forces, leaving only 37 B-24s and 53 P-38s available on 29 October for their final visit until after the Bougainville landings.

During this time, the Japanese 11th Air Fleet at Rabaul managed to keep about 200 planes continuously in operation. Without awareness of Halsey's imminent attack, Koga made the fateful decision to reinforce Kusaka with 173 carrier planes and inaugurate the Operation RO aerial offensive planned earlier. With augmented resources, the Japanese administered a rude shock when, after days of bad weather, Kenney's fliers next visited Rabaul the day after the Bougainville landings.

On 2 November, in what he would call "the toughest, hardest fought engagement of the war,"[3] Kenney sent out 80 B-25 strafers escorted by 80 P-38s. Part of the force raked the harbor defenses with machine-gun fire and used phosphorous smoke bombs that blinded anti-aircraft positions. The smoke, however, also hampered target selection and later damage assessment. Postwar analysis found that three small merchantmen and a minesweeper were sunk, with some damage to other vessels. This was a far cry from the official communique that claimed the sinking of three destroyers, eight merchantmen, and four coastal vessels, plus damages to many other ships including imagined hits on two heavy cruisers.[4]

Raid by New Guinea–based bombers against Japanese shipping in Simpson Harbor, Rabaul, 2 November 1943. Heavy cruiser *Haguro*, in foreground, damaged at the Battle of Empress Augusta Bay (see chapter 13), sustained no further damage. Smoke in background is from a smokescreen laid down by the American planes. (USAAF)

While Kenney expected opposition from about fifty enemy fighters, the skies were swarming with Japanese aircraft, many of them from the carrier fleet. Kenney's pilots, not surprisingly, "reported that the caliber of the Japanese pilots was considerably better than anything they had recently encountered."[5] As later determined, twenty Japanese aircraft were destroyed, not eighty-five definites and twenty-three probables claimed by Kenney.[6]

Fifth Air Force casualties were heavy. Eight bombers and nine P-38 fighters were lost and many other aircraft were badly shot up, including four that crashed returning to base. Casualties included a B-25 flown by squadron leader Major Raymond H. Wilkins that, according to his Medal of Honor citation, sank a destroyer and a transport. With his plane damaged, including the loss of his stabilizer, Wilkins made a strafing run on what was thought to be a heavy cruiser. Unable to maneuver his aircraft to avoid enemy fire, Wilkins was downed while enabling his other aircraft to withdraw safely.[7]

With the additional aircraft acquired from the carriers and the limited results obtained by Kenney after a promising beginning, Japanese air power at Rabaul had grown more formidable since Kenney's campaign began. Halsey was unhappy that more was not accomplished, especially since MacArthur had offered maximum possible support.[8] But the mere threat of air attack by Kenney's fliers tied the Japanese planes to Rabaul, relieving much of the pressure on Halsey.[9]

Halsey had no cause for complaint with respect to AirSols. Almost daily from mid-July through October, medium, dive, and torpedo bombers operating from Guadalcanal, the Russells, New Georgia, and Vella Lavella intensively worked over Japanese airfields in the northern Solomons. The Kahili and Kara fields near Buin were especially hard-hit, with Buka, Kieta, Ballale, and airfields on Choiseul and the Treasury Islands receiving considerable attention as well. By sustained low-level strafing and high-level bombing during twenty-one days of October, AirSols rendered the enemy airfields virtually useless by D-day.[10]

During one notable operation on 17 October, 21 Corsairs from Major Gregory "Pappy" Boyington's "Black Sheep" squadron were attacked by 55 Zeros over Kahili. Enjoying the advantages of altitude and superior aircraft, Boyington's fliers fell upon the enemy aircraft in an action that ultimately spread over hundreds of miles. Without loss to the Corsairs, nine Zeros were downed, less than the spectacular count then claimed but impressive enough. Between aircraft caught on the ground and those lost in such one-sided actions, probably no more than 150 airworthy Japanese planes remained in the Solomons by invasion day to oppose AirSols' 489 operational aircraft.[11]

Five days before the scheduled landings on Bougainville, the Treasury Islands and Choiseul operations got under way.

The Treasuries consisted of two islands, mountainous Moro and little flat Stirling, separated by Blanche Harbor. Before going into Bougainville, Halsey's planners wanted the islands, Moro for a radar station, Stirling as an airfield site, and Blanche Harbor as an anchorage. Reconnaissance missions indicated only about 135 Japanese troops there, all on Moro.[12]

The attack force, under IMAC operational control, consisted of 4,608 New Zealanders from the New Zealand 3rd Division's 8th Brigade plus 1,966 supporting IMAC troops. All ground forces for Operation Goodtime were subordinate to Brigadier Robert A. Row, commander of the 8th Brigade. Previously, the New Zealanders had occupied Fiji and New Caledonia when those islands were threatened, then moved to Guadalcanal for jungle training. While such a large force was seemingly excessive, a counterlanding by the enemy only seventeen miles away in the Shortlands could not be ruled out. Probably, too, for political reasons, Halsey wanted to make maximum use of his New Zealanders. As the first opposed landing by New Zealand forces since Gallipoli, the Treasuries provided an opportunity to introduce the untried troops to combat with little risk. The New Zealand troops were reportedly amused by IMAC's instructions: "Shoot calmly, shoot fast, and shoot straight."[13]

Admiral Fort, who had commanded part of the New Georgia invasion force, was the amphibious commander. In the face of a serious shortage of transports, Fort assembled thirty-one craft including eight APDs and a variety of beaching craft that could carry 3,795 men. The remaining 2,800 would be moved forward in four waves during the next twenty days. Troops and equipment were loaded at Guadalcanal, the Russell Islands, and Vella Lavella, arriving early on 27 October at Blanche Harbor. The invasion beaches were then brought under fire by two destroyers and two newly developed LCI(G)s, infantry landing craft capable of providing fire support from close to shore.

Just after 0630, the 8th Brigade's 34th Battalion landed on unoccupied Stirling Island. Across Blanche Harbor, landing abreast in the Falami Point area of Mono Island, the 29th and 36th Battalions encountered only light machine-gun and small arms fire and quickly established a perimeter. One intrepid Seabee turned his bulldozer on a machine-gun pillbox, used the blade as a shield and buried the position in coral sand.[14] The most serious ground opposition encountered on Mono was from mortar fire directed against the beaches that hit two LSTs before destroyers silenced the mortars.

Concurrently, D Company from the 34th Battalion, with IMAC Seabees and technicians, landed at the mouth of the Soanotalu River to establish a radar station. The expected enemy air attack occurred in the afternoon, when twenty-five bombers attacked and damaged the destroyer USS *Cony* at a cost of having half their force downed by the thirty-two-plane AirSols patrol.

Yet the battle was far from over, as the few Japanese on Mono were determined fighters. The New Zealanders established a defensive perimeter including a small blockhouse around the prospective Soanotalu radar station. Hoping to break through and seize a landing barge for escape to Bougainville, 80 to 90 Japanese mounted a desperate attack centered on the blockhouse. By the end of the action, only three of the nine blockhouse defenders remained unwounded, while 40 Japanese were killed and the remainder withdrew. The last significant fighting occurred four days later when 12 Japanese were driven from a cave near Soanotalu. The New Zealanders and Americans incurred 226 casualties in the Treasury Islands, including 52 dead, while killing 231 Japanese and capturing eight.

Operation Goodtime proved well-named. An airstrip was built on Stirling Island for P-38s and B-25s, a PT boat base was established, and a radar station became operational in time to provide warnings for the Bougainville invasion force. Particularly important, the Treasuries became a valuable way station for funneling supplies to the Bougainville landing beaches.[15]

As noted by Morison: "The Japanese were caught flatfooted at the Treasuries. Although they had an important seaplane and naval base only 25 miles away at Shortlands, they did not catch on to what was happening until our troops were well ashore."[16] After the war, a Japanese intelligence officer commented about American strategy: "The Americans, with minimum losses, attacked and seized a relatively weak area, constructed airfields and then proceeded to cut the supply lines to troops in that area. . . . Americans flowed into our weaker points and submerged us, just as water seeks the weakest entry to sink a ship."[17] This was the successful strategy followed earlier by Halsey at Vella Lavella, was employed in the Treasuries, and would subsequently be followed on Bougainville, the Green Islands, and Emirau. Together with parallel moves by MacArthur, it would bring about the demise of Rabaul and collapse of the entire Japanese position in the South Pacific.

Along with the Treasuries, the Choiseul raid was an important preliminary to Bougainville, described by Geiger as "a series of short right jabs to throw the enemy off balance and to conceal the real power of our left hook to his belly at Empress Augusta Bay."[18] It was hoped that the raid, optimistically code named Blissful, would be interpreted by the Japanese as a prelude to an attack on the south or east coast of Bougainville or against the Shortlands. The operation would be conducted by the Marine 2nd Parachute Battalion commanded by the diminutive and pugnacious Lieutenant Colonel Victor H. "Brute" Krulak, eager to live up to his nickname in this first combat with his paramarines.

Like other paramarine units, the 2nd Parachute Battalion would never jump in combat. Because an opportunity to use their airborne training never arose, paramarines were employed for operations that made use of their skills as a select, hard-hitting force able to fight behind enemy lines using guerrilla tactics.[19] Since leaving the United States in October 1942, the battalion trained intensively in New Zealand and later on New Caledonia. Fully prepared, the men were anxious and ready for combat.

In addition to the regimental machine-gun platoon, an IMAC rocket detachment accompanied the raiders, to the displeasure of Krulak, who disliked being burdened with such heavy equipment. The rockets were included at Vandegrift's insistence to create the impression that a major invasion was under way. It was hoped that the Japanese would mistake the rocket fire as coming from 155-mm artillery, standard armament in an American division. Vandegrift instructed Krulak: "Make sure they think the invasion has commenced."[20] Air support would be provided and PT boats at Vella Lavella could be called upon in emergencies.[21]

Useful intelligence had earlier been gathered during reconnaissance operations. In addition, invaluable information was provided by C. W. Seton, an Australian coast watcher who left Choiseul to share his extensive knowledge and then returned to guide the paramarines. To assist in the landings and later, Seton recruited two hundred island natives.

As the canopy of trees was particularly thick even by South Pacific standards, trails and other important features on Choiseul were unmapped. Another major problem was mountain spurs that in places extended from the interior to the sea, making land movement at many points extremely arduous. Also, the island was teeming with Japanese evacuated from Kolombangara and elsewhere in the Central Solomons who were en route to reinforce Bougainville.

Operation Blissful began on 27 October when the 725-man reinforced battalion with Seton departed Vella Lavella on board landing craft, mechanized (LCMs). That evening the troops transferred to four APDs that had raced to the rendezvous point after discharging forces in the Treasuries. In the first minutes of 28 October, the vessels arrived near the village of Voza on the northwest coast of Choiseul, where the troops landed without opposition. Aided by natives recruited by Seton, supplies were brought ashore and concealed on high ground selected for the base camp. Also concealed nearby with their Navy crews at offshore Zinoa Island were four landing craft, personnel, ramped (LCP(R)s), thirty-six-foot Higgins boats that Krulak intended to use in moving along the coast.

As the raid developed, there was no difficulty attracting the enemy's attention. While still under way, the little fleet was spotted and bombed by a single aircraft without effect, and later another aircraft attacked an escorting destroyer during the landings. Afterwards, when the base camp was set up, there was another bombing attack, again without loss. The red herring operation was then announced to the press as a full-scale invasion, a rare instance during the war when false information was deliberately given to the American public.

A Japanese barge base at Sangigai, eight miles south of Voza, had been identified from native reports and patrol activity as a promising objective. To soften the target, a bombing mission of twelve TBF Avenger torpedo bombers and twenty-six fighters hit Sangigai early in the morning of 30 October. In the process, the boats Krulak intended to use in the attack were misidentified, strafed, and damaged. Krulak immediately changed the plan to an overland march to the Vagara River just north of the target, from which he launched a pincer attack using E and F companies. Advancing on Sangigai along the coast and finding the village abandoned, E Company methodically destroyed everything of use to the Japanese. Documents and charts were discovered, including one marking the minefields off southern Bougainville. These were immediately forwarded to Halsey, who ordered mining of the indicated ship channels, resulting in the sinking of two enemy vessels.

Meanwhile, Krulak led F Company into the interior to strike the rear of the village. Although the difficult jungle slowed movement and prevented a simultaneous attack with E Company, the result was even better than planned. Japanese flushed out by E Company's attack fell back behind the town, only to land in the lap of F Company, which took position in time to block their path. The Japanese then wasted their numerical advantage in a fruitless banzai charge, resulting in seventy-two dead and many wounded.

Moving in the other direction from the base camp, the battalion executive officer, Major Warner Bigger, led a force of eighty-seven men from G Company in a raid by water against an enemy base at Choiseul Bay. After the LCP(R)s ran aground several times well short of their destination, the troops landed at the Warrior River and embarked on an overland march. Soon caught in a swamp, the force was finally extricated by a native familiar with the area who was dispatched by Seton after he learned of their plight. Still hoping to surprise the enemy at Choiseul Bay, Bigger was thwarted when a Japanese soldier escaped an outpost attack to sound the alarm. The raiding force then moved against the secondary target selected by Krulak, a supply depot on offshore Guppy Island. The 60-mm mortar platoon of G Company unloosed 143 shells that hit a fuel dump and caused other damage.

Withdrawing for a pickup at Warrior River, the paramarines had to fight their way through Japanese forces between them and the river. It was then discovered that the enemy occupied the east bank, leaving them surrounded. Just in time, as pre-arranged, two LCP(R)s arrived, and Bigger's men boarded for a return to Voza. The adventure was far from over, however, as one boat sprang a leak and began to sink before clearing the reef. As in a suspenseful action movie, two PT boats suddenly appeared. Fifty-five men crowded on board PT 59, commanded by Lieutenant John F. Kennedy, for the return to base. By this point, the landings on Bougainville had begun, so it was no longer necessary to continue the ruse. With large Japanese forces descending on Voza, the paramarines boarded three LCIs and returned to Vella Lavella the night of 3 November.

As a feat of arms, Choiseul was a brilliant success. At Sangigai, an enemy base with its barges was destroyed and valuable intelligence for the coming Bougainville invasion was obtained from captured charts. Also, substantial Japanese supplies were destroyed at Guppy Island. At a cost of 13 killed, including one man captured and executed, and 12 wounded, the raiders killed an estimated 143 Japanese and wounded many others. As for the primary purpose of the operation, it is uncertain whether the Japanese changed their dispositions appreciably in direct response.[22]

Choiseul provided a perfect launch pad for the illustrious career of Krulak, who received the Navy Cross for the remarkable operation. His most significant and lasting victory, however, would occur on a very different battlefield. In the halls of Congress, during the bitter postwar debate over military unification, Krulak's brilliant defense of the Marine Corps would be instrumental in preserving its established role in the nation's defense.[23]

In the first minutes of 1 November, as Wilkinson prepared to land the Bougainville invasion force, "Tip" Merrill's light cruisers and destroyers struck at Buka Passage. Aided by specially equipped AirSols spotter aircraft, Merrill thoroughly blasted the Buka and Bonis airfields while Japanese aircraft struck back without success. His work done, Merrill raced south for a similar performance before dawn against the Shortland airfields. Later that day and the next, carriers USS Princeton and Saratoga hit the Buka Passage fields again. This time no Japanese aircraft responded, as Merrill's bombardments had rendered the airfields unusable.[24]

Thus, through a variety of operations, the groundwork for the invasion of Bougainville was carefully laid while leaving the Japanese with no idea where the blow would fall.

# CHAPTER 12

# "Guadalcanal—
# Minus Most of the Errors"

Although Halsey's planners studied Bougainville for months before the invasion, much remained unknown, and there would be many surprises. According to the 3rd Marine Division history, "Virtually nothing was known of the hydrography, terrain conditions inland from selected beaches, and location of enemy defenses in the immediate area."[1] One reason for the insufficient information was the delayed selection of the landing location.[2] Nor did it help that the island contained what was arguably the most impenetrable jungle in the Pacific.[3]

Nevertheless, with the highly experienced Vandegrift in charge on land and Wilkinson commanding the amphibious phase "as if he had been preparing for it all his life,"[4] Operation Cherryblossom, according to one study "resembled . . . Guadalcanal—minus most of the errors."[5] Perhaps the most important improvement over Guadalcanal was the decision to employ the Marines only for the assault landings and development of a secure perimeter, after which the Army would take over.

Vandegrift wanted to land the entire 3rd Marine Division at once, but a shortage of shipping caused by the upcoming invasion of the Gilberts made it impossible to move more than two-thirds of the division. In fact, it took strenuous efforts by Wilkinson to obtain even twelve transports and cargo ships so that, according to Morison, "the 3d Marines [the division] went up in style."[6] Wilkinson's staff proposed using a shuttle system over a three-week period to lift the rest of the division, the Army's 37th Division reserve, and other IMAC components. Such a lengthy buildup was unacceptable to Vandegrift, who knew how resourceful the Japanese could be in mounting a swift counterattack. Appealing to Halsey, Vandegrift gained approval for the transports to turn around and immediately bring forward the rest of the ground force.[7] Along with the Choiseul raid, this was an important change from Barrett's invasion plan, which was otherwise closely followed.

After rehearsals in the New Hebrides, the reinforced 3rd and 9th Marines embarked on 28 October in separate transport divisions. Sailing from widely separated bases, Wilkinson hoped to avoid revealing too soon that a major operation was in progress. Two days later, other transports departed from Guadalcanal with the 3rd MDB and the 2nd Provisional Marine Raider Regiment. In all, 14,321 troops were committed. On the morning of 31 October, the transports, under the tactical command of Commodore Reifsnider, met up with a covering force of eleven destroyers, eight minesweepers, and small craft. With an umbrella of Navy PBY Catalina patrol bombers and Army B-24 Liberators overhead, TF 31 proceeded up the southwest coast of the Solomons, past Rendova, Vella Lavella, and the Treasuries, to Empress Augusta Bay.

While the minesweepers went to work and masthead navigation discovered many uncharted shoals, the destroyer USS *Wadsworth* used radar to verify the location of the key invasion area landmarks—Cape Torokina and Puruata and Torokina islands. A reconnaissance by the submarine USS *Guardfish* several weeks earlier had found that air and naval charts were off by several miles, and *Wadsworth* confirmed the errors. As the information obtained from the *Guardfish* expedition was incomplete and out of date, another team conducted a reconnaissance before the landings. Because there had been some evidence of recent Japanese activity, Vandegrift was anxious to confirm that there were still no more than three hundred Japanese in the immediate area. There were actually fewer than that, but the reconnaissance team failed to transmit this information,[8] causing Vandegrift undue anxiety.

The overriding concern was the proximity of the Japanese airfields, especially Rabaul, just 210 miles away and Kahili on Bougainville even closer. Like the challenge at Vella Lavella and now of even greater urgency, the invasion force would need to get in swiftly, unload, and depart. To facilitate a fast turnaround, the transports were loaded to half their capacity and the cargo ships to only a quarter of capacity. Also, to minimize handling, a carefully worked out plan was developed involving the loading and delivery to the beaches of supplies in unbroken cargo nets. Follow-up convoys would deliver additional supplies and bring up the 21st Marines, the 1st Marine Parachute Regiment, and the Army's 37th Infantry Division.

The Marines carried just enough for a single day of expected combat, the riflemen toting 80 rounds and the Browning Automatic Rifle (BAR) men 200 rounds. This calculated risk, designed so the Marines would debark and move unimpeded to their objectives, was run on the assumption that few enemy troops occupied the immediate area. In that respect the intelligence was reliable, although the 2nd Company, 1st Battalion, 23rd Infantry of the Japanese 6th Division would prove formidable enough.

To provide space to rapidly absorb the incoming waves of men and equipment, the invasion beaches, averaging only thirty to fifty yards deep, extended a lengthy eight thousand yards from Cape Torokina to Koromokina Lagoon. Eleven of the twelve transports and cargo ships were assigned their own beaches along this strand, and one transport was assigned the north shore of Puruata Island. The 3rd Marine Division regiments would land abreast, the 9th Marines commanded by Colonel Edward A. Craig on the left and the 3rd Marines under Colonel George W. McHenry on the right, with the 2nd Raider Battalion between 1/3 and 2/3. Puruata was to be taken by the 3rd Raider Battalion, minus M Company, which landed on Bougainville with a special mission.

After the transports and cargo ships anchored, Wilkinson waited for first light to commence the landings. The first waves were rail loaded into LCVPs and LCMs for a rapid embarkation and run to the beaches four to five thousand yards away.[9] Other troops descended to landing craft using cargo nets, each LCVP joining a circle before beginning its run to the beach.

A preliminary naval bombardment that drew no response was followed by five minutes of bombing and strafing by thirty-one TBF Avengers from Munda.[10] These attacks were largely ineffective. Most of the nine hundred rounds of 5-inch shells merely hit the palm trees, and the bombs fell behind the defended beaches. Almost immediately after the TBFs departed, at 0726, four minutes ahead of schedule, more than seven thousand Marines hit the twelve invasion beaches.

Marines from the 3rd Division dash from their landing craft across the narrow beach to enter the dense jungle of Bougainville, 1 November 1943. (USMC)

It was fortunate that the 9th Marines on the left flank encountered no enemy opposition, as landing conditions presented enough of a challenge. Landing craft were furiously tossed about in the heavy surf, and steep beaches prevented them from running far enough ashore to beach solidly. Boats broached, swamped, and collided, leaving the beaches and offshore waters terribly strewn so that orderly landing of men and equipment in later waves became impossible. Because of damage to landing craft ramps or inability of boat crews to find clear beach space, many Marines were forced to wade ashore in deep water. In all, sixty-four LCVPs and twenty-two LCMs were lost that would be sorely missed in completing the unloading, the problem exacerbated by the inability of a salvage tug to assist because of intervening shoals. Once aware of the chaos, Vandegrift and Turnage decided to abandon half of the 9th Marines' beaches.

In the 3rd Marines sector, at the far right, 1/3 came up against the main enemy opposition. The Japanese had built twenty-five log and earthen pillboxes to defend both faces of the cape, with the more elaborate defenses on the south face. The northern face contained the heaviest weapon, a 75-mm field gun, defended by two pillboxes, trenches, and rifle pits. This well-concealed defense wall was only slightly dented by the inadequate destroyer bombardment that eliminated only three pillboxes. As observed in the 3rd Marine Division history: "It was one of the first occasions in the Pacific where the amphibious assault troops encountered an occupied and organized immediate beach defense practically untouched by preliminary bombardment."[11]

After thirty-one Munda-based Marine aircraft completed final bombing and strafing runs, the boats carrying 1/3 entered the waters between Cape Torokina and Torokina and Puruata islands. They were immediately caught in a crossfire from machine guns, mortars, and, most deadly, the 75-mm gun, which opened fire at a range of five hundred yards. Altogether, fourteen boats were hit by the gun, of which four were sunk, with casualties that included the boat group commander. Loss of the boat commander, along with evasive action taken by the Coast Guard crews, resulted in great disarray in the landings. While B Company landed correctly at the left end of the line, A Company found itself in the center where C was to land, and C Company landed unexpectedly at the invasion's right flank near the point of the cape. Working his way laboriously across the battlefield, A's company commander eventually brought his men to their intended position on the right flank. Asked by 1/3's battalion commander where he'd been, he answered, "Ask the Navy!" Also unexpected was the hot reception received by elements of the battalion headquarters and reserve. Expecting to land in the wake of the assault troops, they found themselves in the forefront.

Despite heavy fire, 1/3 did not come through too badly, losing fourteen killed in the boats and twelve on the beach.[12] The wounded included the battalion commander, Lieutenant Colonel Leonard Mason, who shouted to his men before evacuation, "Get the hell in there and fight!"[13]

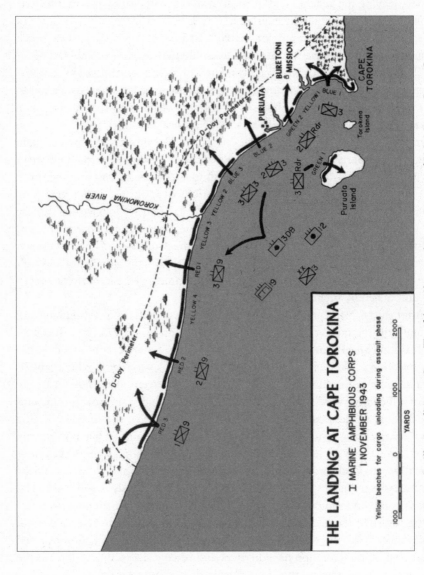

Map 8. Bougainville: Landings at Cape Torokina (Shaw and Kane, *History of U.S. Marine Corps Operations in World War II, vol. 2: Isolation of Rabaul, 212*)

Robert A. Owens, a sergeant in A Company, resolved to silence the 75-mm gun. While others brought fire on two machine guns protecting the weapon, Owens charged through the bunker's fire port, chasing the occupants out the rear door where they were shot down. Killed by fire from supporting enemy trenches as he emerged from the bunker, Owens earned the campaign's first Medal of Honor. The other pillboxes were all knocked out by afternoon using a technique developed from earlier experience. BAR fire was poured into pillbox embrasures, enabling troops to close in and drop grenades into the ventilators or attack the pillboxes from the rear. Some of the most brutal action occurred during hand-to-hand fighting in the supporting trenches. The 1/3 troops nearly used up their limited ammunition during the action, but replenishment was obtained from units less heavily engaged.

Troops from the 3rd Marine Regiment hotly engaged after landing on Bougainville, 1 November 1943. (USMC)

Adjoining 1/3, the 2nd Raider Battalion also took fire from the 75-mm gun, machine guns, and mortars. The battalion commander, Lieutenant Colonel Joseph P. McCaffery, died on the beach while reorganizing his troops.[14] Opposition in this sector was offered by a reinforced enemy platoon fighting from two bunkers and trenches. The battle ended quickly after the destruction of the bunkers, with the remaining Japanese escaping into the jungle. In heading across the bay to Puruata Island, the 3rd Raider Battalion went through the same crossfire as 1/3. A landing point on the northern coast had been chosen to avoid the stoutly sandbagged defenses facing the sea. With the help of 75-mm guns acquired from the 9th Marines, three raider companies went against an enemy platoon fighting from pillboxes, rifle pits, and trees. By afternoon, the fixed defenses were overcome, and the operation, which continued into the next day, was then largely against snipers. Puruata cost the raiders five killed and thirty-two wounded, as against twenty-nine Japanese killed. About forty enemy fighters probably slipped away to fight again. As a final step, two raider platoons landed on tiny Torokina Island on D+3 to deal with a force of Japanese that were bringing small arms fire on Puruata. They found that the enemy had somehow disappeared.

The beaches where 2/3 and 3/3 landed had no fixed defenses, and the few Japanese there retreated into the jungle after brief resistance.

Except for the raiders on Puruata, who would need some additional time, all units took their initial objectives quickly. Even 1/3, which faced the stiffest resistance, took Cape Torokina by afternoon after wiping out their hard-fighting opponents. Of the Japanese defenders, about half the 270-man company died and the rest slipped away. The Marines sustained 182 casualties including 78 killed.[15]

Marines encountering one of their greatest foes on Bougainville: mud. Numa Numa Trail, November 1943. (National Archives and Records Administration)

Units were realigned as necessary, and the Marines advanced to their final objectives. As there were no prominent landmarks immediately behind the narrow beaches, units were ordered to advance a specific distance inland, ranging from six hundred to a thousand yards at Cape Torokina. Meanwhile, two

companies were positioned as advanced guards in areas most vulnerable to counterattack. G Company of the 9th Marines took station south of the Laruma
River to oppose any thrust from the north. M Company of the 3rd Raiders,
detached from the battalion to land with the 2nd Raiders, bounded forward to
an assigned post at the Mission Trail. It was the route the Japanese would most
likely take to approach the perimeter in strength.

With the battle of the beachhead over, a very different struggle commenced
with the wretched environment. It was for one Marine "like running across
30 feet of the Sahara and suddenly dropping off into the Everglades." The
"Everglades" was a swamp extending two miles behind the beaches whose exis-
tence was unknown beforehand. Turnage would later say, "Never had men in the
Marine Corps had to fight and maintain themselves over such difficult terrain as
was encountered on Bougainville."[16]

Invasion-day challenges included bringing forward and emplacing the 12th
Marines' 75-mm and 105-mm guns that, distributed among the front line units,
were essential for defense of the perimeter that night. Making the process more
difficult was the questionable assignment to shore parties of the gunners, who
would better have stayed with their weapons.[17] Fortunately, landing vehicles,
tracked (LVTs) from the 3rd Amphibious Tractor Battalion succeeded in hauling the guns through the mire and setting them up on patches of higher ground,
with ammunition and gun supplies alongside in rubber boats. By nightfall, the
artillery was registered and prepared to fire on areas of possible Japanese concentration. To this was added the firepower of the 3rd MDB's heavier artillery and
90-mm anti-aircraft guns.

While the Marines established themselves ashore, the Japanese command
at Rabaul reacted as expected. At 0735, nine minutes after the Marines hit the
beach, the first attack was unleashed by fifty-three Val dive bombers and Zeros.
Landing operations were suspended for two hours while the ships got under way
and took evasive action. The standing AirSols patrol of thirty-two fighters from
Vella Lavella and Munda then went into action.

Eight RNZAF P-40s surprised the Japanese attackers and within minutes
downed seven planes and possibly one more.[18] Soon after, eight P-38s engaged
fifteen to twenty enemy planes and disposed of seven without loss. Although
twelve Val dive bombers managed to penetrate the air defenses, thanks to skillful
maneuvers and well directed anti-aircraft fire that brought down four planes, the
ships emerged unscathed. Casualties from this morning attack were confined to
two killed and five wounded by a near miss on the destroyer *Wadsworth* and a
few men on the beach hit by strafing. Along with attacks during the afternoon,
the Japanese employed about 120 aircraft that day, of which 26 were claimed
to be shot down.[19] Except for delays they caused in the unloading and a few
American casualties on the ships and beaches, the Japanese had nothing to show
for their efforts.

Before 1730, when unloading was suspended for the day, more than 14,000 Marines and 6,200 tons of supplies were landed.[20] This was a record performance, all the more remarkable considering the interruptions during air attack, the loss of landing craft on the 9th Marines beaches, and the diversion of vessels from those beaches, including one cargo ship that ran aground during repositioning.

While the tonnage brought ashore was a decided success, the disarray on the beaches and the diversion of ships from their assigned beaches caused many supplies to be landed in the wrong places. Units would face extended supply shortages before the mess was sorted out, and in some instances they never recovered much-needed equipment.

Because Wilkinson feared a naval attack, as happened at Savo Island after the Guadalcanal landings, four cargo vessels that had not been fully unloaded were sent away with the others at day's end. Remembering the acute supply shortage that developed on Guadalcanal when ships departed before unloading, Vandegrift tried to prevent their departure. Convinced by Vandegrift that their contents were essential, Wilkinson ordered the four vessels to return and unload on the following day.[21] Their return, and the safety of the entire invasion, would hinge upon the outcome of the naval battle that intelligence reports indicated could be expected that night.

# CHAPTER 13

⦿⦿⦿

# "The Final Outcome ... Was Never in Doubt"

M errill's TF 39 drew a deep breath off Vella Lavella after completing its pre-invasion bombardments at Buka Passage and the Shortlands. That respite lasted just hours, as Army reconnaissance planes spotted a Japanese fleet from Rabaul heading toward Empress Augusta Bay. Halsey immediately ordered Merrill to intercept.

Merrill's force consisted of four light cruisers—*Montpelier*, *Cleveland*, *Columbia*, and *Denver*—escorted by eight destroyers of Destroyer Squadron 23 led by Captain Arleigh A. "31 knot" Burke.[1] Four of the destroyers were commanded directly by Burke, with the other four under Commander Bernard L. "Count" Austin. When the call to action arrived, Burke's destroyers were refueling at Kula Gulf[2] and had to race back, rejoining the task force shortly before midnight.

Merrill would face Imperial Japanese Navy Cruiser Division 5 under Rear Admiral Sentaro Omori. As a destroyer force commander, Omori had participated in the Pearl Harbor attack and later directed the occupation of Attu in the Aleutians. His cruisers were at Rabaul only by chance after escorting a convoy there and were the only big-gun vessels immediately available to challenge the invasion. Although Koga at Truk hoped to conserve his strength for a decisive fleet action in the Central Pacific, he could not allow Halsey to establish himself so near Rabaul without challenge. Thus Omori was put at the full disposal of the 8th Fleet commander at Rabaul, Vice Admiral Tomoshige Samejima.

On 31 October, after Japanese aircraft spotted Merrill's force en route to Buka Passage, Omori set out in pursuit. Through a combination of weather and miscalculation about Merrill's destination, Omori sailed for and reached the Treasuries while Merrill was shelling Buka. Returning empty-handed to Rabaul late the next morning, Omori learned of the landings and received new

111

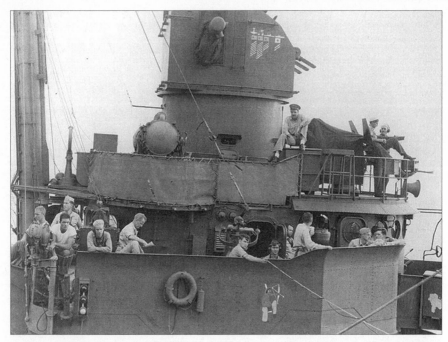

Captain Arleigh A. Burke, reading at left center, on the starboard bridge wing of destroyer USS *Charles Ausburne*, flagship of Destroyer Squadron 23. Note "Little Beaver" insignia on bridge wing and scoreboard on the ship's Mark 37 gun director, 1943–1944. (Naval Historical Foundation)

instructions from Samejima. Reinforced by four newly arrived destroyers, Omori was expected to escort five old destroyer-transports with one thousand troops to Motupena Point immediately south of the invasion beaches. With this reinforcement, Omori's escort force consisted of two heavy cruisers, *Myoko* and *Haguro*, two light cruisers, *Sendai* and *Agano*, and six destroyers. After an extended delay in loading the troops, an encounter with an American submarine, and bombing by an American aircraft, Omori was not certain that the troops could be landed safely. Receiving permission to abort the landing operation, Omori sent back the troop-carrying destroyers and headed for Empress Augusta Bay, expecting to find ripe targets there.[3]

Little would have been found, as Wilkinson withdrew all the transports and cargo vessels in the late afternoon. Reifsnider had turned around the four unloaded cargo ships as urged by Vandegrift, but after word arrived of Omori's approach Reifsnider reversed course to await developments. When a Japanese scout plane misidentified a mine-laying operation as transports disembarking troops, Omori's misconception about what he might find in the bay was confirmed. But regardless of the situation offshore, Omori might seriously disrupt the invasion unless stopped.

The outcome of the coming battle would largely depend on whether Merrill could overcome the superior firepower of Omori's twenty 8-inch guns. Also, though Merrill enjoyed a numerical advantage in destroyers, Omori's ships had torpedoes with greater range and destructive power. But Merrill held a trump card, a highly reliable radar system that could find the enemy in the dark of night. While Omori also had radar, he considered it unreliable and essentially disregarded it in the battle.[4] Also going for Merrill was the preparedness of his cruisers, gained through experience and considerable training.

Merrill was described by one of his captains as "one of those men who thought best under stress," and at that perilous time he made sound decisions that shaped the battle. He resolved to "maintain the cruisers in a position across the entrance to Empress Augusta Bay and prevent the entry therein of a single enemy ship."[5]

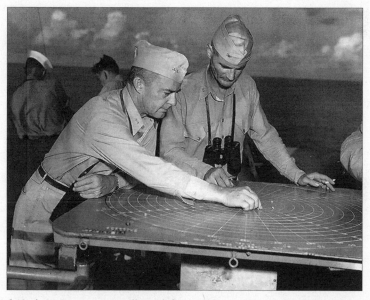

Rear Admiral A. Stanton Merrill (at left) working with a maneuvering board, with Captain W. D. Brown, 23 December 1943. (U.S. Navy)

Kept informed of Omori's movements by two Army reconnaissance planes whose reports he found "phenomenally accurate," Merrill aimed to take position about twenty miles from Cape Torokina. Starting from there, he hoped to push the battle westward, away from the beachhead. At the outset, Burke's and Austin's destroyers would mount torpedo attacks against the flanks of the advancing force. Afterwards, unlike their employment in earlier operations, the destroyers would fight independent of the cruisers. The cruisers would engage at

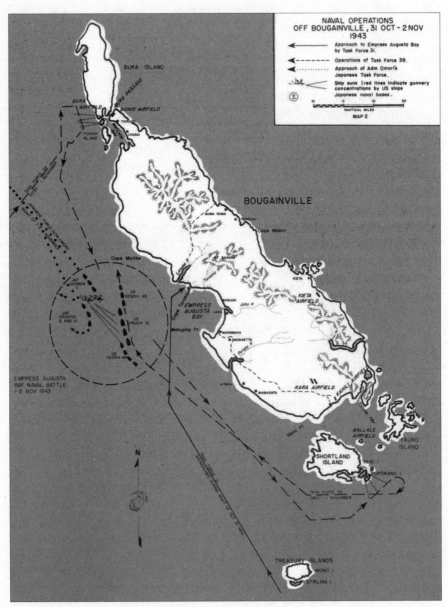

**Map 9. Naval Operations off Bougainville** (Rentz, *Bougainville and the Northern Solomons*, 23)

a range near the limit of the enemy's deadly long lance torpedoes, about 16,000 to 20,000 yards. They would then maneuver to minimize the risk from enemy torpedoes and gunfire while relying on radar to seek out the enemy.

The first blow was struck at 0130 on 2 November by an AirSols plane that bombed and slightly damaged the heavy cruiser *Haguro*. An hour later, speeding north at 0227, Merrill's radar picked up Omori's port (left hand) column at 36,000 yards. Burke's destroyers quickly peeled off on the column's flank and launched twenty-five torpedoes. None struck home, as Omori had just then swung his column southwest. Although this maneuver proved timely for the Japanese, overcomplicated movements ordered by Omori resulted in some loss of formation. Merrill's radar-controlled guns then opened up with concentrated fire on Omori's port column. Hits were registered on the light cruiser *Sendai* that caused multiple explosions and jammed her rudder. Then, while attempting to avoid Merrill's gunfire, destroyers *Samidare* and *Shiratsuyu* collided and were forced to pull out of the fight.[6] Round one decidedly belonged to Merrill.

Omori used brilliant star shells to locate his opponent, to which Merrill responded with a smoke screen. While altering course to maintain a 19,000-yard range, the American cruisers identified and poured fire on the center column that contained the heavy cruisers and on Omori's starboard (right hand) column. Dodging Merrill's shells, destroyer *Hatsukaze* in the starboard column barged into heavy cruiser *Myoko* and lost two torpedo tubes and a section of starboard bow. *Haguro* sustained six hits from Merrill's cruisers, but four were duds and the other shells caused only minor damage.

At 0301, after steering a southerly course, Merrill shook loose Austin's destroyers and led his cruisers in an elaborate figure-8. This enabled him to maintain range while making it difficult for Japanese torpedoes to target his rapidly maneuvering ships. It was not until 0313 that Omori finally sighted his opponent and opened fire. Three 8-inch shells struck *Denver*, all of which failed to explode although the inflow of water forced the cruiser, and in turn the other cruisers, to reduce speed to twenty-five knots. Otherwise, as the cruisers furiously exchanged fire and the Japanese launched ten torpedoes, no hits were scored by either side. Exhibiting far less proficiency in gunnery than in maneuver, Merrill's cruisers fired nearly 4,600 rounds from their 6-inch guns that night but scored no more than twenty hits.[7]

To Japanese observers relying on sporadic star shell illuminations, geysers thrown up around Merrill's cruisers were thought to be torpedo hits and ship disappearances in the dark and smoke were interpreted as sinkings. It appeared to them that as many as three American cruisers were sent to the bottom. At 0337, unaware of the size of his opponent[8] and believing he had done well enough, Omori ordered retirement toward Rabaul.[9] There would be no repeat of Savo Island. But this battle was far from over.

Burke's destroyers had meanwhile run into trouble. After delivering their unsuccessful torpedo attack, his "Little Beavers"[10] became separated and did not reassemble to participate in the attack for an hour. From his initial position in the rear of Merrill's force, Austin could not get a radar fix on the Japanese columns. As his four destroyers separated from the cruisers and swung southwest to seek targets, USS *Foote* misunderstood a signal and went astray. Dashing to resume station, the destroyer blundered into the path of a torpedo intended for Merrill's cruisers that blew off her stern and left *Foote* dead in the water. In a chain reaction, *Cleveland* swerved to avoid *Foote*, forcing USS *Spence* into a sharp turn that caused it to sideswipe USS *Thatcher*. Neither destroyer was seriously injured, but *Spence* then took a shell hit at the waterline that would later cause her to lose speed.

For about an hour and a half, Burke and Austin sought enemy targets in the darkness, mindful that it was as easy to shoot a friend as a foe. At one point, Austin lost a splendid opportunity for a torpedo attack on Omori's heavy cruisers when a combat information center officer identified the ships as friendly. Yet another chance was lost when Burke spotted one of the enemy destroyers that had collided while avoiding Merrill's gunfire, but was deterred from attacking when misinformed by Austin that the target was his own vessel, *Spence*. Burke could also err in the blackness, at one point forcing *Spence* to take evasive action after apologizing to Austin for the incoming projectiles.

While neither Burke nor Austin bagged any fresh targets, they attacked and sent to the bottom two ships crippled early in the action by cruiser fire and collision. They first pummeled light cruiser *Sendai* as it circled helplessly, racked by explosions before sinking at 0400. Admiral Ijuin, who had fought the Battle of Vella Lavella, was rescued, but all except a few others were lost.[11] Closing the action, the American destroyers turned on *Hatsukaze*, which sank at 0539, three hours after the action commenced. The Japanese rescued all but nine of the destroyer's crew.

Eager for more prey, Burke sought permission to pursue Omori's departing force, but Merrill prudently ordered the destroyers to rejoin the cruisers. With dawn approaching, a Japanese air strike from Rabaul was a certainty. TF 39 hurried south, tailed by *Foote* under tow with protective destroyers. An urgent call was sent for air cover, but bad weather allowed only a limited AirSols response.

About a hundred Japanese carrier planes that arrived the day before at Rabaul were thrown into the attack. Disdaining disabled *Foote* and its destroyer escort, they made for the cruisers ten miles farther away. A sixteen-plane AirSols patrol intercepted them, the eight Hellcats, three P-38s, four NZRAF P-40s, and one Corsair downing eight Japanese aircraft at the outset and eight more later. Otherwise, TF 39 had to defend itself during the intense twenty-minute action that began at about 0800.

Merrill described the scene as "an unorganized hell in which it was impossible to speak, hear or even think." Placing the ships in circular anti-aircraft formation, he ordered successive sharp course changes that were as well-executed by the cruisers as their coordinated movements the night before had been. Heavy and accurate fire was unleashed, beginning with the 5- and 6-inch guns that commenced fire at 14,000 yards. Particularly rich pickings were found in sixteen Val dive bombers that obligingly made slow descents in threes. Altogether, Merrill counted seventeen planes shot down including one bagged by a 6-inch gun of flagship *Montpelier*. In return for the sacrifice of precious carrier aircraft and pilots, the attackers could only score two minor bomb hits on *Montpelier's* catapult. Kusaka at Rabaul might have launched further attacks, but he was kept busy defending against a heavy raid by Kenney.

Before returning to base at Purvis Bay near Guadalcanal, TF 39 was called upon to render one more service for Halsey. Reifsnider's four cargo ships were finally unloading and would need protection on the way home. With unloading completed on Bougainville, TF 39 met up with Reifsnider's ships at sea and accompanied them through the night. Off Rendova, Merrill passed along escort duties to a smaller force and headed home for refueling, rearming, and much-needed rest after sixty-three hours of intense operations.

Omori's precipitous withdrawal without attempting to break through to the invasion beaches did not sit well with Koga, who ordered the ships to return to Truk and relieved Omori of command.[12] Nevertheless, Omori would attain the rank of vice admiral months later, first directing the Kaiten human torpedo program and then gaining command of the Seventh Fleet before the surrender, when it remained a fleet in name only.

Like Omori, Merrill greatly overestimated the success of his ships that night. In wording the citations accompanying their Navy Cross awards, Burke and Austin were commended for their roles in sinking five enemy warships and damaging four more, a far cry from the true results. Also, considering that he lost a quarter of his strength before swinging into action, that two of his ships collided and lost efficiency, and that splendid attack opportunities were missed, Austin's commendation clearly overreached in praising how he "hurled the full fighting strength of his ships against the enemy."

Empress Augusta Bay would be the final major surface engagement of the Solomons campaign. Merrill might have achieved more if the gunnery of the cruisers had approached their skill in maneuver and if destroyer attacks had succeeded as planned. Still, Merrill achieved his primary objective of keeping the Japanese out of Empress Augusta Bay. While the fortunes of war might well have shifted in Omori's favor had he continued the battle with his heavier guns, Merrill would nevertheless claim that "the final outcome of the battle was never in doubt."[13]

CHAPTER 14

"The Most Desperate Emergency"

Merrill's victory at Empress Augusta Bay could provide only momentary security for the Bougainville invasion forces. Writing about the ensuing crisis, Halsey called it "the most desperate emergency that confronted me in my entire term as [Commander South Pacific]."[1]

Admiral Koga fully recognized Halsey's vulnerability. Although aircraft carriers and battleships would be too exposed to land-based air attack,[2] heavy cruisers backed by massive air support from Rabaul could annihilate Halsey's less heavily armed warships and devastate the Marine's still fragile foothold. A year earlier, battleship bombardment of the Marine beachhead on Guadalcanal created a crisis that led to Halsey's appointment as South Pacific Area commander. The leader of that bombardment force, Vice Admiral Takeo Kurita, was now assigned by Koga to support Samejima at Rabaul and turn his guns on Halsey's forces at Empress Augusta Bay.

Kurita departed Truk on 3 November with seven heavy cruisers—*Takao*, *Maya*, *Atago*, *Suzuya*, *Mogami*, *Chikuma*, and *Chokai*—plus light cruiser *Noshiro*, four destroyers, and a fleet train. About noon on 4 November, a B-24 bomber sighted Kurita's fleet off the Admiralty Islands, heading toward Rabaul to refuel before sailing for Bougainville.

Even if his ships had not been recovering after their intensive operations, Merrill's TF 39 could not have faced such heavy firepower with any hope of success. But surrendering the waters around Bougainville was not an option. Compounding the immediate threat, a major reinforcement convoy was already at sea with another scheduled to follow three days later. If those ships were not brought in, the troops on Bougainville would be starved for reinforcements and supplies and the entire operation jeopardized—as happened on Guadalcanal after the Japanese dominated the surrounding waters.

Halsey's solution was to employ Sherman's TF 38, built around fleet carrier *Saratoga* and light carrier *Princeton*, then refueling south of Guadalcanal. If surprised while anchored at Simpson Harbor, the Japanese heavy cruisers might be so injured they would be unable to continue their mission. Everything in the rulebook argued against exposing carriers to attack from land-based aircraft, and in that respect the situation was actually far worse than thought. While about 150 enemy planes were believed to be at Rabaul, there were in fact 373 between the base force and the newly arrived carrier planes.

Some factors were in Halsey's favor. Japanese bases along the approach route had all been occupied or neutralized, and there were few shoals to worry about in the eastern Solomon Sea. But the great plus was the men who would conduct the mission. TF 38 was led by Ted Sherman, the Navy's most experienced and aggressive carrier admiral. And there were no better-prepared airmen than *Saratoga*'s Air Group 12, led by Commander Henry H. Caldwell, with effervescent Commander Joseph C. "Jumping Joe" Clifton in command of the F6F Hellcat fighters. Intensively trained as a team, with grandstanding and sloppy flying forbidden, Clifton's pilots were committed to providing close cover for the group's TBF Avenger torpedo bombers and SBD Dauntless dive bombers that were well-schooled in attacking moving ships.[3]

The hastily drawn-up plan radioed to Sherman called for TF 38 to reach a point 57 miles southwest of Cape Torokina after daylight on 5 November and launch its aircraft. The planes would head northwest to Rabaul, 230 miles away. Bomber pilots would make the enemy cruisers their first priority; the destroyers would be second. Everything flyable on board *Saratoga* and *Princeton* would be employed, with AirSols fighters from Vella Lavella providing air cover for the carriers. To inflict additional damage, Kenney's New Guinea–based aircraft would raid Rabaul after the Navy pilots completed their mission.

With the painful knowledge that his son was then on board *Saratoga*, Halsey ordered, "Let 'er go." Halsey later wrote that he "sincerely expected both air groups to be cut to pieces and both carriers stricken, if not lost."[4] Morison described the mission as "one of the most rugged tasks ever handed to pilots in the South Pacific."[5]

Complete surprise would be impossible, as Rabaul had efficient radar that typically could provide at least a half-hour's warning of incoming aircraft. Kenney's bombers had repeatedly visited Rabaul, and with the many major warships in harbor it had become an especially attractive target.

Fortunately, weather conditions were ideal. Overcast skies and squalls shielded TF 38 from enemy reconnaissance aircraft until dawn, when a Japanese plane spotted the ships but misidentified them as a Bougainville reinforcement group.[6] A calm sea made for a rapid run to the launch point at twenty-seven knots, and a favorable five- to seven-knot wind was blowing when launching commenced on schedule at 0900. Ninety-seven aircraft took off: twenty-three

Avengers, twenty-two Dauntlesses, and fifty-two Hellcats. The extraordinary luck continued as the thick cloud cover persisted until the flight neared Rabaul, when the skies cleared to a bright morning with fifty-mile visibility.

After flying up St. George Channel, Sherman's aircraft made a great three-quarter circle to the left, crossing over Crater Peninsula, then swung over Blanche Bay to swoop down on their prey in Simpson Harbor. Below were crowded forty to fifty ships, including Kurita's newly arrived heavy cruisers and about twenty light cruisers and destroyers. Some vessels were refueling or otherwise not in condition to get under way immediately. Those that could leave dashed for the harbor exit or took evasive action within the harbor. Meanwhile, shore batteries lost no time going into action, unleashing an intense curtain of anti-aircraft fire.

Japanese warships in the harbor of Rabaul maneuver to avoid attack from aircraft launched from USS *Saratoga*, 5 November 1943. Photographed from Commander Henry H. Caldwell's TBF Avenger by photographer P. T. Barnett, who was killed during the raid. (National Archives and Records Administration)

About seventy Japanese fighters were airborne when the raiders arrived, flying outside the range of their flak and ready to attack as soon as the Hellcats separated from the bombers. Then came the big surprise. Clifton's Hellcats stayed with the bombers through the flak to provide maximum protection until the last possible moment, flying in three tiers of sixteen planes each. The lowest Hellcats flew just 800 to 1,000 feet above the bombers and the middle tier was 3,000 feet higher. At the top, sixteen Hellcats were positioned to oppose any enemy aircraft that might break into the formation.

Beginning at 14,500 feet, the Dauntlesses descended to release their bombs at about 2,000 feet. On the heels of the dive bombers, the Avengers struck. Flying in low, where they were immune from the guns on shore and not too troubled by ship anti-aircraft fire, they swooped in parallel to their quarry, then executed ninety-degree turns and released their fish some 200 to 300 feet above the water. The torpedoes, with their 600-pound warheads, were set to run at six feet. When the bombers completed their attack, they ran a gauntlet of fire, maneuvering across the harbor at full speed to rejoin their escorts and return to the carriers.

High above the harbor, acting as spotter for the bombers, with a photographer to record the action, was the skipper of Air Group 12, Commander Caldwell. As the operation concluded, eight Zeros closed in on his Avenger and his two Hellcat escorts. During the ensuing desperate fight, his photographer was killed and his gunner wounded as he fought off the Zeros. Although badly shot up during desperate maneuvering, all three planes survived and made it back. One Hellcat landed on board *Princeton* with more than two hundred bullet holes and no flaps, and the other fighter made an emergency landing on Vella Lavella. Caldwell's Avenger returned to *Saratoga*, according to his report, "with one wheel, no flaps, no aileron and no radio."[7]

Of the seven heavy cruisers, four were severely damaged. While *Maya* was attempting to leave the harbor, she was struck by a bomb that either hit the catapult area or plunged down the stack and exploded in the engine room, killing or wounding 130 on board.[8] The resultant fire raged until late the next day. *Mogami*, recently back in service after repair of heavy damage suffered at Midway, was struck by a bomb or torpedo. In the effort to extinguish serious fires in the cruiser's aircraft storage area, two turrets were flooded. *Atago* took hull and other damage from three bomb near misses and lost many on board, including her captain, who was killed by a bomb fragment. *Takao* took a bomb hit on her starboard side that blew a large hole at the waterline and disabled a gun turret. *Suzuya* and *Chikuma* incurred slight damage, leaving *Chokai* as the only one of Kurita's heavy cruisers that emerged entirely unscathed. Two destroyers were slightly damaged, dud torpedoes struck a destroyer and the light cruiser *Noshiro*, and the light cruiser *Agano* took a near miss.[9]

The raid lasted twenty-four minutes, from 1020 to 1044. Five Hellcat fighters and one Dauntless dive bomber were downed. Most heavily hit, proportionately, were the Avenger torpedo planes, four of which were shot down by Zeros while retiring after their attacks. Given the intensity of the opposition, it was almost miraculous that just seven pilots and eight crewmen were lost. Sherman's aviators shot down eleven Zeros, including one bagged by Clifton, with several more considered probable enemy losses.

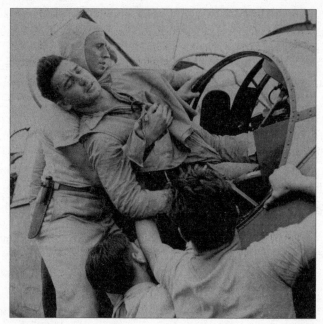

Wounded aircraft gunner Kenneth Bratton is lifted from the turret of Commander Caldwell's plane after landing on *Saratoga*, 5 November 1943. (National Archives and Records Administration)

Immediately after noon, on schedule, Kenney's aircraft hit Rabaul. After losing twenty-two planes there three days earlier when his fliers first encountered the massively reinforced Japanese air forces, Kenney sent just twenty-seven B-24 bombers with sixty-seven P-38 escorts. Because Kenney considered high-level bombing of maneuvering ships unproductive, his planes concentrated on the warehouse area. While much damage was done to Rabaul's shore facilities, the raid provided limited help to Halsey, whose overriding concern was the Japanese ships still afloat in the harbor. This was but one of several instances during the war when Kenney refused to give top priority to targets that would have provided maximum benefit to the Navy.[10]

With many aircraft searching for Sherman's ships, only fifteen Zeros challenged Kenney's planes. American air ace Major Richard Bong shot down two of the Japanese aircraft. Feeling badly let down by Kenney, Halsey would say that he "resented the feebleness of his support at this critical time."[11]

When all aircraft were recovered, TF 38 headed home. It was mid-afternoon before the Japanese sighted the ships, and a flight of eighteen B5N2 Kate torpedo bombers was dispatched. Remarkably, the planes mistook some small craft en route from the invasion beaches to the Treasury Islands for the carrier task force. Unable to sink even these lightly armed vessels, the pilots wildly claimed sinking a large carrier and other major vessels. Radio Tokyo broadcast news of a great Japanese victory.

To the Americans, the most disappointing aspect of the raid was the performance of the Avengers. The torpedo planes had scored only a few hits, and some of those involved duds. While in other respects America's airmen and their equipment far outclassed the Japanese at this stage of the war, torpedo-plane performance continued to lag until 1944, when new techniques made high-speed attacks at one thousand feet possible.

Sherman left Kurita in no condition to continue his mission. Most of the Japanese cruisers returned to Truk immediately, and the others were soon withdrawn. Four would go to Japan for repairs and be sidelined for months.[12] Kurita lost the chance to repeat his success at Guadalcanal, but he would gain fame of a different sort. A year later at Leyte Gulf, his decision to withdraw while a decisive victory lay tantalizingly within his grasp would keep Kurita's name alive for naval professionals and armchair strategists ever after.

As "Jumping Joe" Clifton explained, "The main idea . . . was to cripple all of [the cruisers] rather than concentrate on sinking a few," and that was the exact result. Ted Sherman called the raid "a glorious victory, a second Pearl Harbor in reverse."[13]

Rear Admiral Frederick "Ted" Sherman (center) learns the results of the carrier plane raid on Rabaul from Commander Joseph "Jumping Joe" Clifton, 5 November 1943. (National Archives and Records Administration)

Greatly relieved, Halsey radioed Sherman: "It is real music to me and opens the stops for a funeral dirge for Tojo's Rabaul."[14] But Rabaul was not yet ready for interment. It remained a formidable bastion and potential springboard for further threats to the Allied beachhead. A follow-up raid would be necessary, but in much greater strength. For this purpose, Halsey obtained help from Nimitz, who sent a force centered on new fleet carriers USS *Essex* and *Bunker Hill*, with light carrier *Independence*. Commanded by Rear Admiral Alfred E. Montgomery, the three carriers mustered 234 aircraft. Together with Sherman's TF 38 and Kenney's aircraft, Rabaul's air defenses might be overwhelmed and the base neutralized.

Montgomery's carriers had become available 5 November, the day of Sherman's raid, but an inability to find enough cruisers and destroyers for escorts forced a delay in employing them until 11 November. Sherman wanted to organize one massive task force, but Halsey decided on two task forces attacking from different directions, while Kenney mounted his own attack.

The weather, which had fully cooperated on 5 November, was a severe hindrance on 11 November. Socked in by fog and rain, Kenney's planes were grounded. Although Sherman's carrier planes managed to get off a strike from the vicinity of Green Island at a range of 225 miles, between the poor visibility and the reduced shipping in the harbor, little was achieved. Badly damaged *Maya* and unscathed *Chokai* were still anchored there,[15] but neither could be found in the squall. The most material success occurred when a torpedo struck the stern of light cruiser *Agano*, flooding her engine room. A second strike was canceled because of weather, but at least the foul conditions enabled Sherman's ships and aircraft to withdraw without opposition.

Montgomery launched his planes from 160 miles southeast of Rabaul. His 185 aircraft included new SB2C Helldivers that were intended to replace the venerable SBD Dauntless. AirSols provided air cover using Corsairs and Hellcats from New Georgia that landed and refueled on the carriers. Arriving at Rabaul, the attackers were engaged by 68 Zeros. In rain that made ship identification difficult, Montgomery's bombers defied the heavy flak to seek out targets in the harbor. The limited results amounted to the bombing and sinking of one destroyer, damage by torpedo to another destroyer, and lighter damage to other ships from strafing. Again, it was the low score rate of the torpedo planes that was most disappointing.

While preparing to deliver a second strike, Montgomery received word of a massive incoming flight of 119 Japanese fighters and bombers. Gambling that he could withstand the attack, he ordered the second strike to proceed, confident that his combat air patrol and anti-aircraft fire could handle the situation. The task force assumed a newly adopted defense pattern to mass anti-aircraft fire better, enhanced by improved shell fuses. The three carriers were positioned at the center of a two-thousand-yard circle surrounded by nine evenly spaced destroyers in a four-thousand-yard circle.

Montgomery's gamble succeeded, but the action might well have gone the other way. The Japanese attackers were first engaged forty miles from the task force, but Montgomery's fighters were kept so busy by the escorting Zeros that the D3A Val and Kate bombers easily slipped through to attack the carriers. Much of the fault lay with the carriers' fighter directors, who did not coordinate the available air cover effectively. After Montgomery decided to cancel the second strike while the planes were aloft, the accompanying fighters received little direction and were largely left to decide on their own how and where to join the battle. At one point, sixteen desperately needed fighters were sent thirty miles from the task force to attack what turned out to be a flight of Hellcats.

Without well-directed fighter protection, the burden of protecting the task force rested on ship anti-aircraft fire. Montgomery exhorted over his ship's loudspeaker: "Man your guns and shoot those bastards out of the sky."[16] The forty-six-minute action produced ten near misses involving all three carriers. They caused only slight damage and left ten sailors wounded.

A bomb that might have scored solidly on *Independence* was miraculously detonated in the air by a shot from a 40-mm gun. Eleven defending aircraft were lost, but in return all fourteen Kate torpedo planes were downed as well as twenty-four out of twenty-seven Val dive bombers. This was in addition to about twenty Zeros lost earlier in the day at Rabaul.

Although the 11 November raid did not meet expectations, it proved highly successful in the overall equation. Out of 173 aircraft stripped from the Japanese carriers for Operation RO, only 52 remained after the U.S. carrier actions and other operations. Unable to allow the further slaughter of his carrier air fleet, Koga officially canceled Operation RO and withdrew the surviving aircraft. They were replaced with lesser quality planes and pilots from the Marshall Islands. The day after the second carrier raids, the heavy cruisers remaining at Rabaul were withdrawn. Major Japanese vessels would never again anchor in Simpson Harbor.

The great beneficiary of this squandering of Koga's carrier aircraft was Admiral Nimitz, whose long-expected Central Pacific offensive was ready to begin. In a postwar interview, Vice Admiral Shigeru Fukudome, chief of staff of the Combined Fleet, described the consequences. "Although the Gilberts fight appeared to be the last chance for a decisive fight, the fact that the Fleet's air strength had been so badly depleted enabled us to send only very small air support to Tarawa and Makin. The almost complete loss of carrier planes was a mortal blow to the Fleet since it would require six months for replacement. In the interim any fighting with the carrier force was rendered impossible."[17] When the carrier air fleet was rebuilt, it was with less capable fliers than those sacrificed in the South Pacific. Their slaughter in the June 1944 "Marianas Turkey Shoot" would signal the sharp decline of Japan's once overwhelming carrier air power.

Admirals Sherman and Montgomery more than proved themselves in the Rabaul raids and would distinguish themselves further during the Central Pacific carrier offensive. They would command the U.S. Fifth Fleet successively in the postwar years.

A favorite expression of industrialist Henry Kaiser was that, "Problems are only opportunities in work clothes." No better example could be provided than how Halsey dealt with his "most desperate emergency" to dole out to Japan her own Pearl Harbor.

Just as Japanese naval air power had finally been mastered, so too was it soon demonstrated, in what would be the final run of the "Tokyo Express," that Japanese superiority in destroyer operations had also ended. This occurred two weeks after the 11 November raid in the waters between Buka and Kavieng.

To reinforce Buka, three Japanese destroyer-transports escorted by two destroyers safely brought in nine hundred soldiers and evacuated seven hundred aviation personnel. Anticipating such an operation, Halsey ordered Burke with five destroyers to lay in wait thirty-five miles west of Buka. His crisp order was "If enemy contacted you know what to do."[18] Burke's plan, if the enemy appeared, was to deliver the initial attack with his division's three destroyers covered by Austin's two destroyers, after which they would reverse roles.

At 0141 on Thanksgiving Day, 25 November, after radar contact was made at eleven miles on the two escorting destroyers, Burke's three destroyers closed in to launch fifteen torpedoes for a 4,500-yard run. Enemy Captain Kiyoto Kagawa was unaware of Burke's presence until the torpedoes were four minutes into their run. Reacting too late, his maneuvers put his ships squarely in the paths of Burke's torpedoes. Kagawa's ship *Onomi* blew up immediately and *Makinami* was wrecked but remained afloat until dispatched an hour later by gunfire.

After radar picked up the destroyer-transports, Burke pursued with three destroyers, leaving Austin to clean up the Japanese remnants. At one critical moment, operating on instinct, he abruptly altered course and avoided three torpedoes. The Japanese fanned out in separate directions, and Burke pursued what appeared to be the largest ship, *Yugiri*. Only able to bring his forward guns to bear while pursuing at thirty-three knots, Burke scored hits that sent *Yugiri* to the bottom at 0330.

Burke then hoped to catch the other two ships, but they were too far off, and with dawn approaching he had to get as far away from enemy airfields as possible.[19] To Burke's enormous relief, the only aircraft that appeared were AirSols fighters from Munda ordered by Halsey to cover the operation. Burke later said, "Never has the white star on a wing meant so much to tired sailors as those on these Lightnings."

Burke's victory at the Battle of Cape Saint George, named for the southern-most point on nearby New Ireland, would be called by Vice Admiral William S. Pye, president of the Naval War College, "an almost perfect action, that may be considered a classic."[20] Appropriately, this final surface engagement of the Solomons campaign, epitomizing how far American naval ability had come since the humiliation of Savo Island, occurred on Thanksgiving Day. Four months later, Burke would reluctantly leave his beloved "Little Beavers" to become chief of staff to Admiral Marc Mitscher. In that role, he would be at the fore of the carrier offensive, eventually becoming one of the most revered figures in U.S. naval history.

Cape Saint George was the last of twelve surface battles in the Solomons, of which the Japanese won or drew ten.[21] But in compiling this one-sided score, they sustained losses they could not afford.[22] Husbanding their forces for a supreme effort, the Japanese avoided any significant naval confrontation until June 1944, then, in the vain hope of staving off defeat, risked everything at the Battle of the Philippine Sea.

CHAPTER 15

# "The Closest Thing to a Living Hell"

After the Bougainville landings, except for raider operations that contin-ued on Puruata and Torokina islands, the Marines enjoyed five days of relative peace. The four vessels that remained unloaded on D-day returned and discharged their cargoes the next morning. Seabees labored to create roadways and began constructing a fighter strip at Cape Torokina.

Patrols mounted through 6 November found few Japanese, enabling the Marines to move easily more than two miles inland. Turnage took advantage of the lull to rearrange and consolidate his forces, reversing the positions of the 3rd and 9th Marines. After abandonment of the two left-most beaches, where the 9th Marines had floundered in the surf, 1/9 was positioned in direct reserve near Cape Torokina, with 2/9 forward to its left. Continuing left, successively, he placed 2/3, 3/3, and, at the left flank separated from the rest of the 9th Marines, 3/9. In reserve behind 3/9 was 1/3, obtaining a short-lived breather after its inva-sion-day fighting. When operations on the offshore islands concluded, the two raider battalions reunited, one company positioned at the Piva Trail roadblock with the other companies behind in reserve. Because movement was badly ham-pered by the terrain and incessant rain, this redistribution of forces took until 5 November to complete.

In addition to the extensive swamp, the Marines faced, according to Vandegrift, "Jungle worse than we had found on Guadalcanal." Others, includ-ing a veteran of Guam and Iwo Jima, went further: "of all the twenty-eight months I spent overseas nothing compared to Bougainville for miserable living conditions. . . . Bougainville had to be the closest thing to a living hell that I ever saw in my life."[1]

Turnage already mustered more than 20,000 Marines, and in the next days these forces would be substantially augmented. On 6 November, when the first elements of the 21st Marines arrived, 1/21 was attached to the 9th Marines and placed in reserve. As a vanguard of the Army's 37th Infantry Division, the 148th Regiment landed on 9 November, followed over the next eleven days by the division artillery and 129th and 145th regiments.

While Halsey's now substantial and well-supplied forces rapidly settled into a secure perimeter, Japanese commander Hyakutake reacted slowly, not convinced the invasion was more than a feint or perhaps a prelude to a descent on Buka or Buin.[2] Still, something had to be done, and in usual fashion the Japanese developed an intricate and ambitious plan. Forces would land well north of the Allied perimeter and form up before attacking. They would then engage the left of the perimeter to draw the Marine reserves there. In the main thrust, troops dispatched from Buin would strike the weakened Marine right at the Piva Trail roadblock and attempt a breakthrough to the beach. As happened during Guadalcanal and would recur with even greater importance on Bougainville, the Japanese badly underestimated the strength of their opponent.

For the seaborne operation, Imamura sent from Rabaul four destroyers with 475 members of the 17th Infantry Division's 53rd and 54th regiments. Twenty-one small craft including a motorboat were used for the two-mile run to shore. Since such a Japanese move should have been expected, it was remarkable that the landings made between 0400 and 0600 on 7 November were completed without incident under the nose of a PT boat flotilla based on Puruata. Although the landings were clearly observed by a 1/9 antitank platoon, fire was withheld in the belief the landing craft were American.

But Japanese luck did not hold in other respects. Now it was their turn to be disorganized by the same pounding surf that created chaos during the 9th Marines' landings. Nor had they realized how far north the Marine's position extended. Thus, instead of the planned compact landing distant from the Marine lines, the landing craft were widely scattered from just north of the front lines near the Koromokina River to the far side of the Laruma River. Forced to choose between delaying to consolidate forces or taking advantage of the element of surprise, the Japanese chose immediate action. An estimated one hundred Japanese went into action immediately, well-armed with knee mortars and Nambu machine guns.

The Japanese fell upon 3/9's K Company, which held down the western flank with only two platoons, the third platoon having been cut off by the attack while patrolling near the Laruma River. A machine-gun ambush beside a probable path of enemy advance eliminated thirty Japanese attackers and resulted in a Silver Star for the enterprising machine gunner, Private First Class Challis L. Still.[3] With support by a regimental weapons platoon, anti-aircraft guns of the 3rd MDB and 12th Marines artillery, K Company responded to a counterattack order from 3/9's commander, Lieutenant Colonel Walter Asmuth Jr. Fighting through swamp water sometimes waist deep and employing a double envelopment, the Marines forced the Japanese onto the defensive about 150 yards west of the Koromokina River. But there the Japanese held fast in prepared positions, some developed quickly and some provided courtesy of the two battalions of the 9th Marines that had occupied the area days earlier and left their foxholes behind for the new tenants.

Exhausted after a five-hour fight with seven Marines dead and eleven wounded, K Company was relieved at 1315 by 1/3, which deployed with B Company in the assault and C Company in close support to its right. Unable to deeply penetrate the Japanese defense, 1/3 called up tanks, the 37-mm guns of which searched out and destroyed many emplacements. At the forefront of the action, B Company's commander, Captain Gordon Warner, filled a helmet with grenades and led a tank against six machine-gun nests, which were wiped out. During the action in which he lost a leg and for which he received a Navy Cross, Warner employed his fluency in Japanese, crying "Fix bayonets and charge!" which resulted in further enemy losses.[4] Another B Company hero was Sergeant Herbert J. Thomas. After eliminating two pillboxes and while attacking a third, Thomas threw himself on an errant grenade to protect his squad, earning a posthumous Medal of Honor.[5] With C Company making little headway in the swamp to its front, and recognizing that even more force was needed, the newly arrived 1/21 Marines were brought in. In preparation for renewed attack, 12th Marines artillery and mortars from 1/3 conducted a concentrated bombardment. By this time, it was considered too late for 1/21's attack, which was postponed until the next morning.

Four separate Marine units were caught behind Japanese lines during the fighting. A K Company reconnaissance patrol operating on the upper reaches of the Laruma River managed to regain the American lines after a grueling thirty-hour detour through the swamps with the Japanese in pursuit. Elsewhere, a sixty-man outpost found itself isolated. After killing many Japanese that stumbled upon them, they disengaged and the officer in charge crossed the lines to obtain a concentrated artillery barrage to blast an escape path. As the Japanese still barred the way, the force was ordered to the beach, where it was picked up in the late afternoon by lighters after suffering only two men wounded. Also rescued by lighter was a 1/3 platoon that was isolated while on patrol; it traversed the swamp to the beach and then spent the night there until spotted by a passing aircraft that summoned aid. In the fourth case, a patrol from 1/3's B Company passed the night without detection behind enemy lines but in an area near the beach that was to be intensively shelled the next morning. Private First Class John Perella would be awarded the Silver Star for swimming a thousand yards through enemy fire to obtain a delay in the bombardment until the patrol could be evacuated by boat.[6]

During the night of 7–8 November, Japanese infiltrators penetrated to the hospital area of the 3rd Medical Battalion. While surgeons worked on the wounded from the day's battle, an assortment of headquarters personnel fought off the attackers.

The next morning, after a renewed bombardment by the 12th Marines, 1/21 attacked with the support of tanks and machine guns and the mortars of 1/3. They encountered little Japanese opposition, as the artillery barrage had effectively done its work. The Battle of the Koromokina ended with a dive-bomber strike near the mouth of the Laruma River to ensure that the enemy was broken. Patrols confirmed full success, discovering three hundred Japanese dead in the battle that cost the Marines sixteen killed and thirty wounded. A firm defensive line was then established beyond the Koromokina River that remained largely undisturbed for the rest of the campaign.

After the Piva Trail roadblock was established, both raider battalions were positioned behind this vulnerable point, rotating companies. The 2nd Raiders brought with them valuable four-footed allies, the first war dogs used in the Pacific. Working in pairs, fifty-two handlers managed thirty-six dogs, mostly Doberman pinschers and some German shepherds. With their acute sense of smell and hearing, the dogs could detect enemy troops hundreds of yards away, making them invaluable as guards and scouts, able to sniff out patrols and detect ambushes before humans were aware of a Japanese presence. The most celebrated dog was Caesar, a German shepherd who repeatedly carried messages to the command post and was eventually wounded in action. Saving the life of a Marine on one occasion, Caesar was commended in a letter from the Marine commandant and promoted from private first class to sergeant. After the value of the dogs was proved on Bougainville,[7] the program was expanded to train dogs to act as sentries, lay wire, carry supplies, and perform other specialized tasks.

To closely coordinate operations at the right end of the battlefront, the raider battalions were placed under Colonel Edward A. Craig, who continued as commander of the 9th Marines. The first indication something was brewing came the night of 5–6 November, when E Company of the 2nd Raiders was hit by two probing attacks. With ample evidence that a larger and more determined attack was in store, Craig ordered the raider reserves into close support.

For this main Japanese thrust, Major General Shun Iwasa arrived from Buin with elements of the 1st and 2nd Battalions, 23rd Infantry. On the early afternoon of 7 November, attacking in company strength, Iwasa's force struck H Company of the 2nd Raiders at the roadblock. H held and, supported by the mortars of the 9th Marines, went forward with E and G companies in pursuit of the attackers. Digging in along the trail, the Japanese maintained their position through the night, peppering the raiders with mortar fire. Early the next morning, 8 November, Iwasa attacked with his entire force supported by a heavy mortar barrage that struck E and G at the roadblock and along four hundred yards of the trail. After the Japanese frontal attack was brought to a halt, 2nd Raider E and F companies attempted flanking movements through the swamp that afternoon. They encountered Japanese on the same mission and fought them to a standstill until nightfall, when the raiders withdrew.

**Marine raiders with war dogs departing for the front lines on Bougainville, November 1943.** (National Archives and Records Administration)

Iwasa had done too well to be left in place, able to prevent an orderly expansion of the Allied bridgehead. Turnage ordered the 3rd Raider Battalion to advance to the junction of the Piva and Numa Numa trails. Their advance was preceded by an artillery bombardment that commenced at 0730 on 9 November along the expected line of advance. Many Japanese, however, had succeeded in moving as close as twenty-five yards from the Marine lines, avoiding the barrage and in position to hit back at close quarters when the barrage lifted.

The advance down the trail by two raider companies inched along, with the Japanese meeting them head-on, neither side able to seriously budge the other. In the course of the action, Private First Class Henry Gurke of M Company, 3rd Raider Battalion, fell upon a grenade to protect his BAR-equipped partner, earning a posthumous Medal of Honor.[8] Attempting to break the deadlock, the Japanese tried a flanking move at midday that the Marines parried. With this failure, the Japanese position collapsed, after which their survivors streamed back through Piva Village. In pursuit, the Marines advanced to the junction of the Piva and Numa Numa trails, then continued farther up the Numa Numa Trail without finding any live enemy. The Marines dug in to hold their gains while AirSols aircraft from Munda blasted a fifty-yard swath on either side of the trail leading to Piva Village. 1/9 and 2/9 then passed through the raiders to take possession of the village, while patrols went forward to the junction of the East-West and Numa Numa trails. Like the landings and the action on the Koromokina, Piva Trail casualties were decidedly in favor of the Marines, who lost 19 killed and 32 wounded versus 550 identified Japanese dead.[9]

On 12–13 November, Halsey visited the Marine perimeter to review operations with his commanders. His presence at the fighting front drew an enthusiastic reception from the fighting men and reporters.

The Japanese had shown themselves highly enterprising in their use of small forces, with a remarkable ability to move in unexpectedly and quickly develop strong defenses. It was equally clear that such light forces were highly vulnerable to massed artillery and air attack, which meant that the key to winning at minimum cost was to remain vigilant and leverage those advantages to the fullest. This would be ignored, at a price, during the next major action, the Battle of the Coconut Grove.

Interviewed by journalists during his Bougainville visit, Halsey looks every inch the old sea dog, his tattoo dating from student days at the Naval Academy, 12 November 1943. (National Archives and Records Administration)

The Allied command decided to build two additional airstrips, and a survey team identified a favorable area beyond the perimeter. Because problems persisted in moving supplies through the swamps, no expansion of the perimeter could be undertaken immediately. For the time, Turnage wanted an outpost established at the junction of the Numa Numa and East-West trails. Possession of that critical crossroads would keep the Japanese on the eastern side of the perimeter, away from the planned airstrips.

For this operation, Turnage turned to Colonel Evans Ames, commander of the 21st Marines. The initial idea was to send a company to patrol a thousand yards in all directions from the crossroads in preparation for establishing an outpost. Before that movement could be executed, Turnage decided instead to immediately establish the outpost using two companies with artillery observers. With 1/21 employed on the far left flank overseeing the 148th Regiment near the Koromokina River, and 3/21 not yet arrived, the operation was assigned to Lieutenant Colonel Eustace Smoak's 2/21 battalion. Ames requested and was allowed to employ 2/21 in its entirety to provide close support for the two companies at the outpost.

Ames' operation commenced at 0800 on 13 November. While the rest of 2/21 was drawing rations and supplies and waiting for the artillery forward observers to arrive, E Company moved up the Numa Numa Trail to occupy the crossroads. Incautiously, they advanced without scouting, which Smoak considered unnecessary. But the alert enemy had already recognized the crossroads' importance. The day before, a Japanese unit thought to be of reinforced company strength occupied and extensively fortified a coconut grove about two hundred yards south of the trail junction. Upon reaching the grove at 1105, E Company was assailed by rifle, machine-gun, and mortar fire. Hurrying forward with the rest of the battalion on receiving word of the attack, Smoak ordered G Company to support E by taking up a position on its left. Meanwhile, H Company was to provide mortar-fire support and F was to stand by in reserve. After Smoak received word that E needed immediate help, he ordered F to pass through E's lines and take over the attack. After reorganizing, E was to take a position at the right of the line.

In advancing, F wandered far to the right, missing E completely and ending up in the rear of the Japanese and out of communication with the battalion. E managed to pull back on its own, but the company ended up far from the right of G. Thus, 2/21's companies became dangerously scattered on the battlefield, out of touch with each other and battalion headquarters. With G now in peril, E was again ordered forward and moved left to link up with G. Meanwhile, F's gunnery sergeant had made it back to battalion headquarters, where he described to Smoak the disorganized state of the company. The sergeant returned and led the company back to the Marine lines, arriving at 1745. The situation further stabilized when communication with the artillery was restored after being broken for some time, after which the guns of the 12th Marines prepared for a morning attack.

Following a night punctuated by Japanese rifle fire, Marine patrols went out to ascertain the enemy positions. After being relieved at the left flank of the perimeter, 1/21 arrived and took station near Ames' command post. At 0915, eighteen Avengers blasted a hundred-yard pathway into the coconut grove, an effort that was largely wasted because Smoak was not prepared to commence the ground attack until water was replenished. Later, a twenty-minute artillery bombardment was conducted, but that too was ineffective. The Japanese were able to reoccupy their positions before the attack began at 1155, nearly three hours after the scheduled start time.

Companies E and G advanced in a frontal attack, with F and H in reserve, supported by five M3 Stuart tanks from the 3rd Tank Battalion. Two Stuarts were soon disabled by antitank fire, and others disrupted the attack by firing at and running over several Marines. E Company commander, Captain Sidney J. Altman, earned a Silver Star by leaping on the turret of the lead tank to redirect the attack. Many troops fired wildly, leading Smoak to go forward and call off the advance until order was restored.

Amid the chaos, it was discovered that the Japanese line had been shattered except for isolated troops, which were destroyed in the next hours. Most of the Japanese, however, succeeded in slipping away eastward on the East-West Trail. After Marine patrols made no further contact, they advanced to occupy the objective by 1530, establishing a perimeter defense. The errors made by the Marines in allowing themselves to be ambushed and not making the best use of overwhelming firepower were reflected in the casualty count. While Japanese losses probably exceeded the forty Japanese bodies that were discovered, the Marines sustained fifty-nine casualties, including twenty killed.

The next day, 15 November, the left flank pushed forward about 1,000 yards and the center about 1,500 yards. The new alignment placed the 37th Division's 129th Regiment, reinforced by 2/3, at the left of the perimeter. In the center, 3/3 was posted to the west of the critical Numa Numa and East-West trail junction, with 1/3 in support. Linked to the right of 3/3, 2/21 held the front with 1/21 in reserve. These four center battalions were placed for the time under Colonel George McHenry, commander of the 3rd Marines. The 9th Marines covered the heavy swamp along the Piva River at the right of the perimeter.

Additional troops were continuously arriving, with the last echelon of the 21st Marines, 3/21, incurring severe casualties before reaching the battle line. First, on 17 November, Japanese planes sank the destroyer-transport USS *McKean*, killing fifty-two men from the battalion and sixty-four of the ship's crew. Later, ashore in a bivouac area, 3/21 lost another five men killed and six wounded in an air attack.

The logistics situation was eased considerably on 16 November when a road starting at the mouth of the Koromokina River was linked with the Numa Numa Trail. Also, all artillery on Bougainville was placed under a single command to obtain concentrated firepower when necessary. The commander of the 37th Division artillery, Brigadier General Leo M. Kreber, continued in that capacity and also headed a newly formed Artillery Group that served as IMAC's corps artillery. Kreber's guns would play a key part in the expansion and defense of the perimeter.

By this point, the American command had changed hands. Unexpectedly fulfilling Holcomb's wish that he might lead IMAC in one operation, Vandegrift spent just one day on Bougainville and then withdrew to Guadalcanal to move the later echelons forward. The land campaign was fully entrusted to Turnage until 9 November, at which point Vandegrift handed over command of IMAC to Geiger and departed. Four days later, with the beachhead secured, Wilkinson turned over command of all forces on and near Bougainville to Geiger.

On 20 November, the shape of the war in the Pacific was transformed with the launching of Nimitz's Central Pacific offensive. When the unprecedented casualties at Tarawa were announced, Vandegrift, as the new Marine commandant, absorbed the flak. He wrote to Geiger, "Many times have I longed, even in this brief space of time, for the peaceful calm of a bombing raid on Bougainville."[10] Vandegrift would preside over the Corps during its growth to six divisions and the postwar military unification controversy.

Vandegrift would also regret that the Bougainville campaign was "kind of put off the front page" by Tarawa.[11] Until then, beginning with Guadalcanal, the Solomons held center stage in the Pacific. Once the Central Pacific offensive got under way and MacArthur leaped to western New Guinea, the public lost much of its interest in the South Pacific. It would never be fully regained.

# CHAPTER 16

---∞∞∞---

# "A Shop in the Japs' Front Yard"

One of Geiger's first decisions was to expand the Bougainville position. Swift action became essential after the discovery of a map on a dead Japanese officer indicated a buildup to the east of the perimeter.[1]

The first step was to eliminate two Japanese roadblocks discovered during patrols. One roadblock was on the Numa Numa Trail, about a thousand yards from 3/3's lines, the second on the East-West Trail between the forks of the Piva River. Operations to clear the roadblocks, and the ensuing seizures of high ground, would result in the most intense Marine fighting on Bougainville.

On 19 November, after being relieved on the perimeter defense line by the 3rd Raider Battalion, 3/3 advanced against the Numa Numa Trail roadblock. Following an artillery barrage and with light tank support, the battalion hit the Japanese right flank, killing sixteen and putting the rest to flight. The Japanese responded the next morning with an attack for which 3/3 was well-prepared. After repelling the attack, the battalion moved eastward, carried an enemy position there, then paused to hold the left of the 3rd Marines. To their right, 2/3 moved against the East-West Trail roadblock. Crossing the west branch of the Piva over a hastily built bridge, the battalion occupied the roadblock by mid-afternoon.

To that point, no high ground worthy of the name had been encountered since the landings. Late in the day, a Marine patrol reported sighting a ridge at left of the trail that the heavy canopy of trees had kept hidden. At four hundred feet it provided commanding view of the East-West Trail and Piva Forks area, an ideal potential overlook and artillery observation post. Recognizing its significance at once, 2/3's commander, Lieutenant Colonel Hector de Zayas, ordered his F Company commander to take it. The assignment fell to First Lieutenant Steve Cibik, who went forward with a platoon, heavy machine-gun section, and wire team. Trailing signal wire behind, the team worked its way up the steep

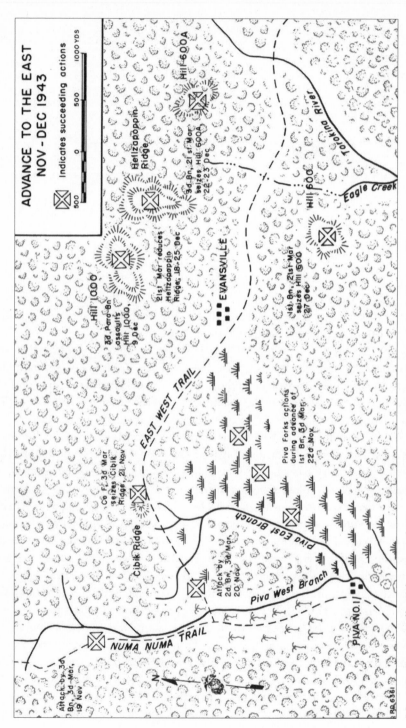

Map 10. Bougainville: Advance to the East (Rentz, *Bougainville and the Northern Solomons*, 63)

slope in the gathering darkness. Hastily placing their machine guns to cover the most likely paths of Japanese advance, the Marines settled in for a tense but ultimately quiet night.

Cibik would later describe the sight the next morning when, after a laborious climb, they reached the summit. "What a view of Bougainville! We were on the tip of a thumb of earth 500 feet high, an oasis in a sea of mist-covered jungle, the only high ground for miles around."[2] A less welcome sight was the well-prepared positions on the ridge, indicating that the Japanese had used it as an observation post and could be expected to return. When they did, the Japanese observation team was swiftly repulsed, and then the real battle began.

The Japanese spared nothing to retake the ridge. Three fanatical charges were made and hurled back that day, a pattern that continued for three days, during which the Japanese at times made it within a few feet of the crest. In desperation, Cibik repeatedly called down artillery fire as near as fifty yards from his position. The little band of defenders received reinforcements so that ultimately there were about two hundred Marines atop the ridge. Equipped with mortars and additional machine guns, the Marines held the ridge until the rest of the front advanced. Cibik wrote of the connection forged those days: "These fellows mean as much to me now as my own family . . . a brotherhood born in blood and battle."[3] Cibik was awarded a Silver Star and the ridge was named in his honor.

Marines eliminate a Japanese pillbox on Bougainville, November or December 1943. (USMC)

On 21 November, Cibik's first full day on the ridge, the rest of the 3rd Marines were also heavily engaged. After crossing the Piva River, 3/3 on the left of the regiment's front was hit by heavy mortar fire and found shelter in foxholes abandoned by the Japanese. At the same time, 2/3 to its right came up against an elaborate pillbox position on the East-West Trail.

After direct assault and flanking maneuvers failed, de Zayas withdrew the battalion through the lines of 1/3, which had meanwhile advanced. While the withdrawal was in progress, the alert enemy sprang forward and attempted a double envelopment of 1/3. But the next round belonged to the Marines. Following the most obvious path of attack, the Japanese charged and were cut down by machine guns positioned at the trail.

Elsewhere that day, as part of the plan to widen the Allied perimeter, the 21st Marines were inserted between the 3rd and 9th Marines, 1/21 at left and 3/21 at right. During this movement, a 1/21 platoon led by a gunnery sergeant seized and held a small rise at the 21st Marines' boundary with the 3rd Marines that thereafter became known as Puckett's Point. Meanwhile, the 9th Marines advanced a thousand yards across the Piva River and then encountered an impenetrable swamp. The easiest movement was at the far left of the Allied perimeter, where the Army's 129th Regiment advanced a thousand yards without opposition.

During a two-day pause on 22–23 November, preparations were made for a renewed Marine attack, to be preceded by a massive artillery bombardment of the Japanese facing the 3rd Marines. Employing the massed artillery of the 12th Marines, the 3rd MDB, and the 37th Division, 75-mm and 105-mm guns concentrated on an eight-hundred-square-yard area, with sectors farther back racked by 155-mm howitzers and guns. Also contributing were the zeroed-in mortars of 1/3, that battalion being held in reserve while the other two battalions prepared to advance. On 24 November 5,600 rounds rained on the Japanese for twenty minutes, the heaviest artillery bombardment in the Pacific until then.[4]

After the barrage lifted and just before the two battalions advanced to occupy the cleared area, a Japanese battery on a forward slope opened up with deadly accuracy. Heavy casualties were taken before forward observers on Cibik's Ridge pinpointed the enemy guns, which were then destroyed by 155-mm howitzer fire. When 2/3 and 3/3 finally advanced they moved through an area of utter devastation, where bodies, shattered trees, and remnants of defensive positions intermixed. Penetrating farther, 2/3 met considerable mortar and artillery fire before coming upon well-developed bunkers supported by trenches and foxholes that poured out effective fire. The advance went no easier for 3/3, which first encountered fierce sniper fire and then faced a flanking attack that they beat off in hand-to-hand combat.

Despite stronger resistance than expected, both Marine battalions reached their objectives by midday. After brief reorganization and an intensive renewed artillery and mortar barrage, the advance resumed but again encountered fierce opposition. On the far left, 3/3's L Company, which had taken high casualties during the morning, came under heavy fire from higher ground, but with support from I and K companies they rushed and took the Japanese position. Stubborn resistance was also met by 2/3 in this final stage, but by the end of the day's fighting the 3rd Marines had penetrated three-quarters of a mile beyond the day's objective. The battle-weary Marines could not then even enjoy the luxury of foxholes, as they found themselves in swampland. Still, there was one special pleasure the next day, Thanksgiving. Cooks had prepared holiday turkeys, which, in the absence of refrigeration, had to be consumed without delay. So in those inhospitable circumstances, Marines in the front line enjoyed a welcome feast.

The Japanese 23rd Infantry Regiment was seriously harmed in the Piva Forks fighting, leaving 1,071 on the battlefield and carrying off many wounded. The Marines fared better, taking just 115 casualties.[5] Still, between this and earlier actions, the 3rd Marines found itself seriously depleted and in need of relief.

That the Japanese still had plenty of fight was shown on the following day, 25 November. Stepping off from Cibik's Ridge after a preparatory ten-minute bombardment, 1/9 headed for a height commanding the East-West Trail supported by the 2nd Raiders. Coming under intense machine-gun fire from seventy Japanese defenders, the troops repeatedly attempted to gain the height, the lines being too close to employ mortars or artillery. One Marine company nearly made it to the top before being hurled back under a shower of hand grenades so intense that they dubbed the knoll Hand Grenade Hill. Inexplicably, the Japanese vacated the strong position that night, leaving thirty-two dead behind. Meanwhile, the 2nd Raiders at the left of 1/9 took a well-situated hill with comparative ease. This fighting cost the two battalions five dead and forty-two wounded.

In the next days, while operations were mostly limited to patrols, units on the front were repositioned. Flanking the 21st Marines, the 3rd Marines moved to the relatively quiet right flank and the 9th Marines took the left of the Marine front, linking up with the 37th Division. While the exhausted 3rd Marines rested and reorganized, a makeshift force of Marines from other units and the 37th Division held the front, which remained quiet in that sector.

Before undertaking any further advances, it was thought necessary to deal with a Japanese buildup near Koiari, about ten miles below Cape Torokina, from which a counterattack against the Marine right was feared. A raid similar to the one on Choiseul was decided on, with penetration possibly as far as the East-West Trail. As on Choiseul, paramarines would be employed, this time the newly arrived 1st Parachute Battalion, veterans of Guadalcanal.

Faulty intelligence doomed the operation from the start. A scouting party that reported finding no Japanese in the planned landing area may have examined the wrong place. Disembarking from LCMs and LCVPs in the early hours of 29 November, the raiders found themselves in the middle of a Japanese supply dump facing forces double their number in well-fortified positions. A sixteen-hour ordeal then began during which mere survival became the only objective. Raked by intensive rifle and machine-gun fire, the raiders asked to be withdrawn. Fortunately the lines were within reach of the 3rd MDB's long-range guns, which broke up Japanese attempts to storm the position.

Rescue came at 2040. Under cover of destroyer fire and the guns at Cape Torokina, the raiders withdrew by sea. The cost to the 614-man force was 22 killed and 99 wounded in an abortive operation that might have turned out even worse. Japanese casualties were estimated at 291, which would seem high under the circumstances.

To secure the perimeter and protect the airfields from shelling, the Marines now needed to occupy hills two thousand yards to the east of their lines. As spearhead for the thrust, Geiger called upon the 1st Marine Parachute Regiment. Their objective was a ridge whose principal features were Hill 1000 at the north end extending to Hills 600 and 500 on the south side of the East-West Trail. Also, to the east of Hill 1000 near the Torokina River was another height that the Marines would come to know well, Hill 600A.

When the battle commenced, paramarines had already established outposts on Hill 1000 and southward across ravines and ridges to the East-West Trail and the Torokina River. Since 27 November, 2/21 had held an outpost on Hill 600, and on 6 December 3/3 easily occupied Hill 500. Aside from the Hill 500 operation, the campaign came to a temporary halt on 6 December when the area was hit by a violent earthquake. With giant trees crashing down, the event was as terrifying as a heavy artillery shelling. The next day, a patrol scouting the ridge discovered a previously unknown spur of Hill 1000 with well-developed defenses showing recent enemy occupation. Unfortunately, the commander of the 1st Parachute Regiment, Lieutenant Colonel Robert H. Williams, did not act immediately as de Zayas had when Cibik's Ridge was discovered. When 3/1 paramarines attempted to occupy the spur the next morning, they were met by a hail of fire from a reinforced company of the Japanese 23rd Infantry. From that commanding height 280 feet above the jungle floor, 235 Japanese troops beat back two attacks, wounding eight, including Williams.

Ultimately, eleven days of intense fighting were needed to win a position that had once been available for the taking. From the title of a popular Broadway show that expressed the mayhem on stage, the spur became known as Hellzapoppin Ridge. It was the story of Cibik's Ridge but in reverse, with a company-sized enemy force steadfastly clinging to the height. On 9 December, the day after Williams was wounded, three paramarine patrols closely engaged the Japanese. Later that day, the Japanese attacked Hill 1000, but were beaten off with the help of artillery. Artillery was less effective, however, in loosening the enemy hold on Hellzapoppin Ridge, where the Japanese were well dug in on the reverse slope. As the lightly armed paramarines had only been expected to lead the way forward to cover the flanks of the 9th and 21st Marines, not to sustain the unexpected battle, the 21st Marines relieved them on 10 December.

After attempts during the next two days by 1/21 and 3/21 to pierce the enemy front were repulsed by machine-gun, rifle, and mortar fire, Geiger called on Marine aircraft. On 13 December, three dive and three torpedo bombers operating from the newly activated Torokina airstrip attacked with limited success. Despite the use of smoke shells to demarcate the front lines, errant bombs claimed seven Marines, including two killed. In the next days, torpedo bombers repeatedly bombed and strafed the ridge. To this was added shelling by a battery of 155-mm howitzers positioned near the mouth of the Torokina River. Firing almost due north, the battery raked the difficult-to-reach reverse slope where the enemy sheltered. The weight of fire finally broke the Japanese defense on 18 December. When the aerial and artillery bombardments lifted, 1/21 and 3/21, operating from Hill 1000, took the ridge with ease from the surviving stunned defenders, discovering more than fifty dead Japanese. Hellzapoppin Ridge cost the 21st Marines twelve dead and twenty-three wounded, a remarkably low cost given the intensity of the action. The 3rd Marine Division history credits the air attacks as "the most effective factor in the taking of the ridge," with the final strikes "the most successful examples of close air support thus far in the Pacific war."[6]

One last operation remained for the 21st Marines. Immediately east of Hellzapoppin Ridge, close by the Torokina River, a patrol on 21 December encountered and drove off a small Japanese force from a hill designated 600A. Following an all-too-familiar scenario, the Marines withdrew to their lines for the night, providing the Japanese an opportunity to reoccupy the hill. When a reinforced platoon from 3/21 with a forward observer team attempted to claim the position the next day, they were hit by small arms fire and withdrew. A double envelopment in company strength was then attempted. But I Company took heavy fire while unsuccessfully seeking out the enemy flanks and then pulled back to allow an artillery bombardment. Afterwards, a renewed attempt by the company failed, as the guns made no great impression on the enemy well dug in on the reverse slope. The following day, 23 December, three frontal attacks by K Company, punctuated by heavy artillery bombardments, failed to dent the enemy defenses. Then, just as mysteriously as at Hand Grenade Hill, the Japanese pulled out that night, leaving Hill 600A to the 21st Marines on 24 December.

The taking of Hill 600A marked the completion of the Marine mission on Bougainville. The Marines, with Army support, had attained their planned final defense line that extended inland for 22,500 yards.[7]

Geiger relinquished command to Griswold, passing responsibility for the ground battle from IMAC to the Army's XIV Corps. Replacing the 3rd Marine Division would be the Americal Division. Formed in New Caledonia during May 1942 from National Guard regiments from Massachusetts, Illinois, and North

Dakota, the division had seen heavy combat on Guadalcanal. On Christmas Day, the 3rd Marines departed for their base camp on Guadalcanal, followed on 28 December by the 9th Marines and the 21st Marines on 9 January 1944. Supporting IMAC units were removed as well except for the 3rd MDB, whose firepower would be needed on Bougainville for another half year.

The 3rd Marine Division had performed splendidly in its battle debut, a tribute to Barrett, who formed the division and oversaw its development. At a cost of 423 killed and 1,418 wounded,[8] in the harshest of environments, a secure position was established at the doorstep of the enemy's great South Pacific base. The Marines were helped by Hyakutake's slow reaction, the piecemeal employment of his troops, and the remoteness of the area. The Japanese left behind about 2,500 dead and carried off an indeterminate number of wounded. Only 25 Japanese were captured.

The 3rd Marine Division would go on to fight on Guam and Iwo Jima. Geiger and Turnage would serve in the same capacities on Guam and, later in succession, would lead all Marine forces in the Pacific as commanders of the Fleet Marine Force.

All raider and paramarine units were disbanded in early 1944, their highly trained and experienced members needed to form the core of new Marine divisions. The Marine high command eliminated the raiders without regret, having unwillingly maintained that elite force within what was already an elite force.[9] The raiders would acquire a new home in the 4th Marines, a regiment captured on Corregidor and revived by name in early 1944. After the bloodless occupation of Emirau Island for Halsey, the 4th Marines would fight on Guam and later on Okinawa as part of the 6th Marine Division.

As for the paramarines, dedicated aircraft and other essential resources for an airborne force were never obtained and operations did not arise that could provide a full scope for their skills. Paramarines helped to form the core of the 5th Marine Division. Five ex-paratroopers from that division were awarded the Medal of Honor for heroism on Iwo Jima.

AirSols underwent a change of command on 20 November with the departure of Twining to lead the Fifteenth Air Force in Europe. In the postwar years, Twining would rise to become chairman of the Joint Chiefs of Staff. Major General Ralph J. Mitchell (USMC), while continuing in command of the Marine component of AirSols, succeeded Twining as AirSols leader.

Construction of the Cape Torokina fighter airstrip began on 10 November and went forward rapidly. Challenged by jungle, wetlands, and constant sniper activity, the Seabees pushed the work day and night to meet MacArthur's Cape Gloucester timetable. Torokina became fully operational on 10 December, in time for dive and torpedo bombers to participate in the Hellzapoppin Ridge battle.

Cape Torokina area, showing newly developed Torokina airstrip at center rear, with Puruata Island in the foreground and small Torokina Island behind, December 1943. (National Archives and Records Administration)

On 26 November, work started on the bomber and second fighter airstrips, Piva Uncle and Piva Yoke. In addition to serving aircraft based there, the three Bougainville strips would become valuable staging fields for aircraft flying from the Central Solomons. It now became possible for Rabaul-bound bombers to arrive early enough at their target to avoid the heavy cloud cover that typically rolled in by afternoon. Always ready with the bon mot, Halsey said to Griswold at completion of the Piva Uncle bomber airstrip on Christmas Day: "In smashing Jungle and Japs to build that strip there has been neither bull nor dozing at Torokina."[10]

Rabaul had not been seriously disturbed by Allied aircraft for a month after the 11 November carrier raids by Sherman and Montgomery. Kenney was unable to participate that day, and thereafter let AirSols deal with the great Japanese base. The respite ended 17 December with inauguration of the air campaign against Rabaul. As Halsey exulted in his bon voyage message to Geiger: "You have literally succeeded in setting up and opening for business a shop in the Japs' front yard."[11] It would be left to AirSols to operate the "shop" and to the Army defending the Bougainville perimeter to ensure that it stayed open for business.

CHAPTER 17

———— ∞∞∞ ————

# "More Nerve-Racking Than . . .
# Tobruk or El Alamein"

Afortter the defeat of the Japanese counterattack at Finschhafen in October 1943, General Wootten intended to follow his original plan to advance on Sio at the north coast of the Huon Peninsula. To secure the 9th Division's flank and rear, however, Wootten first had to eliminate the threat posed by 12,500 enemy troops in the Sattelberg area.

The core of the Japanese defense was the 20th Division's 80th Infantry Regiment, entrenched at five key points in and around Sattelberg. For Sattelberg's capture, Brigadier David Whitehead's 26th Brigade was brought in along with nine Matilda tanks. After a delay in the buildup caused by heavy rains, three regiments advanced on 17 November by separate routes. Progress was slow on terrain marked by razor-backed ridges and dense jungle that slowed the infantry and limited tank movements. Katagiri, the Japanese 20th Division commander, however, was suffering acute supply shortages that prompted him to request withdrawal to his Wareo supply base by the fifth day of the battle. Adachi approved the withdrawal.

To throw the Australians off balance, Katagiri attacked the Scarlet Beach area beginning 23 November using forces northeast of Sattelberg, one group attacking southeast and a second southward along the coast. These counterattacks were contained by the second day and sputtered out afterwards.

After Sattelberg was bombed intensively, eliminating most of the Japanese heavy guns, 2/48 Battalion discovered a steep slope that was left lightly defended in the belief it could not be scaled. Two platoons made the climb but were beaten back, followed by another platoon led by Sergeant Tom Derrick. Derrick also failed but was persistent, requesting another twenty minutes from his company commander before having to withdraw for the evening. Attacking and eliminating seven gun posts himself with grenades while clinging to the hillside, Derrick then led his men in eliminating three more posts, and they took the ridge. The next morning, following the discovery that the Japanese had pulled out, Derrick was given the honor of raising the Australian flag over Sattelberg. Adding a Victoria Cross to other laurels that made him the best-known Australian soldier of World War II, Derrick would later be commissioned, and, permitted by special authority to serve in his old battalion, he was killed on Borneo in 1945. Honors won in Africa and the Pacific would make 2/48 the most highly decorated Australian battalion of World War II.

Contributing significantly to the taking of Sattelberg and blunting the Japanese counteroffensive was the seizure during the battle of a height dubbed Pabu Hill by 2/32 Battalion of the 24th Brigade. Besieged there and under continuous attack, the small Australian force severed a principal Japanese supply line from the coast to Wareo and inflicted many casualties on enemy carrying parties.

Australian casualties during the nine-day Sattelberg battle were 49 killed and 118 wounded against 553 Japanese dead.[1] But the casualty count does not tell the full story. The 26th Brigade diarist wrote, "Many of the lads consider it to have been harder and more nerve-racking than any 10 days at Tobruk or El Alamein."[2]

Urged by the II Corps commander to hasten up the coast to Sio, Wootten cautiously opted for a measured movement with three brigades abreast, 26th Brigade toward Wareo, 24th Brigade at the coast, and 20th Brigade in the center. With twelve battalions and a squadron of Matilda tanks available for the pursuit, prospects were good that the 9th Division might overrun the weakened Japanese. But the Australians encountered many problems, including dreadful weather, supply problems, difficult terrain, widespread disease, and a highly determined defense. Although Wareo was only six thousand yards from Sattelberg, it was four times that far by the only practicable route, and twelve days of fighting were necessary before its capture on 8 December.

After Sattelberg fell to the Australians, Katagiri and Adachi recognized that there was no further hope of retaking Finschhafen and that Wareo could not be retained. The 79th Regiment would march to Sio along inland trails while the 80th Regiment withdrew along the coast. On 5 December, Wootten's newly introduced 4th Brigade set out on the coast road toward Sio, which was taken on 15 January. Before Sio fell, Adachi arrived by submarine to direct the retreat after narrowly escaping death from a depth charge attack.[3]

In the four months between the landings at Finschhafen and the seizure of Sio, an estimated 7,800 of the 12,600 Japanese troops in the area were killed or wounded, and about 4,500 escaped westward. Casualties in the 9th Division during their three and a half months in combat were 284 killed and missing and 744 wounded.[4]

Before Sio fell, the threat to Adachi's forces was compounded by the 2 January landing at Saidor of the 126th Regimental Combat Team (RCT) of the

American 32nd Division, thoroughly reformed since Buna. Situated seventy-five miles west of Sio and fifty-two miles east of Madang, Saidor was wanted by the Allies for use as a fighter base and supply port, and to block the Japanese retreat from the Huon Peninsula.

Encountering virtually no opposition, Barbey delivered 7,200 men and their equipment on D-day, then departed with all ships and beaching craft before a feeble Japanese air attack materialized in late afternoon. No significant opposition was encountered in the next days on land or in the air. In having Alamo Force execute the operation, MacArthur sidestepped the understanding that the Australians would conduct operations in northeast New Guinea. Employing Alamo made sense, however, as Australian forces were then deeply committed and American troops were immediately available.

While the invasion gained an important strategic position nearly without cost, the Allies missed the opportunity to snare Adachi's retreating forces. Brigadier General Clarence Martin, 32nd Division assistant commander and leader of the Saidor Michaelmas operation, wanted to move eastward to trap and destroy the retreating Japanese. Krueger, however, was unwilling to commit large forces fearing that Martin might become overextended.[5] By 6 February, when air observation disclosed that the Japanese were moving westward on inland trails, it was too late to stop them. On 10 February, fourteen miles southeast of Saidor, American forces met the 5th Australian Division that had taken over from the 9th Division after the capture of Sio.

The Saidor landing prompted Imamura and his staff at Rabaul to take stock of the 18th Army's situation. While some urged an attack on Saidor by the 20th and 51st Divisions, others, including Imamura, favored reuniting those divisions with the rest of the 18th Army for the defense of Wewak. It was finally decided that both divisions would follow inland tracks to Madang. That plan entailed a terrible two-hundred-mile march by the weak and starving troops through dense jungle and across the steep Finisterre Range, a retreat that would claim much of their force. The official American Army history observed, "That the Japanese would make such marches in retreat and in the advance are tribute and testimony to the patient fortitude and iron resolution of the Japanese soldier . . . he was a formidable opponent."[6]

In the Ramu Valley, General Vasey's 7th Division had been in a virtual stalemate since the taking of Dumpu. Shaggy Ridge, a considerable height six miles north of Dumpu, barred an Australian advance to the coast at Bogadjim. In late December the 21st Brigade's 2/16 Battalion attacked four hills called "pimples" that formed part of the enemy defensive network. The pathways were just two to three feet wide, there were 300- to 500-foot drops on both sides, and the ground was honeycombed by machine-gun nests and foxholes. Aided by the imaginative use of RAAF Boomerang aircraft to mark enemy positions by strafing, followed by Kittyhawk dive bombings and then intensive artillery bombardment, the hills were taken through hand-to-hand fighting, opening the way to the highest point of the ridge, Kankiryo Saddle. For the attack, Vasey replaced the worn 21st Brigade with the 18th Brigade, veterans of North Africa, Milne Bay, and Buna. He also called forward the 15th Brigade, which had fought at Salamaua, to relieve the 25th.

Australian troops from C Company, 2/9 Infantry Battalion, dig into a newly occupied feature on Shaggy Ridge, New Guinea, 23 January 1944. (By authorization of the Australian War Memorial: 064255)

Although the Japanese position on Kankiryo Saddle was very strong, it was thinly held without reserves, as the defenses were stripped to meet the threat at Saidor.[7] Once again, the ground operation was preceded by a heavy air attack. Operation Cutthroat involved three days of bombings by Nadzab and Port Moresby–based B-25s followed by two days of P-40 strafing and bombing. Finally, an intensive artillery bombardment preceded the infantry attack. Twelve days of heavy ground fighting then followed until the ridge was occupied on 31 January, at which time the 15th Brigade relieved the 18th. The battle of Shaggy Ridge cost the Australians 46 killed and 147 wounded, while approximately 500 of the estimated 800 defenders were killed.

On 18 February, a patrol from the 15th Brigade made contact with American forces at Saidor. Before then, MacArthur's headquarters announced that about

14,000 enemy troops had been trapped, although the Japanese largely avoided encirclement and would need to be faced later. On 25 March, with the Japanese high command anticipating MacArthur's next amphibious move, Adachi was ordered to withdraw westward to defend Wewak. One casualty during the retreat was Katagiri, killed on board a landing craft in a PT boat attack.

The once formidable 105,000-man Japanese 18th Army that fell back toward Wewak and Hollandia had by this point been reduced to 54,000. An estimated 13,000 died during the early battles in Papua, and about 38,000 fell in later battles, at sea, by disease, and exhaustion during the successive retreats.[8]

With the Japanese in full flight, Blamey decided to withdraw the veteran 6th, 7th, and 9th Australian divisions for rest and refit, replacing them with the 3rd, 5th, and 11th militia divisions. After relieving the 7th Division, the 11th Division entered Bogadjim on 13 April and ten days later reached Madang, the ultimate New Guinea target specified in Cartwheel. In the next two months, Australian forces continued on to the Sepik River, Wewak's outer defense line. By this point MacArthur had begun his celebrated leapfrog campaign, beginning with a spectacular leap to Hollandia that left Wewak far behind.

This would be Vasey's last campaign. Sidelined with illness and then performing duties off the battlefield, Vasey died in an aircraft crash while on his way to take command of the 6th Division.

Thus ended nearly two years of desperate fighting, during which Australian forces won eastern New Guinea under some of the most terrible conditions ever faced by fighting men. While historians rightly laud MacArthur's New Guinea campaign as a military classic, too easily overlooked are the indispensable Australian victories that came first.

CHAPTER 18

# "Nature Proved to Be a Worse Enemy
# Than the Japanese"

C ape Gloucester was included in Cartwheel as a stepping-stone to Rabaul.
Once it was decided to bypass Rabaul, the question arose of whether a
landing on New Britain was necessary.

Admirals Carpender and Barbey believed it was essential to gain full possession of the Vitiaz and Dampier straits to ensure safe passage to and from the Bismarck Sea. Krueger, too, considered the operation essential before they continued westward. Kenney, however, thought it unnecessary and believed that airfields could not be developed quickly enough to be worth the time and effort. MacArthur had the last word and insisted that Cape Gloucester be taken.

Many authorities now consider that Cape Gloucester was unnecessary.[1] Unable to bring long-range guns to the area, the Japanese had no means of interfering with Allied movements in the straits. But that is hindsight. Believing that Japanese strength in the Bismarcks was still considerable, Allied possession of Cape Gloucester seemed only prudent.

Operation Dexterity, Alamo Force's first major campaign, consisted of two separate operations. After a diversionary landing by Army forces on the south coast of New Britain, Marines would take Cape Gloucester. The Army operation was built around Colonel Alexander M. Miller's dismounted 112th Cavalry Regiment, a Texas National Guard unit whose experience was limited to the peaceful occupation of Woodlark Island. Leading the task force that included several reinforcement elements was the 112th's former commander, Brigadier General Julian W. Cunningham. For Cape Gloucester, MacArthur was given use of the 1st Marine Division that had recovered and retrained in Australia after its ordeal on Guadalcanal. Major General William H. Rupertus, former assistant division commander, assumed command in July 1943 when Vandegrift replaced Vogel at IMAC.

The original Army plan called for a landing at Gasmata on the south coast. That idea was discarded when it was discovered the area was unsuitable for an airfield and the Japanese had brought in reinforcements. Instead, Arawe, ninety miles farther west, was chosen. As it would never be developed as an air or PT boat base, Arawe's sole value came down to its ability to draw Japanese attention away from Cape Gloucester. The Arawe attack was scheduled for 15 December, eleven days before Cape Gloucester.

To encourage belief that Gasmata was the objective, Kenney's aircraft intensively blasted it, then hit Arawe the day before the invasion. Landings began just before sunrise with the launch from APDs of two raider forces, each consisting of 152 troopers in fifteen rubber boats. One force landed on Pilelo Island, at the head of the waterway leading to the main invasion beach, and swiftly eliminated the defenders.

The other force intended to land east of the main landings to block enemy reinforcement or retreat. But an unfortunate decision was made to dispense with naval gunfire to obtain surprise. While still a hundred yards from shore, the boats were hit by heavy rifle and machine-gun fire. Twelve boats were punctured and sank, sixteen men were killed or went missing, and the rest, including seventeen wounded, were rescued by small craft.[2]

After a fifteen-minute destroyer bombardment followed by B-25 bombing and strafing, the cavalrymen headed for the beaches on board EBSR-manned LVT-2 Buffalo and slower LVT-1 Alligator armored amphtracs. In the dark, there was much confusion assembling the landing craft, which caused the first wave to arrive long before the following three waves that crowded together. Fortunately, opposition from the two Japanese companies in the area was overcome quickly and more than 1,600 men were landed by afternoon.

The principal opposition that day and throughout the month came from the air, beginning at 0900 with an attack by thirty to forty Japanese Vals and Zeros. Eluding the standing air patrol, the Japanese strafed and bombed the beaches and shipping without inflicting serious damage. Daytime air attacks continued through December, yielding few results and costing the Japanese twenty-four bombers and thirty-two fighters.[3] Unable to sustain mounting air losses, the Japanese afterwards fell back on annoying but unproductive nighttime attacks.

Imamura had expected the invasion and sent battalions from the 81st and 141st Infantry regiments overland and by barge under the command of Major Masamitsu Komori, who arrived at Arawe on 26 December. Komori quickly retook the airfield that Cunningham had easily occupied, unaware that the Americans considered it valueless. Several attempts by Komori's forces to pierce the well-fortified American front resulted in heavy Japanese losses from registered artillery and mortar fire.

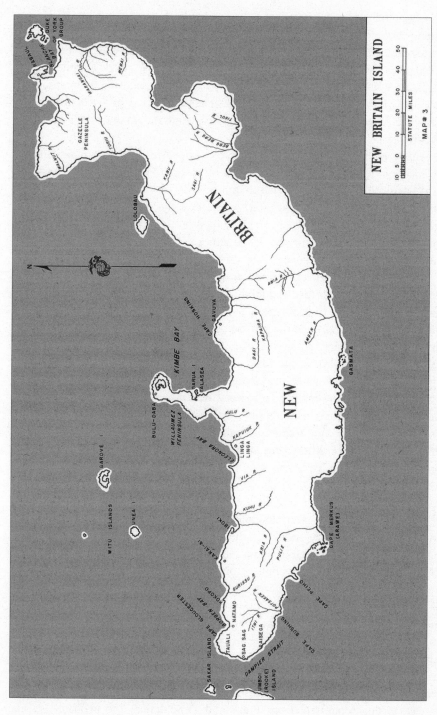

Map 11. New Britain (Hough and Crown, *The Campaign on New Britain*, 5)

Cunningham next attempted to root out the Japanese, but initial infantry attempts could not penetrate the enemy network of foxholes and trenches. He then obtained tanks from the Marine 1st Tank Battalion plus infantry from the Army's 158th Regiment to operate with them. The attack commenced on 16 January with heavy bombing of the Japanese lines, followed by intense artillery and mortar shelling. With five tanks each supported by an infantry company, the American forces broke the Japanese front and attained their objectives by afternoon.

After ending Komori's ability to offer serious resistance and fulfilling his diversionary role, Cunningham withdrew his troops to their defense line. Komori held fast until 24 February, when Imamura ordered him to link up with forces withdrawing from Cape Gloucester. Arawe cost the Army 118 killed and 352 wounded,[4] not a heavy price yet high in relation to its limited value. Better use might have been found for the 4,750 American troops that tied down about 1,000 Japanese.

Meanwhile, the main operation at Cape Gloucester had begun. The plan developed by Krueger's staff involved landings on two widely separated beaches plus an airborne drop, the three forces then converging to seize the Japanese airfield at the cape. Probably relishing the prospect of another high-profile airborne operation like Nadzab, MacArthur was taken aback when a Marine operations officer told him point blank that the Marines disliked the entire plan. Unenthusiastic about an operation in which the Japanese might overwhelm any one of the three prongs, and finding a supporter in Kenney, who disagreed with the airborne plan, the Marines developed their own plan with Krueger's approval.[5]

Through detailed photographic analysis, two narrow beaches seven miles east of Cape Gloucester at Borgen Bay, designated Yellow Beach 1 and 2, were chosen for the landings. The 7th Marines would land first and secure the beachhead, followed by the 1st Marines, which would immediately head for the airfield at the cape. Also, a 1st Marines battalion would land six and a half miles southwest of Cape Gloucester at a point designated Green Beach to block Japanese headed to or retreating from the airfield. In the four weeks before D-day, Kenney's fliers hit Cape Gloucester with four thousand tons of bombs, giving rise to the term "Gloucesterizing" to denote obliteration of a target.[6]

Defending western New Britain was Major General Iwao Matsuda's 65th Brigade from the Japanese 17th Division. Matsuda's command included the 53rd and 141st infantry regiments plus many smaller units, for a total of 9,500 troops, of whom 3,883 were in the general invasion area. He left the Yellow Beach area undefended, believing the Americans would avoid the extensive swamplands immediately behind the narrow beaches. As at Bougainville, the Marines would learn the inconvenient fact of inland swamps only after landing.

Departing separately from Buna and Finschhafen, the invasion vessels, under Barbey's command, joined up at sea and arrived without incident off

Cape Gloucester early 26 December. Observed by a Japanese reconnaissance aircraft, it was thought the ships were headed for Arawe and an air strike was misdirected there.

The invasion commenced with intensive shelling by cruisers and destroyers and bombing runs by eighty-one B-24s and B-25s until the landing craft were five hundred yards offshore. Then, to prevent observation from a nearby height overlooking the beaches, aircraft blanketed Target Hill with phosphorous smoke.

Supported by rocket-firing LCIs and DUKW amphibious trucks, the Marines' landing craft made for shore. An errant wind then blew the phosphorus smoke over the shoreline, making it nearly impossible to make out the intended landing points. Fortunately, there were no Japanese there to take advantage of the disorder; the only opposition occurred when an element landed too far west and had a brief firefight.

1st Marine Division troops wade through the three-foot-high surf to land at Cape Gloucester, New Britain, 26 December 1943. (USMC)

Against light opposition, Colonel Julian Frisbie's 7th Marines seized Target Hill within hours, firmly anchoring the beachhead's left flank. On the right, heading for the airfield along the coast road, Colonel William Whaling's 1st Marines encountered the only serious ground opposition on D-day. In a fight that cost the life of the K Company commander, a well-supported bunker held up the advance until it was rammed and destroyed by an amphtrac.

At Green Beach, the 2nd Battalion, 1st Marines landed unopposed and established a perimeter five hundred yards inland. The 1,500-man battalion met no serious opposition until 30 December, when approximately one hundred Japanese attacked and nearly all were killed. Once it became obvious that no substantial enemy forces intended to traverse the area, 2/1 left by sea starting 5 January to rejoin the regiment. Although both operations made some tactical sense, Green Beach, like Arawe, proved of little practical value.

Unable to seriously oppose the Marines on land, the Japanese struck back from the sky. Evading the air patrol, twenty Val dive bombers escorted by fifty to sixty fighters went after the destroyers at Bogen Bay. USS *Brownson* was mortally hit, losing 108 men. USS *Shaw*, whose magazine spectacularly exploded at Pearl Harbor, had three near misses that showered the vessel with shrapnel, killing four and wounding thirty-one. Near misses on USS *Mugford* killed one sailor and wounded many others.[7]

The Japanese attackers lost heavily when eighty-one P-38s, P-47s, and P-40s in the area struck back, downing twenty-two dive bombers and at least twenty-four of their escorting fighters against the loss of two P-38s and two P-47s.[8] During the action, B-25s on a strafing mission entered the area and were fired upon by LST gunners. Two were downed and two others were badly damaged. Completing the fiasco, the aircraft bombed the Marines, killing one and wounding fourteen. Later in the day, all but one of fifteen Betty torpedo bombers were downed along with two escorting fighters while attempting to attack an LST convoy. Weather and unsustainable aircraft losses[9] would thereafter severely limit Japanese air attacks.

D-day afternoon also signaled the onset of the monsoon, which brought torrential rains and hurricane velocity winds that persisted nearly unabated for three months. Cape Gloucester would be remembered for its dreadful conditions that included the danger of death from toppling trees and electrocution by lightning, which claimed many Marines. Morison would say, "This was one operation in which nature proved to be a worse enemy than the Japanese."[10]

Matsuda had somehow concluded that only about 2,500 Americans had landed, and he confidently ordered 141st Infantry commander Colonel Kenshiro Katayama to come forward from inland to wipe out the intruders. Meanwhile, with the 2nd Battalion, 53rd Infantry at hand, regimental commander Colonel Koki Sumiya was ordered to attack immediately. Pushing through the swamp backing the landing beaches, 2/7 had found solid ground on the far side and was well-prepared to beat off Sumiya's attacks, which continued from 0300 to 0700.

In the next days, the 7th Marines consolidated the beachhead while the 1st Marines drove toward the airfields. On 28 December, D+2, the major Japanese defense before the airfield was encountered and swept away in an action that cost nine Marines killed and 36 wounded against 266 Japanese dead. Concerned that the Japanese might make a stand at the airfield with two full battalions, the attack was delayed while the 5th Marines were brought in. The plan called for the 1st Marines to attack airstrip number 1 from the east while the 5th Marines came in from the south toward airstrip number 2, preventing the Japanese from withdrawing in that direction.

Remarkably, the Marines encountered few Japanese as they took possession of the airstrips. On 31 December the American flag was raised and Rupertus radioed Krueger, "First Marine Division presents to you an early New Year's gift of the complete airdrome of Cape Gloucester." Engineers went to work immediately to make the airfield usable. It would be an agonizingly slow task developing a firm foundation while working in the intense rains with continuous Japanese nighttime bombing raids. Not until mid-February could the first fighter squadron be brought in, and the rapid pace of the war thereafter would severely limit the value of the field. Kenney was proved right about that.

Medium Marine tank crossing Suicide Creek, New Britain, 2–4 January 1944. (Dept. of Defense)

At the other end of the front, Rupertus decided to extend the perimeter beyond Target Hill to include Hill 660, two thousand yards to the south. Assistant division commander Brigadier General Lemuel C. Shepherd Jr., who led the attack, would use the 7th Marines plus 3/5. Shepherd's plan called for 3/5 and 3/7, at the right of the perimeter, to pivot southeast and roll up the enemy line facing 1/7 holding Target Hill.

The Japanese also had plans. Still greatly underestimating the size of his opponent, Matsuda decided to employ Katayama's newly arrived 141st Infantry Regiment to wipe out the beachhead. Given full command of all Japanese forces in the area, Katayama intended to begin by seizing Target Hill.

Shepherd was first off the mark. Operating in dense jungle, his attack stalled at a stream aptly dubbed Suicide Creek, stoutly defended by a battalion from Sumiya's 53rd Regiment. Artillery and mortar fire was of little use to the Marines as the rounds largely ended up as tree bursts and bazooka shells had little effect against earth and log fortifications. To bring in tanks, two days were spent building causeways and reducing the steep creek bank that cost the wounding of two bulldozer operators. During this interlude, Katayama launched his attack. After a feeble artillery prelude, a single Japanese company was hurled against Target Hill with the expectation of later exploiting its capture. The attackers were stopped cold by machine-gun and rifle fire that killed about two hundred and ended thoughts of further attack.[11]

On 4 January, preceded by an artillery bombardment, Shepherd's two assault battalions accompanied by three Sherman tanks broke through the Suicide Creek defenses.

Shepherd realigned his front, placing 3/7 in reserve, and resumed the attack on 6 January. With surprising ease, 1/7 on the left took Hill 150, mistakenly thought to be Aogiri Ridge, described in captured enemy dispatches as a critical defensive position. At the right of 1/7, however, 3/5 met such fierce resistance that forward movement became impossible. The Marines spent the next two days preparing for a renewed attack. Lieutenant Colonel Lewis W. Walt, who assumed command of 3/5 after the battalion commander was wounded, correctly deduced that he was up against Aogiri Ridge. It would be the Marines' toughest fight of the campaign.[12]

When Walt's attack resumed on 9 January, 3/5 attempted to take the ridge from the southeast. A 37-mm gun was laboriously pushed up the height by Walt and a volunteer crew, with pauses during the ascent to fire canister. Reaching the top, the gun was aimed against the thirty-seven log and earth bunkers on the crest. The Marines then dug in for the night, during which they faced five charges by screaming Japanese from the reverse slope. Ammunition was essentially exhausted before the last Japanese charge and replenished with only minutes to spare while artillery fire was called in just fifty yards ahead of the front line.

This action cost Matsuda his last reserve, ending any chance for further offensive action.[13] Walt earned the Navy Cross and the height was named Walt's Ridge.

On 11 January, part of the 7th Marines Weapons Company, including tanks and half-tracks, moved down the coast trail to a position between Hill 660 and the sea to block enemy retreat. For the principal attack, 3/7 was brought from reserve. A deep ravine lay at the base of Hill 660, the steep slope of which was difficult to scale under the best of circumstances. After heavy preparatory air and artillery bombardment on 13 January, one company ascended the hill and was soon pinned down by heavy Japanese fire. A second company sent to their aid was stopped as well, and the two companies then extricated themselves with some difficulty. The next day, 3/7 made a half circle of the hill and attacked the south face, accompanied by tanks that were stopped by the ravine. Mortar fire then proved decisive in neutralizing enemy machine guns and artillery, with the crest finally won by day's end.

Many Japanese fleeing the hill were intercepted at the Weapons Company roadblock. After a pause during which the rains increased in ferocity, two Japanese companies assaulted the south slope in a screaming banzai charge early on 16 January. Struck at their front by heavy mortar fire and at the rear by artillery fire, the Japanese attack broke with the loss of 110 there and 48 more who fell at the roadblock.

After losing half of his command and unable to readily supply those remaining, Matsuda obtained Imamura's authorization to evacuate western New Britain. Colonel Jiro Sato, arriving from offshore Rooke Island with about three hundred fresh troops, took charge of the rear guard and was soon joined by Komori's forces from Arawe. With the Japanese again displaying talent for stealthy withdrawal, there ensued "a game of blindman's bluff with the Marines 'it.'"[14] Although copies of the Japanese withdrawal orders were found, localities mentioned there could not be pinpointed on Marine maps. An arduous two-week patrol to the south led by "Chesty" Puller found nothing except sickly stragglers that were promptly dispatched. Meanwhile, the Japanese gained a healthy lead in retreating eastward along the north coast.

Once Japanese intentions became clear, through a series of short coastal leaps made possible by the 533rd EBSR, the Marines pursued to Iboki, fifty miles from the Willaumez Peninsula. Recognizing the vulnerability of the enemy escape route that ran through the base of the peninsula, Rupertus decided to capture that area by amphibious attack using two 5th Marines battalions.

The landings on 6 March were delayed waiting for a preliminary air attack that never materialized. Little opposition was encountered during the landing phase, during which 1/5 landed first, followed by 2/5, which moved immediately to take a nearby hill. Later that day, well-directed enemy 90-mm mortar fire rained on the shallow 350-yard beach, killing thirteen and wounding seventy-one.

In the next three days, at a cost of only forty-seven additional casualties, the peninsula and surrounding area were won. The Japanese captain defending the area also did well. Starting with fewer than 600 men, he prolonged the battle long enough to allow Matsuda and Komori's forces to escape eastward, following with about 450 of his men who survived the fighting.

A PT boat base soon established at Talasea would be employed to disrupt Japanese barge traffic. A day after the base began operations on 26 March, two American boats were strafed and bombed by friendly aircraft, killing five and wounding eighteen. Once again, Americans were as dangerous to themselves as the enemy.

After forcing the Japanese into the Gazelle Peninsula, the 5th Marines conducted mop-up operations against starving Japanese troops interested only in escape. Indicative of the small scale of operations and feeble opposition, from 10 March to 22 April the Marines suffered just three killed and eight wounded while killing 151 Japanese and capturing 68. Matsuda, Katayama, and Sumiya made it safely to Rabaul, but Sato and Komori, the able leaders of the rear guard, were intercepted and killed.

With its mission essentially finished, MacArthur tried hard to retain the 1st Marine Division, insisting he had no troops to replace them. Needing the Marines for the invasion of the Palaus, Nimitz called MacArthur's bluff. To contain the Japanese remaining on New Britain, MacArthur was given the 40th Infantry Division from Halsey's command, with the changeover completed on 28 April.

The official Marine Corps history observed that "At the tactical level, the 1st Marine Division achieved a degree of perfection probably never equaled in jungle operations."[15] The many elements that made for success included careful planning, selection of the best possible invasion beaches, engineering feats to enable employment of tanks and their adaptation for jungle fighting, and effective coordination with Army EBSR units for coastal movements and supply. Above all was the fortitude of the Marines, campaigning in what would be remembered as Green Hell. Cape Gloucester cost the 1st Marine Division 310 killed and 1,083 wounded, against a Japanese loss of about 4,300.[16] The price was small compared to what would be paid by the division in its even less necessary next campaign—Peleliu.

# CHAPTER 19

———— ∞∞∞ ————

# "Keep Rabaul Burning!"

When the air offensive against Rabaul began on 17 December, AirSols was well prepared with a total of 498 operational aircraft including 199 fighters, 200 light and medium bombers, and 99 heavy bombers.[1] The Japanese had just 201 aircraft on New Britain at Rabaul and Gasmata, with another 91 spread between New Ireland and the Admiralties. The disparity would soon shrink, as Koga considered it necessary to preserve Rabaul as flank protection for Truk. Believing he could tie down superior American forces and refusing to recognize Japan's inability to come out ahead in a war of attrition, Koga unstintingly poured in aircraft during the following weeks.[2]

Rabaul was an especially difficult target. With its five widely separated airfields, it could not be neutralized unless all were knocked out. Rabaul's harbor, with its high surrounding peaks, made for bomb runs under heavy fire, both going in and coming out. Also, as a hub for operations in the South Pacific, Rabaul possessed nearly inexhaustible supplies.[3]

By this point in the war, techniques for attacking such a target had become well-refined. They included using two fighters for every single-engine bomber, attacking all enemy base facilities, and nonstop attacks. Mitchell, AirSols commander, planned to hit Rabaul with conventional bombing and to employ fighter sweeps to lure the Japanese fighters to rise to their destruction.[4]

AirSols campaign began with a seventy-six-plane sweep led by Major Gregory "Pappy" Boyington, commander of Marine Fighter Squadron 214. As the Japanese fighters prudently chose not to challenge such a large force, this major effort produced only a small exchange of aircraft. Two days later, B-24 bombers sank one ship and set fire to another in the harbor, but once again the fighter score was essentially even. The most successful operation during that first month was on 23 December, when Boyington led a smaller fighter sweep. Boyington's forty-eight fighters arrived immediately after Liberators bombed two Rabaul airfields, when about forty enemy fighters remained aloft. Attacking together with the fighters that were escorting the bombers, thirty Japanese planes were claimed, including four by Boyington himself.[5] Only four American planes were lost. Most important, Rabaul was brought under attack in sufficient time to divert attention from MacArthur's Cape Gloucester landings on 26 December.

The AirSols campaign against Rabaul was carried out from several air bases in the Solomons. Heavy bombing was conducted by two bombardment groups of the 13th Air Force. Accompanying the bombers in mixed formations were Marine and Navy F4Us, Navy F6Fs, and RNZAF P-40s, the latter especially welcomed by the bombers for the close cover they provided. Best at furnishing high cover were the Army's P-38 Lightnings.[6]

Japanese pilots were still very skilled, and Rabaul's anti-aircraft defenses remained formidable.[7] After it was discovered that fighters had been stockpiled out of bombing reach at Kavieng, a simulated invasion of Buka was conducted to lure them to come forward to Rabaul for fueling and arming. With that accomplished, AirSols used clever tactics to snare them over Rabaul.[8]

Through year's end, Mitchell reported 147 air victories, although the true count was likely nearer the 64 admitted by the Japanese.[9] Those losses were largely made good by new aircraft delivered to Kavieng by aircraft carrier. Bombing tonnage was also disappointing, amounting to only 192 tons, mostly dropped on the Rabaul airfields without serious effect.

As the 1944 campaign opened, photographic reconnaissance disclosed nearly three hundred Japanese aircraft on Rabaul's airfields and a harbor crowded with destroyers, submarines, cargo ships, and hundreds of barges. A prominent casualty on 3 January was the colorful "Pappy" Boyington, downed along with his wingman. After parachuting from his aircraft and landing in the sea, Boyington was rescued by a Japanese submarine, then endured harsh captivity until war's end, when he was awarded the Medal of Honor.[10]

With completion of the Piva Uncle bomber airstrip on Bougainville in late December, the Piva Yoke fighter airstrip on 9 January, and a B-25 medium bomber base on Stirling Island in the Treasuries on 12 January, AirSols was fully poised to intensify its attacks. Mitchell moved AirSols headquarters from Munda to Torokina, conducting daily raids that typically employed four heavy bomber squadrons, three squadrons of medium bombers, and seven torpedo and dive-bomber squadrons.

With the new airfields and an ample supply of aircraft, AirSols sorties increased substantially during January: 443 by B-24s and B-25s, 613 by SBDs and Avengers, and 1,850 by fighter planes. First priority was generally accorded the Rabaul airfields, with shipping secondary. In these attacks, while Dauntless dive bombers dealt with the air defenses, TBF Avengers proved particularly adept at glide bombing airstrips, typically delivering 75 percent of their bomb loads on target.[11]

A notable exception was an attack on 17 January by twenty-nine dive bombers and eighteen torpedo planes escorted by seventy fighters that concentrated on the harbor and sent five ships to the bottom, the most successful shipping strike since November. In the process, seventeen of the seventy-nine Japanese fighters that rose were shot down at a cost of twelve Allied planes, including eight P-38s. Another significant success was scored on 24 January with the sinking of a large freighter, oil tanker, and army transport.

AirSols victories were bought at a heavy price. One week in January, thirty-three planes were lost, mostly to Rabaul's intensive anti-aircraft fire. Also, Kusaka's diminished air forces were restored to about three hundred aircraft by deliveries from Truk.[12] With no apparent shortage of replacement planes, and a marked Japanese ability to swiftly repair bombed airstrips, AirSols' way ahead still looked long and arduous at the end of January.

During February, AirSols attacks accelerated, with 1,400 tons of bombs unloosed in 3,000 sorties during the first nineteen days of the month. The harbor had become so hazardous that all shipping except barges largely disappeared, and these were mostly destroyed by mid-February. The last great air battle over Rabaul occurred on 19 February, when a raid by forty-eight dive bombers, twenty-three torpedo bombers, and twenty B-24 heavy bombers thoroughly devastated two of Rabaul's airfields. Attempts at interception by fifty Japanese fighters were fruitless, costing them a dozen aircraft against AirSols' loss of one Corsair. Postwar analysis revealed that nearly four hundred Japanese planes were downed in the two months after the campaign began. Now in full gear, AirSols would likely have eventually brought down Rabaul by its own efforts, but events elsewhere hastened the process.

A notable advantage of the separate operations of MacArthur, Halsey, and Nimitz was that activities in one area often had far-reaching repercussions in another. In November 1943, when the Gilberts were invaded, Nimitz reaped an important benefit from Koga's squandering of his carrier aircraft against Halsey. In February 1944, Nimitz returned the favor by way of a massive carrier plane strike against Koga's hitherto secure base at Truk.

Conducted by Rear Admiral Marc Mitscher's fast carriers on 17–18 February, 200,000 tons of shipping and more than 250 planes were destroyed, including many aircraft destined for Rabaul.[13] With Truk left seriously short of aircraft, and recognizing that the heavy loss of aircraft at Rabaul could no longer be sustained, the Japanese withdrew all except 30 damaged Zeros and 26 bombers from Rabaul to Truk.[14] An attempt to extricate 350 of Rabaul's ground crews was thwarted when the evacuation ships were attacked and sunk by AirSols planes.

Few Japanese aircraft operated from Rabaul's airfields after 19 February. But with a superbly developed infrastructure, massive anti-aircraft defenses, and a 100,000 strong, well-provisioned garrison deeply entrenched and eager for battle, Rabaul remained too important to be ignored. The Japanese assiduously repaired their airstrip runways in the forlorn hope they might again be used, while AirSols made certain that such a resurrection would never occur. Only in retrospect did it become obvious that Rabaul was finished.[15]

Unrelentingly, from 20 February to 15 May 1944, 7,410 tons of bombs were dropped on the town, the surrounding airfields, and the barges and small cargo ships that continued to venture into the harbor. Heavy bombers accompanied by fighters were employed until 8 March when unescorted "milk runs" began. After the heavy bombers were redirected to Truk later in March, the fighters were fitted with bomb racks, and the task of bombing Rabaul was assumed by Lightnings, Airacobras, and Warhawks, half of them based on Bougainville. Strictly speaking, AirSols slogan "Keep Rabaul Burning!"[16] became obsolete once little remained of the once bustling town. Burrowed in extensive caverns excavated in the volcanic rock, the well-supplied Rabaul garrison could do nothing but await an invasion that never came.

On 15 February, four days before the last significant air battle over Rabaul, Halsey's forces further isolated Rabaul. Situated just thirty-seven miles northwest of Buka and fifty-five miles from New Ireland, the lightly garrisoned Green Islands served as a barge staging point for movements to and from Bougainville. MacArthur and Halsey agreed that the principal island, Nissan, would make a valuable airfield site for the further encirclement of Rabaul and for bombing Kavieng and Truk. In addition, PT boats operating from there could sever one of the few supply lines still available to Hyakutake. The Green Islands invasion was code named Squarepeg.

Because little was known about the target, the attack was preceded by a reconnaissance in late January. Opposition was encountered from some of the few Japanese there that cost the lives of three and wounded five; in addition, an American officer was crushed while attempting to board an APD from a landing craft in heavy seas. The team found conditions positive: few Japanese occupants, friendly natives, adequate approaches, a fine landing beach inside the lagoon, and ground suitable for airfield construction. Tempting as it was to consider immediate occupation, with enemy air power at Rabaul only 115 miles away, Halsey waited until AirSols reduced that threat and a sizable occupation force could be assembled.

The invasion was built around Brigadier Leslie Potter's 14th Brigade of the 3rd New Zealand Division, veterans of Vella Lavella, under the overall command of division commander Major General Harold E. Barrowclough. Altogether, the invasion force totaled 4,242 New Zealanders plus 1,564 Americans in support functions. Part of the rationale for employing such a large force was the possibility that the vast Japanese army at Rabaul might intervene. Doubtless, too, as with the Treasuries and Vella Lavella, Halsey recognized the political value of making maximum use of the New Zealanders.

Despite the treatment Rabaul was then receiving, the operation was the nearest Allied landing to the great enemy base in the war and hence considered dangerous. As with Vella Lavella, speed was essential, and Wilkinson would outdo even himself for operational efficiency.[17] Little was left unsaid in the elaborate written plan Wilkinson issued, which caused the official New Zealand historian to criticize, as his Australian counterpart did, the American emphasis on detailed written plans.[18]

Invasion craft embarked from many points in the Pacific: New Zealanders from Guadalcanal, Vella Lavella, and the Treasury Islands; Americans from Tulagi, the Russells, and New Georgia. The fully assembled force consisted of eight APDs, thirteen LCIs, seven LSTs, and six LCTs, protected by seventeen destroyers and screened by Ainsworth's and Merrill's cruisers. AirSols planes provided overhead coverage in relays from Munda, Sterling Island, and Bougainville. After Japanese aircraft spotted the approaching force during the night, Kusaka immediately responded by sending thirty-two aircraft from Rabaul. Val dive bombers scored one hit and three near misses on light cruiser USS *Saint Louis*, losing twelve aircraft in the nighttime attacks.

Without preliminary bombardment, landing operations commenced at 0620 with the lowering of fully manned landing craft from the destroyer-transports. The first wave left the line of departure twenty-one minutes afterward. Minutes later, fifteen Val bombers swooped down to strike the landing craft, but lacking fighter protection, they were easily dispatched by the thirty-two-plane standing AirSols patrol. Aside from occasional single aircraft nighttime sorties, this was the end of air opposition in the Green Islands. Within days, organized air attacks from Rabaul airfields ceased forever throughout the South Pacific.

Precisely on schedule, the first echelon landed and established a secure perimeter in two hours. All ships delivered their cargoes and withdrew that day, except for LCTs that were left behind for use when an advanced naval base was established.

Barrowclough and Potter planned a methodical advance by three battalions that would clear each area as they moved forward on Nissan. There were then 102 Japanese on the islands, some from the original garrison and others who arrived by submarine and other means. No enemy troops were encountered until reports were received of Japanese on Sirot Island. A small expedition the next morning eliminated 21 at a cost of five killed and three wounded. The main body of the defenders was encountered and eliminated on 19 February. Land operations cost the New Zealanders 10 killed and 21 wounded, while American losses were three killed and three wounded. The heaviest Allied losses were on the *Saint Louis*, where 23 were killed and 28 wounded.

Within the month, more than 16,000 men and 43,000 tons of supplies arrived. The Green Islands almost immediately blossomed into an important PT boat base, from which patrols extended from New Ireland to Choiseul. Also, a radar station on Nissan Island was established for use with Marine Ventura night fighters patrolling from Torokina. But fighter and bomber strips, hurriedly constructed and made operational in March, provided the big payoff. AirSols acquired bases from which Kavieng, second only to Rabaul in importance in the region, was brought under attack. As Koga removed Kavieng's aircraft after the Truk raid, AirSols met no air opposition while pounding down its airfields and cutting off any possible help to Rabaul from that direction. Also, Liberator bombers flying from Nissan Island attacked Truk and other positions in the Carolines. The Nissan airfields would prove highly useful, too, as refuges for Bougainville-based aircraft that were brought under Japanese artillery fire when Hyakutake took the offensive on Bougainville in March.

The Green Islands would be the New Zealand army's final operation in the Pacific. The 3rd Division was withdrawn to New Caledonia in June and then returned to New Zealand and disbanded, except for about four thousand men who joined the New Zealand division in Italy. RNZAF aircraft remained and would continue to play an important part in the air war.

# CHAPTER 20

# "The Worst-Kept Secret of the War in the South Pacific"

In March 1944, Hyakutake was at last ready to launch an all-out offensive against the Bougainville perimeter. He urged his forces, in frenzied rhetoric, to "erase the mortification" suffered at Guadalcanal.[1] Lieutenant General Masatane Kanda, whose 6th Division was Hyakutake's principal fighting force, composed his own exhortation in poetry.[2] Reflecting complete confidence in the outcome, Japanese battle maps marked the location of the planned surrender ceremony.

When Japanese preparations began two months earlier, those ambitions would have been extravagant but not impossible. After the departure of essentially all Japanese aircraft and warships from the South Pacific, the odds became insurmountable.

Hyakutake has been criticized for mounting a hopeless and ultimately costly battle, but it is difficult to see how he could have acted otherwise. Prodded by Imamura to take action after the Marine landings in November, he delayed, believing that the lodgment at Cape Torokina was only a stepping-stone to Buka, Kahili, or elsewhere.[3] Once it became clear that Halsey had no such ambitions, and after Rabaul came under attack from Bougainville-based aircraft, Hyakutake could delay no longer. Although Rabaul had lost its key importance in the Japanese defense plan before the attack could be launched, Operation TA still had purpose. If the American position on Bougainville were eliminated, Rabaul would avoid isolation and remain capable of playing an active part in the war. Success would raise the morale of a nation everywhere else in retreat, demonstrating that a reversal of the tide was still possible. Even if the Americans were not driven off the island, the battle would divert resources that otherwise would be employed against Japan. Regardless of the outcome, honor would be preserved. If judged to be ill-conceived, Hyakutake's offensive was no more so than certain Allied operations in the Pacific and Europe.

Hyakutake has also been criticized for his failure to appreciate the strength of his opponent and plan accordingly. Underestimates of American forces plagued the Japanese throughout the war, and particularly so at Bougainville. Although the Japanese held the high ground, which provided an excellent view of the American lines, their intelligence service failed to appreciate the size of Griswold's forces. Believing they confronted a single division, no more than 20,000 troops, the Japanese actually faced forces twice as numerous.[4] Still, even with better intelligence, it is doubtful that Hyakutake could have substantially increased his attack force. Whatever the outcome of the battle, he needed to retain sufficient forces to hold the rest of the island.

What Hyakutake managed to do under the most difficult circumstances was remarkable. Despite severe terrain conditions and without air and sea power, he achieved the greatest concentration of Japanese infantry and artillery that would fight at one place in the South Pacific.[5] Of approximately 37,500 17th Army troops under his command, Hyakutake assembled between 15,000 and 19,000[6] outside the American perimeter and moved his headquarters there to directly supervise the operation. Kanda's 6th Division would deliver the principal attack along with elements of the 17th Division. Considered one of the best units in the Japanese army, the 6th Division had fought in China, gaining notoriety for many atrocities including the infamous Rape of Nanking.

With no possibility of help from the air, much reliance was placed on the artillery. Many 75-mm pack howitzers were added to the organic artillery of the 6th and 17th Divisions and laboriously moved over mountain trails onto ridges commanding the American positions. In addition, four 150-mm and two 105-mm howitzers were brought in by barge at night and hauled to the high ground. Their value would be severely limited, however, by the availability of just three hundred rounds for each piece.[7]

While the equation of men and material was severely weighted against the Japanese, Hyakutake possessed one great intangible—the *bushido* spirit of his troops. On New Georgia, Sasaki amply demonstrated how determined fighters could throw more numerous opponents into disarray. Even against Marines, small Japanese units had given a good account of themselves on Bougainville. Perhaps the American Army troops would flee from Hyakutake's toughened 6th Imperial Division regulars,[8] and he would have been doubly heartened knowing his opponents were National Guard soldiers. He would, in fact, come up against two of the ablest and best-led American Army divisions in the Pacific.

With nearly three months to prepare for the attack after the Marines departed, Griswold's troops made good use of the time. Along the horseshoe-shaped front measuring 23,000 yards, extensive pillboxes, trenches, and rifle pits were prepared with clear fields of fire to a minimum depth of a hundred yards. Wherever possible, defenses were developed in depth, mutually supporting, and backed by reserve positions. Double apron or concertina wire and antipersonnel mines covered the front line that could be illuminated at night. Roads radiated in all directions to facilitate supply and movement of forces, especially in the 37th Division's sector, where road building was a special passion of division commander Beightler, a civil engineer by profession. In the infantry regiments, additional machine guns were issued and rifle squads were provided with two BARs to maximize firepower.

Artillery played a key role in Griswold's defense plan. In addition to eight battalions of 155-mm and 105-mm howitzers his two divisions had brought with them, six 75-mm pack howitzer companies arrived shortly before the battle and were assigned to the infantry regiments. Further, Kreber controlled the formidable provisional corps artillery, including two 155-mm gun batteries and eight 90-mm anti-aircraft batteries that were no less potent against ground targets. The guns were registered to fire upon likely assembly areas and approaches.

A change in dispositions at the center of the perimeter would become particularly significant in the battle. Hill 700, to the left front of the American sector, was occupied in January by a battalion of the 164th Infantry after an arduous jungle trek and ascent of the hill's precipitous slope. The boundary between the divisions was then moved east by more than a mile, with the 37th Division's 145th Infantry taking over this highest point on the expanded perimeter.[9] To the left of the 145th, on lower ground, was the 129th Infantry and, next on the left, the 148th Infantry, whose front extended to the beach.

Mortar emplacement of the 145th Infantry, 37th Division on Hill 700, Bougainville, on 15 February 1944, showing steepness of the hill the Japanese would scale in their March offensive. (Dept. of Defense)

Changes also occurred at the far right of the perimeter. Seeking better ground than the swampy area inherited from the Marines, America's 132nd Infantry moved up to the Torokina, straightening the line and establishing outposts east of the river. Concerned about a Japanese buildup near a bridgehead at the river's mouth, Hodge decided to expand that position in January. After preparatory artillery and tank fire, the infantry advanced and encountered heavy fire from a concentration of twenty-one pillboxes.

Tanks sent to assist were ineffective after their hatches were shut because of heavy return fire. Staff Sergeant Jesse Drowley then leaped on board a tank and guided it using tracers from his submachine gun, resulting in the destruction of two key pillboxes. Persisting despite his serious wounds, Drowley encouraged his company to destroy the other nineteen pillboxes. This heroic action earned Drowley the single Medal of Honor awarded in the Americal Division during World War II, the presentation made in a White House ceremony after Drowley's recovery.[10]

In another move to secure his right flank, Griswold decided to occupy the Magine Islands about a mile south of the coastal village of Mavavia, three thousand yards east of the Torokina. Because Hyakutake's offensive might include a thrust by way of the village, Griswold wanted the islands as an observation post. Occupation was achieved in February without opposition, another instance in which the Japanese failed to appreciate and occupy a strategic position.

To the left of the 132nd was the 182nd Infantry, whose front included Hill 608, next to Hill 700 the highest point on the perimeter. The 182nd maintained an outpost on Hill 260 that, like Hill 700, would become a focal point in the coming battle. At the left of the 182nd, linking with the 37th Division immediately east of Hill 700, was the 164th Infantry. Despite its central position, the 164th sector would remain relatively quiet in the coming battle except for artillery activity.

Beightler's and Hodge's troops continuously patrolled their fronts, including expeditions in strength far beyond the front lines that provided clear evidence of a Japanese buildup. Especially adept at intelligence gathering was the 1st Battalion of the Fiji Infantry Regiment under XIV Corps command. Tapping into their special abilities as jungle fighters, on 2 January the Fijians established a base at the village of Ibu on the Numa Numa Trail twenty miles north of Cape Torokina. Supplied by air, the Fijians monitored activity on the east coast, disrupted communications, and inflicted heavy losses while incurring few casualties. When Japanese intentions to eliminate the outpost became clear, the Fijians were evacuated.

Meanwhile, Hyakutake prepared a plan that involved the usual Japanese penchant for complexity and deception. Kanda's forces were organized in three groups, each named for its commander. First to attack would be the Iwasa Unit, under Major General Shun Iwasa, whose forces the Marines first encountered

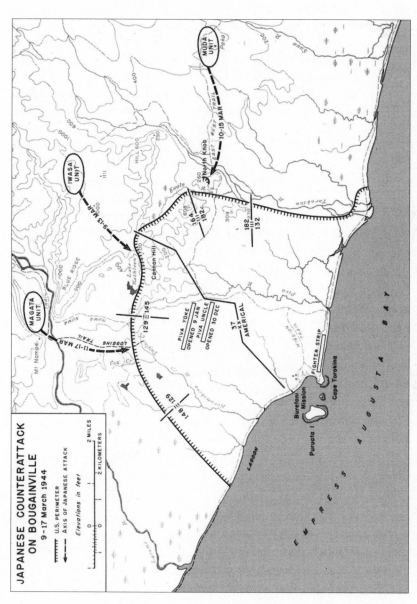

Map 12. Bougainville Perimeter: The Japanese Counterattack (Miller, *The U.S. Army in World War II—The War in the Pacific: Cartwheel*, 353)

at the Battle of the Piva Trail. This 4,150-man force included the 23rd Infantry Regiment from the 6th Division and the 13th Infantry Regiment's 2nd Battalion, plus artillery and other supports. Iwasa would strike one of the least accessible positions on the American front, precipitous Hill 700. After piercing the 37th Division line, Iwasa was to move on the Piva airfields.

At the same time, Colonel Toyoharei Muda's 1,350-man force, consisting of the rest of the 13th Infantry Regiment plus engineers, would strike the east of the perimeter and take another formidable height, Hill 260, in the Americal sector. From there, the Muda Unit would seize additional positions within the perimeter to secure Iwasa's left flank. After attracting the American reserves to this sector, 4,300 of Kanda's best troops, the 45th Infantry Regiment supported by artillery and mortars under Colonel Isashi Magata, would attack the 37th Division front along low ground west of Hill 700. Following the breakthrough, the Iwasa and Magata units would overrun the Piva airfields, after which all three units would thrust south to take the Torokina airstrip. The troops would carry rations for two weeks, which was thought to be sufficient time to achieve final victory.[11]

A great deal was known about Japanese plans and deployments from a wide variety of sources, including observed movements by ground and air patrols, coast watcher reports, interrogations of prisoners, radio intercepts, and documents carelessly lost or found on bodies during patrols. Particularly useful was the detailed Japanese artillery plan, discovered on the body of a dead officer, which enabled American artillery to target enemy positions and inundate them with fire when action began.[12] Japanese intentions were, according to Bergerud, "the worst-kept secret of the war in the South Pacific."[13] Nevertheless, Hyakutake would spring some rude surprises and fully test the mettle of his opponents.

The dramatic situation was appropriately described by the 37th Division's historian in theatrical terms: "The stage was set, and the curtain about to rise on one of the bloodiest, most fanatical Banzai attacks made by the Japanese in the South Pacific War. The players were the boastful warriors, the cream of the Jap militarists, pitted against a civilian army of battling clerks, farmers, mechanics, schoolboys, business men, molded into an army by the blood-letting of New Georgia."[14]

CHAPTER 21

# "But for the Stern Resistance . . . of the XIV Corps"

T he long wait for Hyakutake to attack ended the evening of 7 March when American patrols came upon wire-cutting parties, the customary prelude to a Japanese infantry attack. But Kanda's infantry did not attack that night or the next day, probably because deployment was delayed by artillery fire on their assembly areas. Instead, at 0545 on 8 March, the battle opened with the heaviest Japanese artillery bombardment up to then in the Pacific.

As many as three thousand rounds were fired that day from the Blue Ridge hills north of the perimeter and from hills along the Saua River to the east, with the Piva airstrips the principal targets. One B-24 bomber and three fighters were destroyed, and nineteen aircraft were damaged, prompting relocation of the planes to New Georgia except for six TBFs kept for local support. This hardly affected air defense, as AirSols coverage was readily obtained from Munda and other Solomons fields. While the American front lines were largely ignored, fire was directed against artillery emplacements, supply dumps, and road junctions.

Forward observers and scout planes had spotted many Japanese gun positions, some even before the action commenced, and they called down heavy and accurate counterbattery fire.[1] Relying entirely on direct fire, Japanese artillerists were unable to fight as equals with howitzers firing unseen from reverse hill slopes. Further, by midmorning and increasingly during the day, fighters and torpedo bombers sought out and pounded the Japanese guns.[2] It was thus soon clear that the artillery so laboriously assembled was entirely outclassed. Finding they could not fight openly and avoid swift destruction, the Japanese guns mostly suspended bombardment in the afternoon, then resumed firing at dusk when they were less visible.

After a second day of uncoordinated Japanese fire during which the Torokina airstrip became the target, shelling slackened over the course of the battle. Lacking effective artillery support and without air cover, Kanda's infantrymen would fight with little in their favor except blind courage, with even that quality offset by the tenacity of their opponents.

With the unequal artillery fight under way, Iwasa's men massed in front of Hill 700, at the far right flank of the 37th Division's front. The Japanese 2nd and 3rd battalions of the 23rd Infantry had stealthily moved in close to the hill, but the movement was detected and caused a heavy bombardment of their assembly area. The Japanese, however, were largely sheltered at the base of the hill, waiting for the signal to scale the height.

Occupied by the 2nd Battalion of Colonel Cecil Whitcomb's 145th Infantry, Hill 700 was configured like a camel's back, the highest point at the far right held by E Company with F Company in reserve. From there, a saddle occupied by G Company extended westward, ending at a projection called Pat's Nose. With a precipitous 65 to 75 percent grade, Hill 700 was a difficult target, but that feature presented a problem for the defenders too, as the guns could not be depressed to cover the steep slope. According to the 37th Division history, "it was difficult to reach an enemy hiding literally under the front lines."[3] The narrowness of the crest also prevented a defense in depth, so that the front was covered by a single line of bunkers connected by trenches, with supporting infantry behind in foxholes.

Shortly after midnight on 9 March, in fog and a driving rainstorm, the attack on Hill 700 began. On all fours with rifles slung across their backs, Japanese troops worked their way up the slope. After two preliminary attacks were repelled by E and G companies, Iwasa made his main effort. At 0230, the saddle was stormed in a terrifying charge, the Japanese yelling and singing in English to unnerve the defenders. American artillery swept the slope and thoroughly racked the follow-up attackers of the 3rd Battalion, none of whom are known to have reached the crest. Blasting their way through the wire using bangalore torpedoes, however, the 2nd Battalion gained the crest, seizing one pillbox whose four courageous occupants passed up an opportunity to escape, resisting to the end.[4]

Through the night and morning, the Japanese expanded their position, seizing six more pillboxes by noon. From the salient driven into the 145th's position, Iwasa's troops were able to bring McClelland Road, the single lateral truck route to Hill 700, under machine-gun and mortar fire. This threat to his supply line made it essential for General Beightler to quickly eliminate the salient. 1/145 was withdrawn from division reserve and attacked that afternoon with mixed results. While C Company was stopped in its tracks attempting a frontal attack, F Company retook five pillboxes by striking the flanks of the salient.

The next morning, withering fire prevented Iwasa from reinforcing and expanding the salient, then measuring about one hundred by fifty yards. Much time was spent by the 145th reorganizing units intermixed in the fighting, but later a coordinated attack was made by elements of 1/145 and 2/145. Pillboxes were won back and lost, but by day's end the length of the inroad was reduced to forty yards. An additional success that evening was the recovery of papers from a dead Japanese officer that provided complete plans for the operation.

At daybreak on 11 March, unable to make headway on the saddle, Iwasa launched a banzai-style charge farther west against Pat's Nose, employing an entire battalion on a platoon-sized front. Wave after wave of Japanese charged up the steep slope. Saber-wielding officers shouting *"chusuto!"* (damn them!) led the attack followed by their troops, who responded in kind for mutual encouragement. This display of blind courage gained them nothing, as G Company cut them down with help from 37-mm guns positioned at the flank. After an hour of meaningless sacrifice, Iwasa withdrew.

Intent on eliminating the salient before commencement of the Magata attack, which intelligence showed was imminent, Beightler withdrew 2/148 from reserve for a fresh attack. Also, Beightler temporarily replaced Whitcomb after learning that he was suffering from exhaustion. Following a massive artillery and mortar bombardment, 2/148's E Company struck the salient flanks and gained and held ground by the end of the day's fighting. The Iwasa battle ended the next day, 12 March, when 2/148's E and F companies, using grenades, rifles, and flame throwers, eliminated the last Japanese positions and restored the front. Thoroughly defeated, Iwasa withdrew the remnant of his force to the security of the Blue Ridge hills, two miles distant.

Meanwhile, the Muda Unit went into action against the Americal outpost on Hill 260, a half-mile in advance of the perimeter position held by Colonel William D. Long's 182nd Infantry. Hill 260 consisted of a South and North Knob connected by a small saddle. Its value stemmed from the panoramic view afforded by an observation post atop a 150-foot banyan tree on the South Knob, a highly valuable asset to whichever side possessed it. That tree was regarded as "the most expensive tree in the world."[5]

The South Knob was occupied by a platoon from 2/182's G Company with an artillery observation team, eighty men in total. Disdaining easier approaches with the same elan exhibited at Hill 700, two Japanese 13th Infantry companies scaled the precipitous eastern slope of the South Knob. Gaining the crest, they killed some defenders and sent the rest fleeing to the North Knob, with the exception of six defenders who found security in a pillbox and held out in hope of relief.

Hodge was prepared to leave the hill in Japanese hands, but Griswold, apparently fearing its use as a base for attack on the perimeter, insisted that it be regained. Through that day and the next, four 182nd companies tried various approaches to gain the hill, all of which failed, with the aggressive Japanese even mounting counterattacks. Fighting on the second day gained nothing except an opportunity for the six beleaguered pillbox occupants to escape to safety.

The third day, 12 March, would become known as "Bloody Sunday" in the annals of the Americal Division. Action began with Japanese artillery and mortar fire that was answered by a massive counterbombardment. Hodge's assistant division commander, Brigadier General William A. McCulloch, placed in immediate charge of the Hill 260 battle, then tried to win the hill using two 182nd companies involved in the earlier fighting.

At 1300, with F Company providing a base of fire from the North Knob, B Company attacked the South Knob from the west and northwest. While one platoon was stopped by two new pillboxes, a heavy blanket of retaliatory fire it laid down enabled the other assaulting platoon to reach the crest without loss. The Japanese on the east slope of the hill struck back fiercely, pinning down the platoon with heavy machine-gun fire from the base of the great tree.

With the small force atop the hill low on ammunition and badly in need of reinforcements, and all 182nd forces committed, McCulloch reached into Americal's only battalion not already in action or occupying the thinly held perimeter. It was hoped that A Company of 1/132, approaching from the southwest, could join the force clinging to the hilltop and hold through the night. But it took time for the company to arrive, and when it went forward the attack was disrupted when the company commander was killed. Recognizing that the relief force could not make it to the top before dark, McCulloch made the painful decision to vacate B Company's dearly bought foothold and withdraw A Company as well.

Once again, Hodge asked permission to withdraw his outposts to the perimeter but Griswold still refused.[6] "Bloody Sunday" was followed by attacks over the next three days that went much the same way, with dearly bought gains finally given up for lack of support. The use of tanks in this action was considered and rejected because of difficulties bringing them forward and the steep South Knob slope they could not traverse.

As it had finally become apparent that the Japanese lacked sufficient strength to threaten the perimeter, Griswold allowed Hodge to break off his attacks. In the next days, Americal activity was limited to patrols and artillery and mortar fire, including a bombardment on 17 March that brought down all but a remnant of the costly banyan tree.

Muda's force on Hill 260 had meanwhile been sharply reduced. To reinforce the Magata Unit, whose battle had begun on "Bloody Sunday," Hyakutake and Kanda sent to that front Iwasa's survivors and the entire Muda Unit, except for a small number that remained to hold the South Knob. Thus, Hyakutake discarded his original plan in favor of trying for a single breakthrough.

Magata's attack at dawn on 12 March was particularly ill-timed, as Beightler could turn his full attention there when the Hill 700 position was restored later that day. Thanks to documents found on a dead Japanese officer on Hill 700, Beightler knew the intended target and avoided drawing on troops from that sector.

Magata's attack hit the center of the 37th Division front, an area of low ground held by the 2nd battalion of Colonel John Frederick's 129th Infantry. Although the terrain was far easier than that faced by Iwasa and Muda in their attacks, Magata came up against some of the perimeter's strongest defenses.[7] Fully aware of the vulnerability of 2/129's position, whose lines could be readily reached by way of the Numa Numa Trail, Frederick had prepared an elaborate defense in depth. Behind a double apron of barbed wire and antipersonnel mines, a network of mutually supporting pillboxes had been established with interlocking lanes of fire covering all possible approaches. Supplementing the regiment's 75-mm pack howitzers were 37-mm and 40-mm guns able to strike attackers with devastating flat-trajectory direct fire.

Magata's initial attack was delivered on a one-hundred-yard front by two battalions of the 45th Infantry Regiment. Incurring heavy casualties from machine-gun and BAR fire, the Japanese broke through the first line of defense and took seven pillboxes held by 2/129's G Company. Beightler responded by bringing in 1/129 from reserve. C and G companies won back two pillboxes and beat off a Japanese attack before the day closed. In the early morning hours of 13 March, after a night in which American artillery hit Japanese concentrations, Magata launched a fresh attack that took one pillbox. At Beightler's request, Griswold released Sherman tanks from corps reserve to assist the infantry in retaking the pillboxes. After initial difficulties, all the pillboxes were retaken, restoring the front to its opening position.

Rebuffed after his initial attempt, Magata spent 14 March reshuffling his forces in preparation for a renewed attack, moving his artillery for close support. At 0400 on 15 March, F Company, covering the Cox Creek area left of G Company, was hit by an attack that penetrated about one hundred yards and captured one pillbox. Counterattacks won back the pillbox, but meanwhile the Japanese had dug in. Pausing to rest and regroup, Magata resumed the attack at 0400 on 17 March, striking east of Cox Creek and driving seventy-five yards into 2/129's lines.

Beightler personally led the infantry and tank attack that restored the F Company position, his first opportunity to personally command troops in combat. He wrote to his wife, "I had more fun than I ever had in a battle. I shot Japanese at not more than ten feet, helped capture 4 prisoners, and in fact had one hel[l] of a good time generally." Griswold and Harmon were not happy about having their division general risk his life by "acting as a 2nd Lieutenant," but Beightler was nevertheless awarded a Silver Star.[8]

From 18 to 22 March, Magata paused and prepared for a final attempt at a breakthrough. For this operation, Iwasa's and Muda's remaining forces, except the few still manning Hill 260, were employed to replace the heavy losses incurred by the 45th Regiment. With this reinforcement, Magata's force was built up to 4,850 men. Meanwhile, Beightler's troops used the respite to repair and strengthen their defenses.

During this time, heavy fighting resumed at Hill 260. With unwarranted optimism, McCulloch judged that the South Knob could be retaken with relative ease. Thus, from 18 to 20 March, while the rest of the American front remained alert but unengaged, A and B companies of 1/132 were sent against the hill. Much as in the earlier fighting, each drive started out promising but failed for lack of support. After three days of futile attacks, activity was once again limited to patrols interspersed by artillery and mortar bombardments.

Major General Robert S. Beightler, commander of the 37th Division, personally directs a tank-infantry attack on Bougainville, 17 March 1944. (U.S. Army)

While Magata's troops readied for a last attempt to penetrate to the air-fields, once again the plan became an open secret. In addition to considerable information gleaned from prisoners and reconnaissance, an intelligence unit at MacArthur's headquarters intercepted a message from the 17th Army to Tokyo reporting when the attack could be expected.

Late on 23 March, assisted by darkness, the Japanese mounted a furious attack against F Company in the Cox Creek area. Though many were cut down by mortar and machine-gun fire, they managed to take three pillboxes and pen-etrated within twenty-five yards of 2/129's command post. Beightler promptly organized a counterattack using two companies from the unengaged 148th Infantry sector with antitank gun and tank support. This composite force was ready for action by 0725, and within twenty minutes, after the position was softened by tank fire, the infantry regained most of the lost ground. At mid-morning, two infantry platoons accompanied by the Sherman tanks set out to regain the rest. Using smoke grenades, the infantry pinpointed enemy locations, after which the tanks blasted the pillboxes, banyan roots, and other positions where the Japanese had established themselves. By noon the enemy was fully eliminated.

Much of the fighting up to this point had been too close to permit extensive use of artillery. With the Japanese withdrawal well to the front of the division, and a renewed attack expected, Beightler seized the opportunity and secured Griswold's authorization for an all-out bombardment.[9] Kreber responded with the heaviest concentration of artillery fire in the Pacific until then. In three coordinated bombardments on 24 March and one early on 25 March, 14,882 rounds were unloosed on Japanese troop concentrations.

Hyakutake did not require the bombardment to recognize the futility of continuing the battle. He had already obtained Imamura's authorization to withdraw. After Magata broke off the battle, only Muda's small force on Hill 260 needed to be dealt with. On 28 March, an American patrol found the hill unusually quiet. Further probing revealed that all the defenders had pulled out, another puzzling instance where the Japanese gave up a strong position.

There were even greater surprises for the Americans when they advanced into the zones vacated by the Japanese. Many of the enemy guns so laboriously brought forward had been abandoned with large stores of ammunition. But most surprising was the visible evidence of the potency of the relentless American artillery and mortar bombardments. In areas where Kanda's troops had assembled and advanced to attack, remains of many Japanese who never reached the front lines were encountered, as well as some severely shell-shocked survivors. Estimates of Japanese casualties during the three weeks of fighting vary greatly, one reasonable estimate being 5,500 killed and 3,000 wounded, indicating that a 50 percent casualty rate was incurred without the troops ever penetrating beyond the perimeter. Remarkably, given the intensity of the fighting, XIV Corps dead amounted to just 263.[10]

The official U.S. Army history theorized that the Japanese might have obtained better results by attempting a breakthrough at just one point on the perimeter.[11] Hyakutake belatedly came around to that view by finally investing everything in his Magata force. In retrospect, the most promising approach might have been enlargement of the attack on the Americal Division front in sufficient strength to swiftly carry, by weight of numbers, one or more hills on the perimeter along with Hill 260. Even if they had been unable to advance beyond the perimeter, the Japanese would have been well-positioned to disrupt the American position, with a strong observation post and base of operations at Hill 260 and a line of communication extending to Buin by way of the East-West Trail for reinforcement and resupply. Had he been willing to forgo unrealistic expectations of conquest and desisted from wasteful banzai attacks, Hyakutake might have tied up American resources in a protracted battle and not led away a shattered force that was never again able to launch a major attack.

Of the American commanders, Beightler turned in the most impressive performance. Trusting his regimental commanders to directly conduct the battle, he provided them with maximum air, artillery, and tank support and responded immediately to the threat to his supply line. Maintaining division reserves under his direct control, Beightler committed them where most necessary after Kanda's intentions became known. At the conclusion of the battle, he called for the massive bombardment that wrote *finis* to Hyakutake's aspirations.[12]

It is more difficult to render a firm judgment about the fighting on the Americal front. Certainly, Hodge deserves good marks for correctly recognizing that Hill 260 might best have been left to the Japanese after it was lost. At the same time, before Japanese plans and strength became clear, Griswold's insistence that the hill be regained was reasonable, recognizing that the enemy might use Hill 260 as a base for serious attacks on the perimeter. What is surprising is the lack of a clear understanding by Griswold and Hodge before the battle was joined about the necessity of holding a highly exposed outpost described as "a sore thumb stuck into the poison ivy."[13] Troubling too was McCulloch's repeated attacks on the hill with forces that were insufficient to take and hold it. If Hodge approved of these attempts, he should have provided adequate forces by cobbling together from his quiet sectors an adequate force, much as Beightler did on 23 March.

Given the American preponderance of manpower and equipment, it is easy to overlook the human dimension in the outcome. As observed by the division historian, "At no time in their campaigns in the Pacific did the 37th Division meet enemy soldiers equal to these in valor or ability."[14] While the 6th Imperial Division would otherwise have merited admiration and sympathy, such sentiments were forfeited by its conduct in China against a helpless population, and its drubbing was hailed by Beightler as a partial repayment for those crimes.[15]

For the victors, their greater numbers and tools of war would not have sufficed if employed less capably. Morison observed, "Kanda's forces could have captured the Perimeter and the Torokina airdrome, wiping out the gains of the Bougainville campaign and raising new hopes at Rabaul, but for the stern resistance offered by the infantry and artillery of the XIV Corps."[16] In what had become a backwater of the Pacific war, few then noticed and far fewer now remember this hard-won victory over elite Japanese troops by the citizen soldiers of Ohio, Massachusetts, and Illinois.

# CHAPTER 22

---— ∞∞∞ —---

# "They Wanted to Fight"

The Japanese retreat on Bougainville began on 28 March. Iwasa's and Muda's survivors headed south toward Buin, covered by the 4th South Seas Garrison and the 6th Cavalry Regiment. Meanwhile, Magata went north with 1,500 men by way of the Numa Numa Trail. Before Hyakutake admitted defeat, Griswold had readied a follow-up plan.

Recognizing that the beaten and isolated Japanese troops posed no significant threat if adequately contained, Griswold saw no point pursuing them to their bases to obtain total victory. He instead ordered his forces to harass the enemy's line of supply and attack their rear, preventing buildup for a possible renewed attack.[1] These planned actions included the occupation of key hills and establishing trail blocks to exercise control over territories far beyond the perimeter. He also singled out for attack the enemy flank anchored on Empress Augusta Bay. The operations would be conducted primarily by the Americal Division, which acquired a new commander, Major General Robert B. McClure, as Hodge departed to command the new XXIV Corps destined for Leyte.

Participating with Griswold's divisions for training and support would be the first African American troops introduced to combat in the Pacific. They included the 1st Battalion of the independent 24th Infantry Regiment and, from the African American 93rd Infantry Division, the reinforced 25th Infantry Regiment.

First to be employed in a combat role was 1/24, a battalion led entirely by white officers from the Army's single African American regiment. After garrison duty in New Caledonia and working as service troops in the Solomons, 1/24 was detached from the regiment and sent to Bougainville, arriving 30 January 1944. Assigned initially to the XIV Corps reserve, 1/24 was later attached to the 37th Division. Operating with the 148th Regiment's reserve, one company moved to the perimeter on 11 March, losing two men that night, the first African Americans killed by grenade and rifle fire during the war.[2] The first patrol conducted by an African American unit occurred the next day, when a clash with eight Japanese resulted in one death on each side. Eager to report success, the press blew this minor action entirely out of proportion. As reported by the New York Times, the battalion had "infiltrated several thousand yards within the Japanese lines, killed some of the enemy, threw others off balance . . . evaded a Japanese ambush . . . [and] out-fought the Japanese in their chosen medium—the jungle."[3]

Pressure immediately built for the further employment of African Americans in combat, inducing the War Department to declare it a "national policy."[4] It was in this atmosphere of high expectation that the 93rd Division's 25th Regimental Combat Team arrived on 28 March. Having undergone considerable training after activation in May 1942, the 93rd was judged "in fine shape" by the deputy chief of staff of the Army and better prepared for employment than the 92nd Division, the other African American division.[5]

Had it been left up to the War Department and the Army high command, African Americans would not have been considered for use as Army combat troops regardless of their unit designations and training. It required pressure from the African American leaders and the press, and finally from the president, who needed support in the upcoming election, for action to be taken. Army chief of staff General George C. Marshall and secretary of war Henry L. Stimson, both predisposed to doubt the fighting capacities of African Americans but unable to prevent their use, were anxious that they not be employed in serious combat until fully prepared. Mostly they feared the negative publicity if unready units failed in combat. Sharing their outlook, Harmon reluctantly accepted African American combat troops in the South Pacific. He promised Marshall that the 93rd Division troops would be carefully eased into combat. Initially, they would conduct patrols and mop-up operations with experienced units, their performance carefully monitored and reported on in detail to the highest command levels. As noted in the official Army study, it was "a klieg-lighted atmosphere" that no other troops experienced before or since.[6]

Anticipating the need for manpower to occupy several outposts that Americal planned to establish outside the perimeter, the three 25th Infantry regiments were assigned to that division, each battalion attached to a different regiment. Also, 1/24 was reassigned from the 37th to Americal, its first assignment after the occupation of Hill 260.

During April, Americal units moved against hill masses to the east of the perimeter where much of Hyakutake's heavy artillery had been concentrated. On 1 April, patrols from the 164th Regiment advanced into the hills north of Hill 260 and west of the Torokina River. After clashing with small enemy forces, four principal heights were seized and occupied by the next day. Atop Hills 250, 600, 1000, and 1111, much of the heavy artillery that had been so laboriously brought forward and hauled into position by the Japanese was discovered and destroyed.[7] Active patrolling, including by elements of the 25th Infantry, was then conducted eastward and along the west fork of the Torokina toward Mount Bagana, near the base of which was a Japanese evacuation trail. The consequences from one of the patrols, insignificant enough from a military standpoint to be ignored in the Americal Division's official history, would decisively affect the Army's attitude toward the further employment of African American troops.

On 6 April, 3/25's K Company was ordered to advance eastward about two miles from Hill 250 and establish a trail block. Unlike the other 25th Infantry companies, 3/25's companies had never accompanied Americal troops on patrol. The party was led by a white company commander, with African American platoon leaders and noncommissioned officers (NCOs) and reinforced by a machine-gun platoon from M Company. Accompanying the patrol was an experienced sergeant from the 164th who acted as guide and two members of a signal photographic unit prepared to take pictures for distribution to the press.

After an uneventful march to within a quarter-mile of their destination, they encountered an abandoned Japanese hospital compound. While pausing to check the huts, the patrol came under fire from what was later estimated as no more than a Japanese squad. Initially all went well as the two trailing platoons came forward to flank the leading platoon. Soon, however, indiscriminate fire broke out, with the lead platoon caught in a crossfire. An attempt by the company commander to impose fire control was fruitless, and his efforts to conduct an orderly withdrawal failed. No help was forthcoming from the platoon leaders and sergeants, including the company's first sergeant and a platoon sergeant, who immediately fled back to base. After much difficulty, the patrol withdrew with twenty wounded, most of them casualties from friendly fire, leaving ten dead behind including the weapons platoon leader.[8] Such performance was not unprecedented for a unit in its first action, but what followed made it clear that there was a more serious problem involved.

Much equipment had been abandoned in the headlong flight, including BARs, M-1 rifles, and a machine gun, mortar, and radio. Despite repeated efforts, it required three days to retrieve the bodies and equipment. First, an L Company patrol retreated after meeting light opposition before reaching the site of the engagement. The following day, a forty-man carrying party from L Company led by a K Company platoon leader found six bodies. But despite threats of disciplinary action, only two NCOs and two privates were willing to assist with the dead, so that help had to be obtained from K Company to retrieve just three bodies and part of the equipment. Only on the third day were the other bodies and the rest of the equipment retrieved by a carrying party led by the battalion commander. An investigation was immediately ordered by Griswold, during which virtually everyone involved in the incident was interviewed, resulting in a far-reaching report in May.

Meanwhile, along the coastline, the vulnerable Japanese left flank anchored on Empress Augusta Bay was attacked. On 5–6 April, a concentration of pillboxes in front of the 132nd Regiment's bridgehead at the Torokina River was subjected to massive shelling, primarily by destroyers with follow-up howitzer and mortar fire. The infantry attack began on 7 April, when 2/132's E Company left the perimeter, skirted the pillboxes, and established a roadblock to their rear. The advance on the pillboxes progressed slowly, as the palm trees and undergrowth were thoroughly torn up by the bombardments. Arriving at the objective, E Company found only a few Japanese occupying the pillboxes and they were soon wiped out.

The next morning, advancing along the beach toward the village of Mavavia, the company discovered well-concealed enemy positions at the fringe of the jungle. 2/132's battalion commander asked for tanks, which were promptly delivered by LST. The attack conducted two hours later by a platoon from 1/132's C Company and the newly arrived tank platoon eliminated all the pillboxes within ninety minutes, after which a company from the 25th Infantry occupied the ground gained.

The following day, 9 April, 1/132's C Company advanced past shattered and abandoned pillboxes to enter the ruins of Mavavia. During the three-day attack, sixty-two pillboxes were destroyed, although not many more than forty Japanese were killed. The operation concluded with the arrival of 1/24 to occupy the Mavavia area. That African American battalion, which had occupied Hill 260 since 29 March, turned over the hill's defense to elements of the 93rd Division.

In later operations during the month, 1/24 would again be under fire. On 19 April, a platoon operating near the mouth of the Mavavia River was pinned down by Japanese fire but succeeded in extricating itself. Then, after a bombardment lasting several days, one company participated with a tank platoon in a push that claimed thousands of yards of beach, after which elements of the 24th held the ground.

The 132nd next dealt with the hills on the west bank of the Saua River. Attached for the operation was 1/25 and the Fiji 3rd Battalion. After saturation artillery shelling and air strikes, 3/132 advanced on 15–16 April to take possession of Hills 165 and 155 without opposition. Resistance was encountered, however, when the north base of Hill 500 was reached. An artillery bombardment sufficed to weaken the Japanese sufficiently so that the crest of the hill was gained by midday. It was then that the enemy struck back with determination and was repelled only after a sharp firefight. Fighting then shifted to the low ground southwest and west of the hill, where the Japanese were firmly entrenched. After the area was saturated with artillery and mortar fire, 3/132 advanced to discover that the Japanese had fled. The last height in the hill mass, Hill 501, fell without opposition and, as was done to hold the other hills, was occupied by troops from

1/25. Fighting on this front continued during April against enemy concentrations near the Saua River, but resistance largely ended by month's end.

In the months after April 1944, America's 164th and 182nd Regiments on Bougainville probed far to the east to the headwaters of the Tekessi and Reini rivers, encountering few Japanese. Clashes were so infrequent that division casualties in the sector from May to November amounted to only twenty-one, including seven killed.

In a reversal of the situation during Hyakutake's attack when the 37th Division bore the brunt of the fighting, that division would have the easier time beginning in April. Early that month, a force composed of a company from 3/148, two Fiji companies, and 2/25 went northward up the Numa Numa Trail. After meeting and overcoming some opposition, the expedition reached the forks of the Laruma River five days later. To control the ground gained, trail blocks were set up on the Numa Numa and secondary trails. Thereafter, there was continuous patrolling against little or no opposition, including long-range operations north of the Laruma forks and to Cape Moltke.

The African American troops of 2/25 performed well during these operations, which included a river crossing involving a sixty-foot descent by rope. During one action, Private Wade Foggie set up his rocket launcher under heavy fire, then knocked out three enemy pillboxes, killing about ten Japanese, for which he was awarded the Bronze Star. On its return to the perimeter, 2/25 was commended for killing about thirty Japanese while sustaining only four minor casualties.[9]

African American soldiers of the 93rd Infantry Division on the Numa Numa Trail, Bougainville, 1 May 1944. (National Archives and Records Administration)

The report by the K Company investigation committee was released on 10 May. Predictably, because the company had been given no opportunity to patrol with troops from the 164th Regiment, inadequate training was cited as a problem. More worrisome, because more difficult to correct, were charges of insufficient initiative and inability to control their men on the part of the African American officers and NCOs. Low officer morale was considered one contributory cause of the problem. Significantly, the sergeant from the 164th who guided the patrol reported, "They would listen to me because they thought I had more experience. They wanted to fight."[10]

By the time the report was issued, however, two warring narratives developed. African Americans came to believe that the white company commander deserted his men and caused the African American officer's death, after which the affair was covered up by pinning the blame on the troops. An equally false and destructive account was circulated among the white troops that inflated the panic of one company into the failure of the entire 93rd Division.[11]

In transmitting the report, Harmon pointed out "a lack of proper discipline, and small unit leadership" and recommended additional training to correct the deficiencies. On receiving the report, the regimental commander pointed out that the situation might have been averted if the company had "been given prior instruction and been accompanied by an experienced platoon . . . in its initial action." He observed that similar situations, including firing by troops at each other, had often occurred among unseasoned troops in the jungle.

When the report reached the War Department, undersecretary of war John J. McCloy appended a transmittal note to Stimson expressing his feelings. He wrote, "on the whole I feel that the report is not so bad as to discourage us." Noting that considerable improvement had been achieved by an African American air squadron after unfavorable initial reports, McCloy opined, "It will take more time and effort to make good combat units out of them, but in the end I think they can be brought over to the asset side."[12]

But Stimson was unconvinced. Based on this report and reports about other incidents involving the 93rd Division, he rendered what would be the final verdict on the employment of African Americans in combat. In his opinion, "I do not believe they can be turned into really effective combat troops without all officers being white."[13]

With a shortage of available white officers and a great need for labor, the experiment on Bougainville quietly closed with the relief of the 25th Regiment between 20 May and 12 June. Sent first to the Green Islands, where it performed security and service duties, the regiment with other 93rd Division units did much the same elsewhere in the Pacific. Despite continuous training in the course of such activities, and lip service given by MacArthur as to their further employment in action, the 93rd would have few additional contacts with Japanese forces.

The 24th Infantry fared better. After advancing farther beyond Mavavia, the battalion was relieved by 2/132 and later patrolled in the Reini River area. On 25 June, the battalion, which had incurred twenty-six casualties, half of whom were killed in battle, was sent to the Russell Islands for labor and guard duty. However, befitting the "good" rating rendered by Griswold for its Bougainville service, the 24th was sent to Saipan and Tinian for garrison duty during December 1944. The regiment would kill or capture 722 of the enemy remaining hidden in caves and elsewhere, earning the highest commendation by the inspector general. The report remarked that "the morale of this Regiment is high and its discipline is well worthy of emulation and praise." Further, members of the 24th were deemed eligible for the Combat Infantryman's Badge and a battle star, and their performance was cited for consideration in future questions about the employment of African American troops.[14]

Not all African American units were removed from Bougainville. The 93rd Division's reconnaissance troop remained longer, participating in a battle on the East-West Trail during July before rejoining the division. That left the 49th Coast Artillery Battalion as the single African American unit remaining on the island. Fully integrated into XIV Corps artillery, the battalion performed to a high standard during Hyakutake's attack in March, earning a commendation from Kreber. It continued to provide important support during later operations in the Laruma Valley and would be retained until February 1945, when it left for New Guinea.

In July 1945, the chief historian of the Army analyzed with great perceptiveness the problem of employing African Americans effectively in the military. In a letter, he said that "when a man knows that the color of his skin will automatically disqualify him for [sic] reaping the fruits of attainment it is no wonder that he sees little point in trying very hard to excel anybody else. To me, the most extraordinary thing is that such people continue trying at all. . . . We cannot expect to make first-class soldiers out of second or third or fourth class citizens. The man who is lowest down in civilian life is practically certain to be lowest down as a soldier."

Further, the historian regretted the unavoidable assignment of African Americans to southern U.S. training camps, where "unfamiliar Jim Crowism was exceedingly unacceptable to northern Negroes."[15] Recognizing that the serious underlying problems could not be readily corrected in the midst of war, he concluded that "the War Department must deal with an existing state of affairs." Looking out further, he hoped "that in the long run it will be possible to assign individual Negro soldiers and officers to any unit in the Army where they are qualified to serve efficiently."[16]

By that point, the War Department had gathered substantial information about the performance of African Americans in both the Pacific and Europe, and would ultimately face up to the impossibility of obtaining maximum performance from a segregated army. It would require the desegregation of the armed forces and profound societal changes in the postwar years to meaningfully address a seemingly insoluble problem.

CHAPTER 23

# "The South Pacific Campaign Was Finished"

At the August 1943 Quadrant conference in Quebec, the Combined Chiefs of Staff agreed to bypass Rabaul. To complete its encirclement, MacArthur was ordered by Marshall to capture the Admiralty Islands and Kavieng.[1]

Situated 200 miles from New Guinea and 117 miles from Rabaul, the Admiralties were as tempting a target as existed in the South Pacific. Possession would sever a key line of supply to Rabaul and provide flank protection for MacArthur's planned New Guinea operations. Further, fifteen-mile-long Seeadler Harbor could provide a superb alternative to Rabaul as a fleet anchorage, and aircraft based in the Admiralties could control a 1,000-square-mile area that included Wewak and Truk.

The Admiralties consisted of two principal islands and many surrounding islets. Largest was Manus, forty-nine miles long and sixteen miles wide, separated at the east by a narrow waterway from smaller Los Negros. Had the original invasion plan involving a full divisional landing on 1 April 1944 been followed, the assault would probably have occurred on the shores of Seeadler Harbor. That plan changed entirely when a photo reconnaissance mission over the Admiralties on 23 February encountered no ground fire and observed no enemy activity. Concluding that the Japanese may have pulled out, Kenney rushed to MacArthur urging that a reconnaissance-in-force be mounted.

If the invasion force could get ashore and hold, additional troops could be rushed in. If the Japanese were found in great strength, the force could be withdrawn. Kenney's immediate goal was possession of the overgrown Momote airstrip on Los Negros that could be made operational quickly to receive men and supplies. For him, "That coral strip on Los Negros . . . was the most important piece of real estate in the theater."[2]

Kenney was recommending a dangerous course of action. As shown by the abortive Koiari raid on Bougainville and similar operations, extricating a hard-pressed force by sea can be difficult and costly. Barbey would later say that withdrawal would not have been possible. MacArthur pondered the situation and found the opportunity irresistible. Anxious to keep up with Nimitz's progress in the Central Pacific and enhance his chances to gain approval for a return to the Philippines, advancing the Admiralties timetable seemed well worth the risk. MacArthur embraced the idea, saying, "That will put the cork in the bottle."[3]

Chamberlin, MacArthur's operations officer, and Kinkaid readily bought the idea, but Willoughby, the intelligence chief, disagreed. He doubted that the Japanese would have vacated such a strategically important area. His estimate, based primarily on Ultra interceptions, indicated that more than 4,000 Japanese were still there. They were even known, specifically, to consist of the 51st Transportation Regiment, a battalion of the 1st Independent Mixed Regiment, and elements of the 38th Division.[4] Imamura had with difficulty built up the garrison to 3,646 in the face of American submarine attacks that claimed many troop transports.

Kenney's idea also did not sit well with Krueger, whose own intelligence staff told him there were about 4,500 Japanese present. Krueger cared deeply about his fighting men and considered the assignment unnecessarily risky. And, not expecting the invasion to begin for another month, Barbey would need to scramble to collect vessels that were dispersed on supply runs and in repair yards.

Colonel Yoshio Ezaki, commanding the islands, expected an invasion. He ordered his forces not to fire at aircraft or otherwise disclose their presence, and Kenney was taken in. But Ezaki had a large area to defend, and he guessed wrongly that the Americans would strike directly at Seeadler Harbor.

Instead, with the Momote airstrip the immediate objective, Hayne Harbor on the eastern coast of Los Negros was targeted. Ezaki had rejected the possibility of an attack there since the harbor was too narrow to accommodate a large invasion force. To learn something of the area, a six-man patrol was dispatched. They were unable to complete the scouting mission because, as they reported on the afternoon of 27 February, the place was "lousy with Japs."[5] However, with the landings scheduled for the morning of the 29th, cancellation was impossible.

The dismounted 1st Cavalry Division at Oro Bay, New Guinea, was selected to take the Admiralties. This last square division in the U.S. Army was organized in two brigades, each with two regiments, with two squadrons in each regiment. Rated one of the top divisions in the Army, this would be its first combat in World War II. When concern was expressed as to its inexperience, MacArthur sentimentally fell back on a childhood recollection from the Indian Wars about the performance of the 5th Cavalry that would lead off the invasion. He observed, "They'd fight then—and they'll fight now. Don't worry about them."[6]

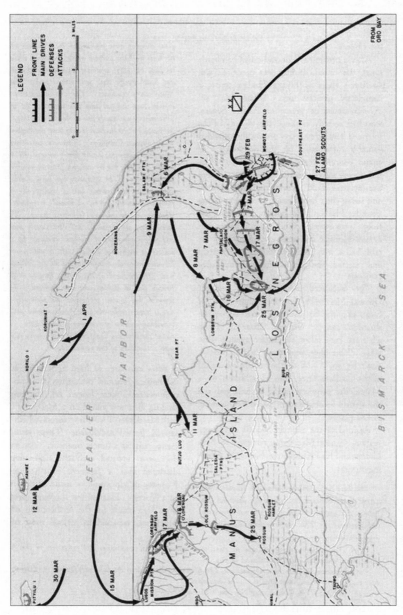

**Map 13. Admiralty Islands Campaign** (U.S. Army—Center of Military History, *The Campaigns of MacArthur in the Pacific*, 139)

Three APDs and eight regular destroyers transported the 5th Cavalry Regiment's 2nd Squadron, together with artillery and anti-aircraft support, a total of 1,026 men, from Oro Bay to Los Negros. Barbey chose his deputy Rear Admiral William M. Fechteler to command the naval attack group. Rear Admiral Russell S. Berkey was ordered by Kinkaid to cover the approach and conduct the bombardment with cruisers USS *Phoenix* and *Nashville* plus four destroyers. To decide on the spot whether the force would stay or withdraw, MacArthur accompanied the expedition on board *Phoenix* along with Kinkaid.

General Douglas MacArthur (center), with Vice Admiral Thomas Kinkaid, on board cruiser USS *Phoenix*, observes the landings on Los Negros, Admiralty Islands, 29 February 1944. (National Archives and Records Administration)

Bad weather on invasion day allowed only three bombers to get through, leaving it up to the Navy to soften the target with a half-hour bombardment. By that point, nine B-25s arrived and strafed the beaches. From a transport area five thousand yards from the harbor, the troops debarked into twelve LCP(R)s for a run to the beach starting at 0830.

The first wave made it to shore with relative ease, but heavy fire forced the second wave to turn back while destroyers silenced the enemy positions. Afterwards, the third and fourth waves took fire from 25-mm guns, causing some casualties and damage to four of the boats. On shore, resistance was negligible, with the Momote airstrip in American hands just an hour and a half after the first wave landed. The cost up to completion of the landings at 1100 was two sailors and two soldiers killed and three sailors and three soldiers wounded.

Landing by the first wave of troops from the 5th Cavalry Regiment, 1st Cavalry Division on Los Negros, Admiralty Islands, 29 February 1944. (U.S. Army)

Brigadier General William C. Chase, commander of the 1st Cavalry Brigade, came ashore during the afternoon and took charge of what was called the Brewer Task Force. MacArthur and Kinkaid arrived too. Pleased with the results, especially the effectiveness of the naval gunfire, MacArthur decided the invaders would stay and be reinforced. He told Chase, "You have your teeth in him now—don't let go."[7]

MacArthur's willingness to expose himself to enemy fire at Los Negros went far to dispel the "Dugout Doug" image. Although the strategy of bypassing areas of enemy strength called "leapfrogging" had already been employed effectively by Halsey, MacArthur later wrote, "Probably the first time it attracted general public attention was the Admiralty landings."[8] And the successful operation went far to convince the Joint Chiefs of Staff that MacArthur had the ability to effectively lead the return to the Philippines.

Lacking barbed wire and recognizing that his force was too small to defend the area gained, Chase withdrew from the airstrip and drew his force in tight. That night and the next, small numbers of Japanese attempted to infiltrate the American lines and were beaten back. On 2 March, Chase reoccupied the airfield. The remainder of the 5th Cavalry then arrived, along with Seabees who immediately went to work repairing the Momote runways. To meet the long-expected Japanese counterattack, land mines were laid, automatic weapons positions were prepared, protected by dugouts at their flanks and rear, and artillery was positioned to sweep the front.

Delayed by faulty intelligence and difficulties assembling his forces, Ezaki's all-out attack was mounted the night of 3–4 March. While in some sectors the Japanese attempted infiltration as during the first nights, the main attacks were delivered openly by the Iwakami Battalion at the north of the perimeter. The Japanese came on noisily, in one instance heartily singing "Deep in the Heart of Texas," and fell in droves to the land mines and small arms fire.

At a revetment manned by eight men from G Troop, all except Sergeant Troy McGill and another cavalryman were killed or wounded. After ordering the other man back to safety, McGill continued to fire into the enemy ranks until his weapon jammed, then fought with his weapon as a club until he was killed. McGill was awarded the division's first Medal of Honor in the war.

Especially important was the fire laid down by anti-aircraft and field artillery batteries and particularly by destroyers, about which Chase would say, "They didn't support us; they saved our necks."[9] The Americans lost 61 dead and 244 wounded, including Seabee casualties, while more than 700 Japanese were killed. The Japanese squandered their forces at the last point in the campaign where they possessed adequate offensive strength.

The next morning, the 2nd Squadron, 7th Cavalry arrived and relieved the 2nd Squadron, 5th Cavalry, which withdrew for well-earned rest. Chase now estimated that he faced as many as two thousand Japanese and asked for additional troops. Ammunition supplies were replenished by Flying Fortress airdrop, but a lack of barbed wire proved an impediment in securing the defenses. Still, attacks during the night of 4 March, largely consisting of small Japanese patrols, were beaten back with relative ease.

Brewer Task Force would now take the offensive to secure Seeadler Harbor and the Lorengau airstrip on Manus. The immediate target was Salami Plantation, where a good beach could serve for a shore-to-shore operation.

Command of Brewer Task Force changed on 5 March with the arrival of the 1st Cavalry Division commander, Major General Innis P. Swift. Intensely devoted to Krueger, who was willing to overlook his advanced age, rugged sixty-two-year-old Swift had once served as John J. Pershing's aide-de-camp in the Philippines and campaigned alongside George S. Patton against Pancho Villa. Swift's primary interest was to evaluate Chase, who showed signs of fatigue and taut nerves that concerned Krueger. Pleased with the performance of the troops but gaining the same impression as Krueger, Swift took over operations.

Swift ordered an immediate advance northward by the 2nd Squadron, 7th Cavalry. In good spirits after its baptism by fire the night before, the squadron moved slowly on the heavily mined road, gaining only five hundred yards that day. The arrival the next morning of the 12th Cavalry, with light tanks and amphibious LVTs, provided extra punch for a renewed movement. Once again, the 2nd Squadron, 7th Cavalry moved slowly, this time hindered by mud, felled trees, and mines. The 12th Cavalry, however, swung west and, with the help of the tanks that knocked out defended buildings and bunkers, took Salami by afternoon.

Seeadler Harbor could not be used by Allied ships until enemy positions were eliminated on the promontories of, from west to east, Lombrum Plantation, Papitalai Mission, and Papitalai on the western shore of Los Negros. Separately attacked on 7 and 8 March, Lombrum Plantation and Papitalai were easily taken with only a few casualties, but Papitalai Mission, assaulted by the 2nd Squadron, 12th Cavalry, proved far more difficult. Preceded by air and artillery attacks, the cavalrymen crossed Seeadler Harbor using just two available LVTs. During the crossing of nearly a mile, the boats took fire from mortars, machine guns, and a 75-mm howitzer. The twenty men in the first wave landed in the face of enemy fire from bunkers and held out alone for forty-five minutes until the second wave arrived. By nightfall, the LVTs had brought in just G Troop, which then had to defend a 150-yard-wide beachhead alone. After a night in which three enemy counterattacks were broken up by artillery fire 50 yards ahead of the front line, the Japanese withdrew. Papitalai Mission cost the cavalrymen seven dead and twenty-seven wounded.

Seeadler Harbor could now be used after it was cleared of mines dropped months earlier by Kenney's fliers, but much of Los Negros was still in Japanese hands. Employing light tanks, the 12th Cavalry swept through the Mokerang Peninsula, quickly eliminating the few Japanese at the north end of the island. To the south on Los Negros, stronger opposition was encountered. On 11 March, lacking mortars and flamethrowers that were not brought forward in time, the 5th Cavalry's attack against Hill 260 was repulsed. With support from the 12th Cavalry, the hill was taken three days later, essentially ending the fight for Los Negros. Small numbers of Japanese remained that were mostly hunted down and killed during March.

Lorengau airstrip on Manus was now the key remaining objective, and the 2nd Cavalry Brigade was brought to Salami on 9 March to take it. Borrowing an idea that worked nicely at Kwajalein, nearby islands would first be occupied, from which artillery fire could be brought on Manus. Native reports indicated that the Japanese may have departed Hauwei and Butjoluo islands, and that was indeed the case at Butjoluo. But Hauwei was another matter.

A twenty-six-man patrol that landed from an LCVP on Hauwei was ambushed, resulting in twenty-three casualties, including eight killed and loss of the boat. The next day a squadron of the 7th Cavalry Regiment, supported by Australian P-40s, destroyer fire, and a tank, captured the island at a cost of fifty-four casualties, including eight killed. The fierce resistance, the cavalrymen discovered, had come from just forty-three steadfast Japanese sailors.

To avoid enemy areas of strength in the Lorengau area, the landings were made two miles to the west near Lugos Mission. While artillery on the newly won islands pounded Lorengau, destroyers and B-25s thoroughly softened up the invasion beaches. On 15 March, in a shore-to-shore operation from Los Negros, the 8th Cavalry crossed the harbor without loss.

Swift's bold plan involved separation of the two 8th Cavalry squadrons for a two-pronged attack. While the 1st Squadron moved against Lorengau on the coast road, the 2nd Squadron would strike south and then east on a road converging with the coast road. This tactic provided an alternative route to Lorengau in case the coast road proved impassable or too strongly defended. Further, American troops on the inland road would prevent the Japanese from retreating into the mountains, from which they might mount protracted resistance.

Poor road conditions impeded both cavalry forces. The coast road had become nearly impassable after heavy rains, while the inland road needed to be cleared by bulldozer to bring tanks forward. Enemy resistance from bunkers near the airfield was so strong and resistant to artillery and tank fire that it was necessary to commit from reserve the 7th Cavalry. It required three days of intense fighting by the 2nd Brigade to finally gain the airstrip and advance to the Lorengau River.

Lorengau was taken the next day with surprising ease. After thorough artillery and mortar preparation, the 2nd Squadron, 8th Cavalry crossed the sandbar at the river's mouth and fanned out. The bunkers that survived the heavy bombardment were swiftly eliminated, and by afternoon the town was occupied at a cost of only seven wounded. From the relatively few enemy troops so far encountered, it became obvious that there were far fewer than the two thousand estimated on Manus.

A captured Japanese map showed heavy troop concentrations on the Rossum Road to the south of Lorengau, flanked by deep, jungle-covered ravines greatly favoring the defense. Because there was some concern that Japanese were filtering onto Manus from Los Negros, the 8th Cavalry was directed to clear eastern Manus, leaving Rossum and the west end of the island to the 7th Cavalry. Six days of fruitless attacks by the 7th Cavalry then followed, during which heavy losses were incurred for a gain of less than two thousand yards.

Having enjoyed a breather finding few Japanese east of Lorengau, 1st Squadron, 8th Cavalry was brought in for a fresh attempt on the Rossum Road. The attack on 25 March was preceded by heavy bombings by RAAF P-40s and intensive artillery fire. Neither proved successful; the P-40s were unable to achieve the bombing precision of B-25s and the artillery succeeding in eliminating just two bunkers after expending 1,455 rounds. Nevertheless, with considerable help from their 81-mm mortars, the troopers got within grenade-throwing range and, employing tanks and flamethrowers, captured the height. The Rossum Road battle cost the two regiments 36 killed and 128 wounded.

That was the last organized Japanese resistance on Manus. Operations thereafter by the 1st Cavalry involved hunting down Japanese stragglers on Los

Negros and Manus and clearing the offshore islets. Although the campaign was not declared over until May, for all practical purposes it ended in March. At a cost of 326 dead, 1,189 wounded, and four missing, American forces accounted for 3,280 Japanese killed and 75 captured,[10] gaining what would become an invaluable fleet anchorage and two important air bases.

MacArthur was proved right in his decision to undertake the risky campaign and by his confidence in the fresh 1st Cavalry Division that would later win further laurels. Swift's reward for the well-fought campaign would be command of the First Corps in August 1944, becoming the oldest corps commander in the American Army in World War II. Nothing further was heard from Colonel Ezaki after he reported the loss of Papitalai Mission.

Unfortunately, victory brought another conflict. An imbroglio resulted when Nimitz proposed that since Halsey's Seabees would constitute most of the workforce for base development and Seeadler Harbor would be used principally by the Fifth Fleet, Halsey's South Pacific Area should include the Admiralties. Interpreting this as part of the Navy's attempt to take over the Pacific war, MacArthur threatened to retire if that happened.

As told by Halsey, during a stormy meeting in Brisbane, "MacArthur lumped me, Nimitz, King, and the whole Navy in a vicious conspiracy to pare away his authority." Until the matter was resolved, MacArthur would allow only his Seventh Fleet to use Seeadler Harbor. But after Halsey charged, "General, you are putting your personal honor before the welfare of the United States,"[11] MacArthur backed down. By June, naval forces operating from Seeadler Harbor would provide important support for Nimitz's leap to the Marianas and MacArthur's advance toward the Philippines.

When it was clear that the Admiralties operation would succeed, MacArthur pressed for the immediate seizure of Kavieng. Halsey disagreed, believing "the geography of the area begged for another bypass," and he was backed by Nimitz. Agreeing with Halsey and Nimitz, the JCS approved Halsey's recommendation that the invasion force assembled at Guadalcanal for Kavieng be used instead to take Emirau Island.[12]

Located halfway between Kavieng and the Admiralty Islands, Emirau would complete the encirclement of Rabaul. On 20 March, Kavieng and its nearby airfields were thoroughly pummeled by air and sea, creating the impression that it was being softened for invasion. Meanwhile, the occupation of Emirau went forward.

Demonstrating how thoroughly Japanese power in the Bismarcks had collapsed, absolutely no opposition was encountered. Wilkinson entrusted the amphibious operation to Reifsnider, who had commanded the Bougainville invasion transports. The troops came from the reconstituted 4th Marines, its ranks including ex-raiders that had recently fought on Bougainville. As with the Green Islands, Emirau became a PT boat and air base. When the airstrips became fully operational, most missions against Rabaul and Kavieng were flown from Emirau and the Green Islands.

Cartwheel's objectives were fully achieved in a remarkable chain of successes recapitulated in the official Army history: "In less than one year MacArthur's and Halsey's forces fought their way from Guadalcanal and Buna through Woodlark, Kiriwina, Nassau Bay, New Georgia, Lae, Salamaua, Nadzab, the Markham and Ramu Valleys, Finschhafen, the Treasuries, Empress Augusta Bay, Arawe, Cape Gloucester, Saidor, the Green Islands, Emirau and the Admiralties."[13]

"Strategically," observed Bergerud, "the Admiralties and Emirau put the cork into the bottle as far as Rabaul and Kavieng were concerned."[14] Reflecting on the vast resources poured into the development and defense of Rabaul, Morison noted "the folly of building up a great overseas base and garrison without a navy capable of controlling the surrounding waters and air." To Bergerud, the Japanese defeat in the South Pacific was even more consequential than El Alamein and Sicily for the Germans. In its long-term impact, it was considered comparable to Stalingrad.[15]

Admiral Koga did not live to witness the outcome of Japan's failed strategy. Like Yamamota, his end would come in an air crash, although not from Allied action but from bad weather while moving his headquarters from the Palaus to the Philippines during March 1944.

Halsey described the situation in March 1944: "The South Pacific campaign was finished . . . encirclement was complete . . . control of the land, the sea, and the air was ours."[16] But the fighting and dying continued.

# CHAPTER 24

---

# "Kicking Around a Corpse"

W ith the objective of the war in the South Pacific achieved by the encir- clement and neutralization of Rabaul, the divided command arrange- ment was ended. On 15 June 1944, MacArthur assumed tactical control of all forces in the South Pacific while Halsey, in Morison's words, "transfer[red] busi- ness to a new location."[1]

Until then, Halsey had worn two hats, as Commander Third Fleet and Commander South Pacific. Halsey retained command of the Third Fleet and departed to join the Central Pacific offensive. Although an American naval com- mand continued at Noumea under Vice Admiral John H. Newton,[2] with the disappearance of Japanese warships from South Pacific waters except for the occasional supply submarine, Newton inherited what had essentially become an administrative command.

After twenty months leading from behind a desk, Halsey returned to sea. Four months later at the Battle of Leyte Gulf, a measure of revenge was exacted by Kurita, whose heavy cruisers had been surprised at anchor by Sherman's great carrier raid. As Kurita's battlewagons descended on the thinly defended Leyte beachhead, Halsey allowed himself to be lured away by a carrier decoy force.

After losing several warships and narrowly escaping greater disaster, Halsey's fleet was caught in two devastating typhoons. Further, Halsey's unme- thodical command style that sufficed early in the war proved unsuitable for large task forces. Carrier admirals that alternately served under admirals Raymond Spruance and Marc Mitscher, and then under Halsey and John "Slew" McCain, were nearly unanimous in preferring the former.[3]

In evaluating Halsey, critics have tended to focus heavily and sometimes almost exclusively on his checkered performance in the last year of war. Too little attention is generally given to his twenty months as area commander in the South Pacific, arguably his most important and brilliant service during World War II.

To his considerable credit, no leader tried harder than Halsey to minimize casualties. He was certainly superior in that respect to MacArthur, who, in order to satisfy his timetable, was heedless of casualties at Buna and Sanananda, and later at the Driniumor River as will be seen. To this must be added MacArthur's plans to capture Rabaul and Kavieng, which would have made for bloody fighting had these operations been allowed to proceed. Learning from the difficult campaign on New Georgia, Halsey avoided well-defended Kolombangara by leaping instead to Vella Lavella, set up "a shop in the Jap's front yard" at Bougainville at minimal cost, then sidestepped Kavieng by occupying the Green Islands and Emirau. After Halsey left the South Pacific, his impulse to avoid areas of enemy strength caused him to urge that the Palaus be bypassed, which would have avoided the needless bloodbath of Peleliu.[4]

Directly connected with Halsey's attempts to minimize casualties was his expectations from his ground commanders. After his unhappy experience on New Georgia, which he swiftly dealt with, Halsey would never again place his forces under an inexperienced commander who did not enjoy his complete confidence. Although he handled the dismissal of Vogel clumsily, Halsey at least was willing to recognize his friend's unfitness for IMAC command and took steps that led to Vogel's removal. In the same vein and unknown until 2007, when the Holcomb papers became available, was Halsey's decision to relieve Barrett. Coming not long after the dismissal of Vogel, removing one of the most highly esteemed Marine generals before a shot was fired took enormous courage and was subsequently proved correct from the evidence.

And, of course, there was the unique Halsey persona, "a swashbuckler of the old tradition"[5] according to historian E. B. Potter. One air crew chief on Guadalcanal expressed the feelings of the fighting men in October 1942, when Halsey assumed command in the South Pacific: "we all feared defeat and capture. . . . We believed that Halsey and Roosevelt saved us."[6] Here was leadership in the mold of the great captains of history, the ability to imbue forces with the sense that they would prevail despite anything they might encounter.

In the June 2011 issue of *Naval History* magazine, Richard B. Frank evaluated thirty-eight World War II naval leaders as demonstrating Outstanding, Average, or Poor performance. Frank felt it necessary to divide Halsey in half for that purpose, as nothing about Halsey could be considered Average. Ideally, historians will strive harder for such nuance in judging Halsey, whose daring usually but not always paid off.

Wilkinson also departed the South Pacific to lead the III 'Phib at the invasions of the Palaus, Leyte, and Lingayen Gulf, followed by planning the unneeded Kyushu landings. After the war, Wilkinson briefly served on the JCS Strategy

"Bull" Halsey personified the fighting Navy for America's troops and public alike, as reflected in this World War II poster. (Naval History and Heritage Command)

Committee before his tragic and ironic death by drowning in 1946, when his car rolled off a ferry at Norfolk, Virginia.

As part of the reorganization of the South Pacific command, AirSols was dissolved and the Army's 13th Air Force became part of Kenney's expanded command, designated the Far East Air Force. As part of a shrunken command renamed Aircraft, Northern Solomons (AirNorSols), other former AirSols units continued their mission of suppressing the bypassed Japanese positions in the South Pacific.

With the disappearance of Japanese air power, retention of the RNZAF squadrons in the theater was for a time uncertain. A New Zealand home front manpower crisis in 1944 resulted in the disbanding of the 3rd New Zealand Division later in the year, and the RNZAF was similarly at risk. Losing these highly skilled pilots made little sense however. Also, with the nation expecting to take a place at the peace table, New Zealand's withdrawal from the Pacific war was politically unacceptable. Thus, the RNZAF planes remained in the South Pacific.

Mitchell retained command of the smaller organization and its Marine component, becoming subordinate to Kenney. Before the changeover, Mitchell met with MacArthur, Kinkaid, and Kenney to explore ways that his fliers' skills might be better employed. Kenney provided his assurance that Mitchell's airmen were performing important work and not "kicking around a corpse."[7] But that was indeed the case, and another direct appeal failed, with Kenney claiming he could not even accommodate the numerous aircraft in his pipeline.

During the Philippines campaign, after Kinkaid complained about insufficient air cover, Halsey proposed using Marine air units since Kenney "was assigning [them] to missions far below [their] capacity."[8] This led to the employment of four Marine air groups for close air support of Krueger's and Eichelberger's forces on Luzon and in the southern Philippines. Winning the highest praise from ground commanders and the men on the firing line, these successes "marked a long stride toward the formulation of Marine aviation's postwar mission."[9]

The many other members of AirNorSols left behind in the South Pacific would indeed be left "kicking around a corpse," principally the bare but still stoutly defended airstrips of Rabaul and Kavieng. Through war's end, 20,600 tons of bombs were dropped on Rabaul, including 3,400 tons by Kenney's bombers that returned occasionally after mid-1944. In Japanese hands but without defending aircraft, Rabaul acquired some value to the Allies as an educational resource. While keeping the base neutralized, fresh air crews gained experience in how to attack a town and airfield complex protected by antiaircraft defenses.

Despite such fringe benefits, according to the postwar Strategic Bombing Survey, "attacks on Rabaul and other by-passed positions were continued longer and in greater volume than required."[10]

# CHAPTER 25

⎯⎯⎯ ⚭ ⎯⎯⎯

# "The Japanese Could Die Where They Were
# or Die Advancing"

L
ittle of consequence occurred on Bougainville during the second half of
1944. In July, the Americal Division took over responsibility for the area
north of the forks of the Laruma River, where movement was limited by high
ridges, deep ravines, and few native trails. Division forces also moved down the
coast to establish a trail block near the mouth of the Jaba River, meeting little
opposition and maintaining that advanced post without difficulty.

America's 182nd and 132rd regiments attempted during October and
November to clear an area around the upper Numa Numa Trail.[1] Activity was
mostly limited to patrolling at the company and platoon levels during which
there were few contacts with the Japanese. Now under MacArthur, the primary
activity of forces on the island was preparing for the Philippines campaign.

With the steady development of infrastructure, conditions on Bougainville
became comfortable by South Pacific standards. At the same time, conditions
steadily deteriorated for Hyakutake's men. Cut off from outside support, mere
survival presented challenge enough. Extensive vegetable gardens were planted,
providing employment for Allied fliers, who eagerly sought out and destroyed
them by napalm. As conditions worsened and morale plummeted, insubordination and desertion became increasingly common. Under the circumstances, the
Japanese were more than willing to accept the tacit truce that set in.

Mid-1944 would be a much more difficult period for American forces protecting MacArthur's rear on New Guinea. After opposing the Australians in the
Huon Peninsula and the Americans at Saidor, Adachi's forces moved westward
to defend Wewak. Everything changed in late April after MacArthur, with support from Nimitz's carriers, leaped past Wewak to seize Aitape and Hollandia.

Once the Admiralties were lost, Imamura was isolated at Rabaul and was no
longer able to effectively oversee Adachi on New Guinea. Consequently, Adachi's

18th Army along with the 4th Air Army was assigned to General Korechika Anami's 2nd Area Army on western New Guinea. Adachi and Anami planned a coordinated attack against Hollandia and Aitape, but that became impossible once Anami was forced farther west. With Adachi and Anami far apart, the 18th Army was subordinated to Southern Army headquarters at Singapore.

To attack Aitape, Adachi's men had traversed hundreds of miles of rough jungle trails, hauling much of their supplies and equipment by hand because of insufficient motor transport and the sinking of their barges by PT boats.[2] Further, aided by Ultra intelligence, Kenney's airmen largely destroyed the 4th Air Army, depriving the marchers of air cover. In the face of enormous problems and great sacrifice, 15,000 to 20,000 men from the 20th, 41st, and 51st Divisions were assembled in the Aitape area by June.

While Adachi and his troops remained eager for battle, the Southern Army decided the operation had lost its purpose and ordered him to instead conduct "delaying action at strategic locations in eastern New Guinea." Adachi was too much of a fighter to accept that order in silence. As his chief of staff put it, "the Japanese could die where they were (i.e., in isolation by attrition) or die advancing."[3]

Actually, attacking Aitape was a practical decision. For the worn 18th Army, a trek to join the Second Army in western New Guinea might well inflict greater losses than a battle would. They would be starved for food and supplies if they remained in place in their isolation, and the capture of Aitape might yield sorely needed provisions. Whether or not he succeeded, Adachi could at least draw forces away from MacArthur's offensive, slowing the American advance toward the Philippines while preserving Japanese honor.

Adachi framed the situation: "The presence of the enemy in Aitape affords us a last favorable chance to display effectively the fighting power which this Army still possesses, and to contribute toward the destruction of the enemy's strength. It is obvious that, if we resort from the first to mere delaying tactics, the result will be that we shall never be able to make effective use of our full strength."[4]

Adachi got his way to fight what would be the last major, and perhaps least-known, battle by American forces in the South Pacific, the desperately waged Battle of the Driniumor River.

After Krueger captured Aitape in April, he was concerned that Adachi might attempt such an attack. Still, it was long thought that Japanese movements westward from the Wewak area were most likely part of an attempt to move the 18th Army to western New Guinea. Ultra intercepts and other intelligence finally made it certain that the Japanese were headed for Aitape, the great unknown being the exact date of the attack.[5] That could not be pinned down because the Japanese themselves were long uncertain because of Adachi's difficulty bringing his forces forward.

To defend Aitape, Krueger assigned the 32nd Division, substantially rebuilt and retrained after its ordeal at Buna, under a new commander, Major General William Gill.[6] To reinforce the 32nd, Krueger added Colonel Edward M. Starr's still untested 124th RCT, a Florida National Guard unit detached from the 31st Division. Also assigned was Cunningham's 112th Cavalry RCT that had gotten its first taste of battle at Arawe, New Britain.[7] The 43rd Division, roughly handled during its drive on Munda, was also called in but would not arrive from New Zealand until July.

To control what would eventually be the equivalent of nearly three divisions, Krueger summoned Major General Charles P. Hall, newly arrived from the states with his XI Corps headquarters. Taciturn and remote, Hall had no battle experience but had greatly impressed Army Ground Forces commander Lieutenant General Lesley J. McNair, who recommended him for the command.[8]

Three defense lines defended Aitape. The outermost lay twenty-two miles east of Aitape along the western bank of the Driniumor River, extending five miles to Afua in the foothills of the Torricelli Mountains. The area contained two principal trails, the Anamo-Afua Trail extending south from the coast just west of the river's mouth, and the Palauru-Afua Trail running westward from Afua. Designated the Covering Force, troops on this line were commanded by Brigadier General Clarence A. Martin, the 32nd Division's assistant division commander. Their mission was to conduct a delaying action if the Japanese attacked.

The main defenses were divided into two sectors. The Eastern Sector, with outposts along the Nigia River about halfway between the Driniumor and Aitape, was directly under Gill's command. The Western Sector defense line covered the Tadji airstrips, the great prize in the area. These fields had become key stops between eastern New Guinea and Hollandia and, for close air support of Hall's forces, were home to RAAF Beaufighters and Beauforts.

As long as Aitape required strong protection, significant forces had to be diverted from MacArthur's westward drive. MacArthur's overriding concern was that this might slow his race to the Philippines, as a delay might cause the JCS to give Nimitz the nod for his very different Pacific plans. By attacking Adachi first, the Americans would gain the initiative and hopefully destroy his army. Such action would also eliminate the possibility that the Japanese might instead strike at an even more critical position, Hollandia.[9]

MacArthur urged Krueger to quickly clean up the situation, and Krueger in turn pushed his Aitape commanders to take the offensive. Uncertain that he had sufficient strength, and regarding his primary mission as defending the airfields, Gill resisted. Remaining within a well-prepared perimeter, with overwhelming artillery superiority and complete command of the air and sea, Gill felt best able to defeat Adachi at least cost.[10] Essentially, this was the tactic that succeeded against Hyakutake on Bougainville in March.

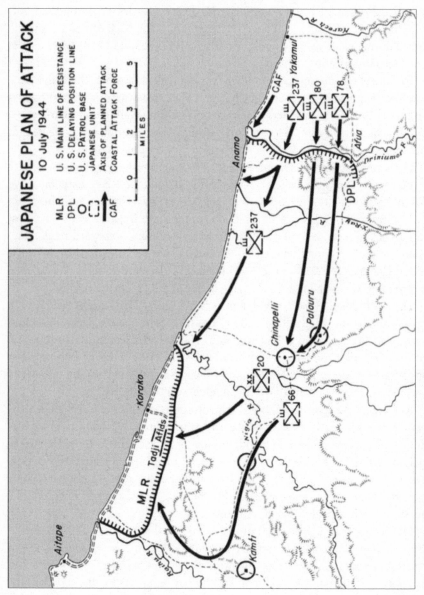

Map 14. Driniumor River: The Japanese Plan (Smith, *The U.S. Army in World War II—The War in the Pacific: The Approach to the Philippines*, 149)

Siding with Krueger, Hall concluded that the Japanese lacked the strength to seriously threaten Aitape and planned to take the offensive. He decided to land the 124th far to the rear of the Japanese line at the Driniumor. Martin's forces at the river would then advance, trapping the Japanese. In readiness for its coastal operation scheduled for 13 July, the 124th was held back near the Tadji airstrips, with the 32nd Division's 126th RCT nearby.[11] Gill did not share Hall's optimism, doubted Hall's fitness as a newcomer to the Pacific, and resented being relegated mostly to administrative and supply duties while Martin played a key role in the battle.[12]

This deployment provided good protection for Aitape and the airstrips but left the forces along the Driniumor seriously overextended and in no position to face a determined Japanese attack. It had earlier been expected that the Covering Force might pull back from the river in such a case. But, under pressure from Krueger, who wanted the Japanese held as far to the east as possible, Hall ordered that the Covering Force could retreat "only in the face of overwhelming pressure."[13] Dangerously spread out along the western riverbank on a five-mile front were two 32nd Division regiments, the 128th on the north with its left at the mouth of the Driniumor and the 127th to its right, and the 112th cavalrymen at the far right near Afua.

In early July, Willoughby predicted the Japanese would attack on 10 July. His warning was received with skepticism because his earlier predictions were wrong and the front had remained quiet for some time.[14] In fact, Japanese patrols were very active, but so successful in infiltrating the porous front that their presence wasn't recognized.

Five days before Hall's planned attack, Krueger ordered Hall to conduct a reconnaissance in force to ascertain Japanese dispositions.[15] Although Hall doubted that the Japanese were readying for battle, he did not like the idea but needed to comply. Closer to the situation, Gill and Martin sensed a pending Japanese attack and feared weakening the already overstretched defense line. Hall gained a deferral to 10 July, but Martin was finally forced to send out two teams, one from the 128th to the north and the other from the 112th Cavalry to the south. That night, while the teams were deep in enemy territory, Adachi struck the depleted front.

Before launching his attack, Adachi appealed to the spirit of his army, exhorting: "I am determined to destroy the enemy in Aitape by attacking him ruthlessly with the concentration of our entire force in that area. This will be our final opportunity to employ our entire strength to annihilate the enemy. Make the supreme sacrifice, display the spirit of the Imperial Army."[16]

Adachi's plan entailed a crossing of the waist-deep, hundred-yard wide Driniumor River by the 41st Division's 237th Infantry in a sector held by E Company, 128th Infantry. After a breakthrough, one wing would move west toward the main Aitape defenses while the other headed northwest to clear the coast near the mouth of the Driniumor. A unit designated the Coastal Attack Force, consisting principally of the 41st Division artillery, would cooperate by pinning down the 128th RCT near the coast. On the left of the 237th, the 80th Infantry opposite the right of E Company of the 128th, and next below the 78th Infantry opposite G Company, were expected to force their way across the river and move west. After pausing to regroup, and joined by the 51st Division's 66th Infantry, the Japanese planned to take the Tadji airstrips by a three-pronged attack.

In the last minutes of 10 July, after a brief artillery and mortar barrage, screaming Japanese troops from the 78th Infantry charged across the river in waves opposite G Company, 128th Infantry. The Americans cut down many attackers with heavy machine-gun and mortar fire, and their artillery took an even greater toll. Twenty minutes later the 80th Regiment attacked E Company at G's left. After being thrown back initially, the Japanese were reinforced and, probably outnumbering the defenders ten to one,[17] broke through E's thinly held line. Penetrating Martin's defenses for 1,300 yards, a follow-up attack expanded the lodgment to 2,000 yards. The attack that night was costly for the 18th Army, which lost about three thousand killed and wounded, but it succeeded in its purpose. Fanning out, the Japanese threatened to encircle Martin's troops along the river.

Unclear about the extent of the breakthrough and without reserves, Martin obtained permission to withdraw the two reconnaissance forces. Remarkably, thanks to the thickness of the jungle, both teams made it back safely. After a counterattack by 1/128 failed, Martin recognized the danger and ordered a general withdrawal to X-ray River and Koronal Creek, about 4,000 yards west of the Driniumor.[18]

The morning of 12 July found Martin's forces defending the new water line. 1/128 and the survivors of 2/128 held the left behind Koronal Creek. On the right, separated from the 128th by an extensive swamp, the 112th Cavalry held the Afua Trail crossing with part of 3/127 at its left.

Not convinced that a withdrawal was necessary, Krueger wanted the Japanese driven back across the Driniumor. To comply, Hall planned an immediate counterattack. The still untested 124th Regiment was called forward and ordered to clear the coast as far as Anamo, then move south on the Anamo-Afua Trail while clearing the Japanese from the west bank.

Having lost confidence in Martin, Hall sent him to the rear and placed Gill in direct charge of the battle. Gill divided the front in two sectors. The North Force, under Brigadier General Alexander N. Stark Jr., consisted of 1/128, 1/124, and 3/124. The South Force, under Cunningham, included the 112th Cavalry and 3/127. Reorganizing near the coast and acting as reserve was 2/128. Gill modified Hall's plan to include participation by his entire force. While the two 124th battalions moved according to the original plan, 1/128 would clear the coast from Anamo to the mouth of the Driniumor, then move south along the river and operate with the 124th. The South Force would join the attack by driving east along the Afua Trail, regaining the river at the right of the 124th. Meanwhile, Australian cruisers and American destroyers would shell Japanese positions up to four miles inland to disrupt enemy supply lines.[19]

The offensive began the morning of 13 July. Advancing at the coast east of Anamo, 1/128 was ambushed by Adachi's Coastal Attack Force. In the course of the fighting, which involved major support by an American artillery battalion, two tank destroyers, and LCMs, the enemy artillery was destroyed.[20] The battalion units then separated, two companies taking positions at the mouth of the Driniumor while the other two pushed south on the Anamo-Afua Trail. Meanwhile, the two 124th battalions also moved along the coast, then struck south, one battalion on the Anamo-Afua Trail and the other farther west. A brief crisis developed when South Force advanced and regained its positions in the Afua area only to discover there was no sign of the 124th battalions that were to have covered its left. The 124th commander had misidentified his position in the heavy jungle, creating a gap of at least 2,500 yards.

Well aware of this situation, the Japanese fought fiercely to keep the gap open during the next days. Inadvertently, efforts by the 124th Infantry to close it were made more difficult by Hall's decision to have 1/127 and 2/127 eliminate the Japanese who were cut off west of the river. Driven from the rear of North Force, many Japanese found their way into the gap and helped to keep it open. On 18 July, the gap was finally closed and a continuous front re-established by Gill along the river. Three days later, 2/169 arrived as vanguard of the 43rd Division and was assigned 1,000 yards of the front on the right of the 124th. Gill then discovered that the battalion had arrived unequipped for combat.

After some attempts to regain the western bank of the river in the area of his earlier breakthrough, Adachi changed direction and decided to roll up the American right at Afua. For the attack, Miyake Force was formed, composed of a variety of units led by Major General Sadahiko Miyake, the 20th Division's infantry group commander. The initial attack, which began the evening of 18 July, forced the 112th Cavalry and 3/127 from their positions, which they regained the following morning. For the next two and a half weeks, desperate hand-to-hand fighting was waged around Afua by forces groping for each other in the thick jungle. At one point, C Troop from the 112th was entirely surrounded, even its location unknown for a time. After fighting continuously for four days against much superior Japanese forces, the cavalrymen were finally extricated.

Bolstered by the rest of the 127th Regiment and other reinforcements, Cunningham succeeded in holding down the American right flank. South Force casualties up to 31 July were almost a thousand, but the enemy lost more. Recognizing their inability to break through on that front, the Japanese withdrew, covered by a last desperate charge on 4 August that was cut down by the 112th cavalrymen, who had carried much of the battle.

While the Afua battle raged, Hall planned a counterattack to clear the Japanese from the Driniumor region. Because the 43rd Division was not ready for combat, Hall turned to Starr's 124th RCT. Hall formed a column code named Ted Force, consisting of Starr's three battalions plus 2/169 from the 43rd Division. The plan called for three battalions to advance abreast at the northern end of the battle line to Niumen Creek, about three thousand yards east of the Driniumor, then move south or east as Hall would direct.

Jumping off on 31 July, Ted Force's eastward movement was slow at first partly because the terrain had been thoroughly worked over by American artillery. Because of a lack of accurate maps for directing artillery fire, the guns had saturated the entire area, expending more ammunition than in any of MacArthur's operations up to then. Even more than in earlier phases of the campaign, heavy reliance was placed on air supply, although for seven men on the ground the deliveries made without parachutes were as lethal as enemy bombs.[21] More friendly fire deaths occurred later when Ted Force was misidentified and hit by artillery fire that killed and wounded thirty-five.

While heavy fighting was still in progress in the Afua area, Hall directed Ted Force to swing to the southwest, cutting across the enemy supply lines. It was difficult for the troops to move cross-country in heavy jungle over terrain intersected by sharp ridges, deep gullies, and swamps. As they slogged forward against sporadic resistance, Adachi withdrew, having suffered heavy casualties and nearly out of food and supplies. Although its movement hastened the Japanese retreat, Ted Force did not cause it.

On 10 August, a month after the Japanese offensive began, Ted Force completed its march by linking up with the 112th Cavalry. It was a fine performance by Starr's 124th Regiment in its first combat mission, extravagantly praised by MacArthur as "a feat unparalleled in the history of jungle warfare."[22] This ignored the fact that Adachi's forces avoided encirclement and got away.

A distinctive aspect of the fighting in heavy jungle was the fragmentation of combat. Significantly, all four Medals of Honor awarded for the campaign involved platoon actions. On the first day of the Japanese offensive, Staff Sergeant Gerald L. Endl of the 128th Regiment was killed near the coast by automatic weapons fire while attempting to rescue seven wounded members of his platoon. The other three awards all involved fighting around Afua. Two 2nd lieutenants in the 112th received posthumous awards, George W. G. Boyce Jr. for smothering the blast of an enemy grenade to protect his platoon and Dale E. Christensen for leading his platoon in a series of actions to destroy enemy machine-gun positions. Also, Donald R. Lobaugh, a private in the 127th Regiment, volunteered to work his way forward and take out a Japanese machine gun blocking the withdrawal of his platoon. Persisting despite serious wounds, he rushed the enemy and was cut down after hurling a grenade.

Leaving behind 8,821 killed and 98 captured along with nearly all its heavy arms, Adachi's army lost its offensive power in the Driniumor battle.[23] American forces suffered 597 killed, 1,691 wounded, and 85 missing,[24] making it their costliest battle on New Guinea after "Bloody Buna." Worst hit proportionately were the 1,500 troopers of the 112th, who lost more than 20 percent of their strength in the intensive fighting around Afua. MacArthur had vowed "no more Bunas" but disregarded that promise to hasten an end to Adachi's threat. Disregarding the true cost, MacArthur's headquarters claimed the victory was gained at "negligible cost to our units."

The adversaries left the battlefield. Adachi and his battered forces trekked back to Wewak, weak with hunger but no longer burdened by the heavy equipment laboriously hauled to the Driniumor. Krueger declared the campaign over on 25 August, leaving it up to the 43rd Division to deal with any Japanese remaining while his other forces prepared for the Philippines.

The situation that had meanwhile developed in the South Pacific was described by Bergerud: "Once the area of operations for the finest troops the warring nations could muster, the South Pacific became a dumping ground for men suffering from battle fatigue and those earning well-deserved leaves. . . . The South Pacific, which for nearly two years was the nexus of a harsh war, had become the rear."[25] Still, the suffering and death went on for another year.

CHAPTER 26

# "Doubtful That He Checked with the Ordinary Foot Soldier"

The American-Australian relationship, as it stood in mid-1944, was described in the official Australian history: "The cooperation of allies produces many difficulties and irritations, particularly when the larger one is established in the territory of the smaller. . . . It would be satisfactory to MacArthur's headquarters if a separate sphere of action could be found for the Australians."[1] That opportunity presented itself when MacArthur needed American manpower for the Philippines campaign. Freeing up American troops that were containing bypassed Japanese forces in the South Pacific and substituting Australians for them was a welcome solution.[2]

While the Australians would enjoy greater freedom of action than Halsey had been given, they were still part of MacArthur's command and subject to his orders, including the size of the replacement forces. Altogether, three Australian divisions plus three separate brigades would be employed, specifically, five brigades on Bougainville and nearby islands, three brigades on New Britain, and four brigades on New Guinea. When MacArthur ordered this deployment, Blamey argued for smaller forces, suggesting that he was then not yet thinking about assuming the offensive in these areas.[3]

The turnover on Bougainville began during October and proceeded rapidly, with most of the American units relieved of front-line duty by Thanksgiving Day. Relinquishing command of Bougainville on 22 November, Griswold took his XIV Corps to the Philippines as part of Krueger's Sixth Army. It would be a contentious situation for Griswold, who thoroughly disliked Krueger and was not inclined to suffer Krueger's callous treatment of his officers in silence. Griswold's able performance on Luzon would earn him MacArthur's nomination to command the Tenth Army after its commander was killed on Okinawa. Although Griswold was disappointed in losing out to General Joseph Stillwell, he at least gained relief with the transfer of his corps to Eichelberger's Eighth Army.[4] Capping his fine career, Griswold commanded in succession the Seventh and Third armies after the war.

Beightler's 37th Division departed Bougainville in mid-December for the landings in Lingayen Gulf. Like Griswold and many others, Beightler hated serving under Krueger, whose negative attitudes included disdain for the National Guard.[5] And he had another axe to grind. Beightler resented the Army's caste system that effectively disqualified him as a National Guard officer from gaining another star and advancing like Hodge to corps command.[6]

The Americal Division left Bougainville on 8 January to join the battle on Leyte as part of the X Corps in Eichelberger's Eighth Army. Before then, the division acquired a new commander as McClure departed to a post in China, replaced by the XIV Corps' chief of staff, Major General William H. Arnold. After Leyte, the division participated in the liberation of the southern Philippines and was preparing for the invasion of Japan at war's end.

On New Guinea, XI Corps turned over the Aitape area to the Australians and left for the Philippines. Hall continued to head the corps, impressing MacArthur, who considered him a possible replacement for Krueger when MacArthur became unhappy with his Army commander's slow progress on Luzon.[7] Of the others who led the Driniumor battle, Gill continued to command the 32nd Division on Leyte and Luzon, bitter about being denied corps command and freely expressing his hatred of Krueger.[8] Martin fared better. Despite being relieved of the Covering Force by Hall, Martin gained command of the 31st Division and disengaged from Krueger to fight under Eichelberger on Mindanao.[9] Cunningham brought the 112th to Leyte and Luzon with many new cavalrymen replacing the regiment's heavy losses. The newcomers included aspiring novelist Norman Mailer, whose Philippine experiences would find their way into his war novel *The Naked and the Dead*.

The American 40th Division, which months earlier had relieved the 1st Marine Division and the 112th Cavalry, handed New Britain over to the Australians on 27 November. The 40th Division would fight with both the Sixth and Eighth armies on Luzon and elsewhere in the Philippines.

The Australians who took over the American positions on Bougainville, New Guinea, and New Britain inherited an unspoken truce that every rule of reason said should be maintained. Although there was no compelling reason why the Japanese should not be left alone, Blamey decided that the war had to go on.[10]

A staff officer during and following World War I, Blamey rose rapidly and made many enemies. He then left the military to become police commissioner of the state of Victoria. Aligned with conservative factions during a period of labor unrest, he was described in the official police force history as "confrontational, readily violent, and generally ruthless,"[11] a not surprising judgment since he broke the police union. Forced to resign after lying about a police incident, Blamey, who had remained a territorial officer, rejoined the regular army.

With the outbreak of war in Europe, he was appointed commander of Australian forces in the Middle East and deputy commander-in-chief of the theater. Although he earned praise from General Wavell, who called Blamey "Probably the best soldier we had in the Middle East," for General Auchinleck "he wasn't a general I should have chosen to command an operation." At that time, according to his biographical entry, "he provoked antipathy towards himself [without] try[ing] to dissipate it."[12]

When the Pacific war began, Blamey returned home to serve as Commander, Allied Land Forces. Blamey's authority, however, was later severely limited when MacArthur organized the American troops in Alamo Force. He suffered another blow when MacArthur denied the Australians a role in liberating the Philippines, leaving them behind to handle the bypassed Japanese forces. Blamey with other senior officers followed MacArthur to the Philippines but was denied a role in strategy decisions. It was a frustrating situation for someone intensely invested in personal prestige, and it explains Blamey's thinking and policies.[13]

As heavy-handed as when with the police, Blamey accused a brigade that had fought hard of running like rabbits from an inferior foe. Adding to the anger and resentment he readily provoked, Blamey had a reputation for heavy drinking and womanizing. The decorous chief of the Imperial general staff, General Sir Alan Brooke, acidly described short and rotund Blamey in his diary as "not an impressive specimen . . . entirely drink sodden and somewhat repulsive . . . as if he had had the most frightful 'hangover' from a debauched night!"[14] MacArthur shared Brooke's sentiments, considering Blamey a "sensual, slothful and doubtful character," but nevertheless "a tough commander likely to shine like a power-light in an emergency."[15]

Abandoning the American policy of containing bypassed Japanese forces, Blamey set out to pursue and destroy the enemy where possible. An aggressive policy could not be pursued on New Britain because of the strength of the numerous, well-supplied, and battle-ready garrison at Rabaul. But there were no such constraints on New Guinea and Bougainville. Although he disagreed with Blamey's aggressive policy, MacArthur, fully absorbed in the Philippines and with little interest in areas no longer of military importance, declined to intervene.

From February 1945, dissatisfaction about the relegation of the Australian army to "mop-up" duties and many other issues resulted in demands from the press and Australian Parliament that Blamey be removed. Lashing back, Blamey shocked even his own supporters by remarks made during a war loan radio broadcast. He railed, "They suggest that we should leave this enemy fruit to wither on the vine. . . . It is no mopping-up to those Australians who have to fight it."[16] This was indeed true, but it was Blamey who chose to fight that battle, and he was more than indelicate to use that occasion to answer his foes.

Blamey survived the onslaught thanks to the support of the Conservative members of Parliament and the Advisory War Council. But by May even his supporters seriously questioned whether Blamey's offensive operations were necessary. The situation was clarified by a letter obtained from MacArthur, who wrote, "These [bypassed] hostile forces are strategically impotent and are suffering a high rate of natural attrition. . . . A local Commander in such situations has considerable freedom of action as to methods to be employed. The Australian Commanders have elected to carry out active operations in effecting neutralisation where other Commanders might decide on more passive measures."[17] No such choice had, in fact, been left to the local commanders, who could only follow the policy laid down by Blamey.

During May, after the aggressive pursuit of the Japanese had continued for five months and with little more than two months of war remaining, Blamey was called upon by the Advisory War Council to fully explain his policy. He maintained that he had been forced to choose between three courses of action: (1) continue a policy of defense, (2) conduct an all-out offensive to destroy the enemy, or (3) force the Japanese from garden areas and bases to starve or otherwise destroy them. For all practical purposes, there was little to distinguish between 2 and 3 since Blamey set out to destroy the Japanese with whatever resources were available.

The rationale given by Blamey was hardly compelling. He claimed that by destroying or tightly confining the Japanese, smaller forces would be required to keep them subdued. But such economy of force was hardly important since MacArthur had no plans to use those Australian troops elsewhere. Blamey also claimed that the bypassed Japanese were not "withering on the vine," but remained strong and well-organized, fed by gardens and drawing supplies through submarine and air deliveries. In fact, the Japanese were appreciably "withering" in their isolated situation and insalubrious environments. Also, having sufficient resources to remain alive didn't mean that the enemy remained capable of mounting serious attacks.

Blamey also expressed fear that if the Australians did not liberate the natives formerly under their administration, it "would lower the prestige of the Australian nation" and "in the native mind . . . lower the prestige of the Government to such an extent that it might be difficult to recover on the termination of hostilities." But the small nation that had given so much of itself since 1939 and earned laurels aplenty from Tobruk to New Guinea need hardly have worried about garnering further prestige. As for the sparse, primitive, and nonpolitical native populations of the South Pacific, there were no significant liberation movements such as faced by other colonial powers in the region to arouse such concerns. The South Pacific was not India. And, whether or not pertinent, these were political matters for others to decide. It was helpful to Blamey that for much the same reasons of personal and purported national prestige and with as little bearing on the outcome of the war, MacArthur was then in process of liberating the southern Philippines.

Most dubious, Blamey insisted that an aggressive campaign was neces- sary to maintain the morale and fighting edge of the troops. But the reaction of the Australian militiamen that would do the fighting must have been quite the opposite. The effective performance of the 37th and Americal Divisions in the Philippines after months of limited action on Bougainville points up the frailty of Blamey's explanations.

Blamey's arguments met with considerable dissent when received by the Advisory War Council. The nongovernment members had been under the impression until then that MacArthur and not Blamey had laid down the strat- egy that was being followed. One member, who refused to take responsibility for the operations as they were being conducted, complained that "insofar as there were political reasons for the change of policy General Blamey had instituted, that was a matter for decision by the Government not General Blamey." Another council member, not believing that the rationale furnished by Blamey justified his course, could not reconcile the necessity of destroying the enemy on New Guinea and Bougainville while it was considered sufficient to merely contain their forces on New Britain.

Blamey's supporters took a very different view, believing their commander had been fully vindicated by operations that were proceeding successfully and with what were considered small losses. Ultimately, the council endorsed Blamey's policy of destroying the Japanese where that might be done with "light casualties." Inflicting suffering and death without any bearing on the outcome of the war seems not to have mattered. In any event, the council's opinion made no difference, as it was not written until 31 July and was not received by Blamey until the day Japan surrendered.

Implementation of Blamey's aggressive policy was the responsibility of the First Australian Army, led by Lieutenant General Vernon A. H. Sturdee, based at Lae, New Guinea. A veteran of Gallipoli and former chief of the general staff, Sturdee commanded Australian forces on New Guinea, New Britain, and Bougainville, and garrisons on certain islands, an area about a thousand miles in length. Included were Savige's II Corps on Bougainville, Major General Alan H. Ramsay's 5th Division on New Britain, and Major General Jack E. S. Stevens' 6th Division at Aitape, with the 8th Brigade west of Madang.

During October 1944, Blamey informed Sturdee that he wanted him "by offensive action to destroy enemy resistance as opportunity offers without com- mitting major forces."[18] Understandably, Sturdee was entirely confused by such a seemingly inconsistent instruction. Seeking clarification, Sturdee noted that "the Jap Garrisons are at present virtually in POW Camps but feed themselves, so why incur a large number of Australian casualties in the process of eliminating them. . . . I should like some guidance as to the extent of the casualties that would be justified in destroying these Jap Garrisons."

Musing about the possible reasons why lives needed to be risked for little obvious purpose, Sturdee continued, "I realize that there may be some question of prestige that makes the clearing up of Bougainville an urgent necessity, or alternatively of the elimination of the Japs in that area to reduce inter-breeding . . . [to] . . . avoid the potential trouble of having a half-Jap population to deal with in the future."[19] It is hard to know if Sturdee was entirely serious about the last possibility as it related to Bougainville, but it is to his considerable credit that he probed for a reason.

In response, Blamey noted that information about the size of Japanese forces and their dispositions was still imperfect. Once clarified, he would "push forward light forces to localities which can be dealt with piecemeal. These light forces would form the nuclei from which patrols would contact and destroy the enemy by normal methods of bush warfare." Blamey allowed that information on Japanese troop strength was "far from exact." He went on to advocate "a complete probe and . . . better knowledge . . . before any large commitment is undertaken," as if sufficient clarity might be obtained by nibbling at the edges of the enemy. Not until the surrender was it realized just how numerous the enemy was. Rather than about 75,000 as had been believed, the actual count in the region turned out to be about 170,000 including civilian workers.[20]

After dwelling at length on how operations might be conducted, Blamey finally addressed Sturdee's question as to the purpose and adduced just one reason, "the undesirability of retaining troops in a perimeter . . . [which is] certain to destroy the aggressive spirit." Historian Harry Gailey commented wryly about Blamey's decision to end the unofficial truce in the South Pacific: "It is doubtful that he checked with the ordinary foot soldier. . . . If given the choice between a relatively comfortable sedentary life in the rear areas or aggressive patrolling in a hot, humid jungle with the very definite risk of being killed, it is likely that most would choose the former, even if it took the edge off combat efficiency."[21]

Acting on Blamey's instruction, Sturdee ordered his commanders during November to conduct patrols and raids to obtain information from which plans "designed to destroy the enemy" would be developed and implemented. The least necessary fighting of the Pacific war would then begin.

CHAPTER 27

———— ⚬⚭⚬ ————

# "No Enemy Can Withstand You"

Lieutenant General Stanley Savige led the Australian forces on Bougainville as commander of II Corps. A soldier with long war experience, Savige had worked for Blamey for several years during the 1930s and was fiercely loyal to him. Popular with his troops, Savige was known to lead from the front.

Savige's principal fighting force was the 3rd Division, under Major General William Bridgeford, composed of the 7th, 15th, and 29th Brigades. He also had two independent brigades, the 11th and 23rd, the latter performing garrison duty elsewhere until April 1945, when it joined the others. All were militia units made up principally of Queenslanders. Attached to Savige's command were artillery and tank units, New Guinea native troops, the Fiji Infantry Regiment, and 2/8 Commando Squadron trained for reconnaissance and long-range patrols.

Just as Hyakutake had grossly underestimated the size of the American forces in March, the actual numbers of Japanese on Bougainville differed substantially from Allied estimates. While Griswold's staff believed there were about 12,000 Japanese in October 1944, and Australian intelligence estimated it was twice that, postwar analysis concluded there were actually between 37,000 and 40,000. A principal cause of the underestimate was failure to appreciate that there were as many as 11,000 naval personnel. For the little more than 30,000 Australians who would campaign there, Bougainville would prove a far more difficult and unpleasant operation than touted by Blamey.

The Japanese were alerted to the arrival of the Australians and rightly assumed this change of opponent might portend a more aggressive policy. They did not expect any change to occur soon, but just one week after the transfer of command, the informal truce was shattered in the Numa Numa sector. On 29 November, Japanese occupying Little George Hill were surprised by a platoon from the 3rd Division's 9th Battalion operating from nearby George Hill, which

**Map 15. Bougainville: The Australian Campaign** (Long, *Australia in the War of 1939–1945—The Final Campaigns*, 91 [under authorization of the Australian War Memorial])

took the height, killing twenty at a cost of two killed and six wounded. During the next week, the battalion captured Arty Hill, named for the intense shelling it had received. These initial operations placed Savige's forces in position to move against the dominating height in the area, Pearl Ridge.

To the south, the Australians pushed across the Jaba River and cleared the south bank by late December in preparation for further advances. Some clashes occurred, but Kanda held back his 6th Division forces, believing that the main attack would come from the sea.[1] Casualties were small on both sides in that first month of renewed activity, but the count would soon climb.

Once reconnaissance yielded enough information about Japanese dispositions, Savige developed his plans. The principal thrust by the 3rd Division would be southeast toward the enemy base at Buin. Initially, Bridgeford's troops would obtain control of the territory between the Jaba and Puriata rivers and of the inland tracks and paths paralleling the coast. In the central sector, where the island is only thirty miles wide, Pearl Ridge would be seized. Affording views to both coastlines, the ridge would provide a lookout point and patrol base to control Numa Numa's hinterland. To the north, the Japanese were to be driven toward and destroyed in the Bonis Peninsula.

The Australian offensive began on 30 December. On the Numa Numa front, the 3rd Division's 25th Battalion attacked Pearl Ridge. Believing the position was occupied by fewer than a hundred Japanese, a single battalion was considered more than sufficient. The Japanese, however, had been strongly reinforced, bringing their numbers to more than six hundred. Employing all four companies of the 25th Battalion on a one-thousand-yard front, the advance began at 0800 after an air strike. Although the attack went well elsewhere, the company on the right, forced to advance along a narrow razorback, was stopped by concentrated fire. After digging in and repelling a Japanese counterattack during the night, the attack shifted to the center companies the next day, and the key height was won by midafternoon.

The inaccessibility of Pearl Ridge posed a special supply challenge, which was met by construction of jeep tracks, the work expedited by a bulldozer that was hoisted by ingenious methods up a precipitous height. Thereafter, the Australians exercised control of the territory beyond Pearl Ridge through patrols, never occupying the ridge with more than a single battalion. Expecting a major advance from that direction or a seaborne attack near Numa Numa that might sever their lines of communication on the eastern coast, the Japanese tied up about 1,600 men in defense of the area. After the battle, Savige's forces were reorganized, with the 25th Battalion joining the rest of the 3rd Division for the march on Buin. The 11th Brigade then assumed responsibility for both the central Numa Numa and northern fronts.

Meanwhile, the 31st/51st Battalion of the 11th Brigade advanced north from Kuraio Mission. While the main force moved along the coast road without meeting resistance, patrols operated inland to force the Japanese into the coastal belt and away from the hills, where they might hold out. Native scouts reported that the main Japanese defenses lay south of the Genga River. This was confirmed when the leading Australian company on the coast road clashed with Japanese forces whose main body rested on curved and wooded Tsimba Ridge, eight hundred yards from the Genga. After frontal and flank attacks failed in the next days, an attempt was made to take the ridge from behind by gaining the north bank of the river. On 25–26 January, a company made it across the Genga, but could only hold out against counterattacks in the next days.

To break the deadlock, the 11th Brigade commander, Brigadier John Stevenson, planned a set-piece battle beginning with intense artillery and mortar shelling. Three platoons attacked the ridge from different directions, gaining the height except for a pocket at the western tip. A Japanese counterattack was defeated, but their force in the pocket remained. Finally, on 9 February, after a mortar bombardment, the Australians took the position without opposition. The 31st/51st spent two further weeks clearing the banks of the river and pressing forward along the coast, encircling and forcing the remaining Japanese to withdraw from a defensive line at the Gillman River. During the Battle of Tsimba Ridge and related operations near the Genga, about 750 Australians were engaged, with 34 killed and 91 wounded; the Japanese lost 148 killed from about 900 engaged.[2]

After taking over from the 31st/51st Battalion on 22 February, the 26th Battalion advanced upon the Soraken Peninsula, which was reached after continuous small actions during the next month. Facilitated by an amphibious landing on the western coast, Australian forces entered the peninsula from the south and moved along both shores. By 26 March, all organized resistance ended on Soraken, the offshore islands were taken, and substantial stores of equipment were captured.

It now became the turn of the 55th/53rd Battalion, taking over from the 26th, to continue the advance toward the Bonis Peninsula and deal with Japanese remaining in foothills to the south. Good progress against limited opposition was made through April and the first days of May, during which Pora Pora was captured and the neck of the Bonis Peninsula was reached without difficulty. At first it seemed possible that the enemy had abandoned the peninsula, but with stiffening Japanese resistance it became apparent that many were there, ready to fight.

Japanese soldiers on this front had in fact withdrawn to Numa Numa, turning over defense of the Bonis Peninsula and Buka to the 87th Naval Garrison Force. At the core were 1,400 highly trained sailors, supplemented by partially armed civilian workers, about 1,800 combatants in all. Their mission was to delay the Australians as long as possible to enable the transfer of valuable equipment to Numa Numa. To accomplish this, the Japanese attacked the Australian supply lines and conducted ambushes along the area tracks, while maintaining a solid defense across the neck of the peninsula.

The Australian line lay immediately to the south in thick jungle on a five-mile front. Serious clashes occurred regularly between patrols; isolated Australian companies were attacked and their supply lines were continuously disrupted. Recognizing the poor condition of the 55th/53rd, the battalion was relieved by the 26th Battalion in late May. The drive on Bonis was then suspended until June, when a fresh attempt was made to break into the peninsula.

In the Kieta region, natives loyal to Australia were waging a war of their own. Using captured weapons and supplies obtained by air drop and led by C. W. Seton, who had played a key part in the Choiseul raid, they controlled much of the countryside. Killing about two thousand Japanese, the natives were poised to attack Kieta itself by war's end.

During December, Hyakutake had moved forces from the Shortlands to reinforce his base at Buin. Recognizing that the Australians were intent on conquering all of Bougainville, Hyakutake adopted delaying tactics. Mystified about the Australian policy, a Japanese officer wrote, "Army staff officers . . . were at a loss to account for the Allied policy and felt that the actions would make no impression on the course of the war and were absolutely pointless."[3] Many Australians felt that way too.

In describing operations toward the south, the official Australian history compared the 3rd Division's movements to a crab moving simultaneously forward and sideways. This was necessary to secure the flanks of forces moving generally southeast in country where the enemy defenses extended well inland and could not be left behind to threaten lines of communication.

Having attained the Jaba River by late December, Brigadier R. F. Monaghan's 29th Brigade proceeded along the coast toward the head of Gazelle Harbour. The offensive began well, as Kanda did not intend to make a serious stand north of the Puriata River. In quick succession during mid-January, the brigade took the key villages of Mawaraka on the coast and Makotowa immediately inland. Also, a landing was made near Motupena Point while other Australian forces covered the eastern flank about six miles inland. By the third week of January, after advancing thirteen miles, the 29th Brigade was relieved by Brigadier John Field's 7th Brigade.

Believing the enemy was "weak and off balance," Savige urged Bridgeford to advance to the Puriata in a "swift and vigorous action." But movement soon became difficult as the troops encountered extensive swamps and heavy undergrowth. Taking full advantage of the terrain, the Japanese conducted ambushes, mined the track, and severed communications. Australian morale sagged, but spirits revived in early February when they left the swamps behind and entered a country of tall trees with light undergrowth. Mosigetta, a key crossroads to the south of the Hupai River, was taken by convergence of the 9th Battalion advancing east from Mawaraka and the 61st Battalion moving south. Kanda had already initiated a withdrawal to the Puriata, which accelerated after the 25th Battalion made a surprise landing at Toko and proceeded inland to take

Barara on 20 February. Toko then became a principal Australian supply base for the 3rd Division.

Meanwhile, the Japanese command was in disarray. Younger reserve officers, unhappy about the tactics of the older professional soldiers, became so vocal in their opposition that many were removed from command. Perhaps as an upshot of both the battlefield situation and the turmoil within his ranks, Hyakutake suffered a stroke during February that left his side paralyzed. Kanda took command of the 17th Army and was succeeded as head of the 6th Division by Lieutenant General Tsutomu Akinage, until then the army's chief of staff. Without means of evacuation, Hyakutake remained on Bougainville as an invalid.

On 4 March, one company from the Australian 25th Battalion crossed the Puriata River and established a perimeter defense at the Buin Road. Two days later the Japanese heavily shelled a knoll near the river, wounding Private Carl R. Slater, who remained at his post until relieved. Thereafter known as Slater's Knoll, the height would later come to symbolize Australian tenacity much as Cibik's Ridge and Hill 700 had taken on special meaning for American forces. Advancing down the Buin Road toward the next principal objective, the Hongorai River, the battalion encountered a well-developed Japanese pillbox and trench system. On 22 March, Sergeant Reginald Rattey, using a Bren gun and grenades, single-handedly eliminated three bunkers and a machine-gun position, earning the Victoria Cross. With growing indications that the Japanese were preparing a major attack, the 25th Battalion halted its advance and dug in on a line anchored by Slater's Knoll, where Lieutenant Colonel John McKinna established his battalion headquarters.

Kanda assembled about 2,400 mostly fresh troops from the 6th Division's 13th and 23rd regiments for a major counterattack. Beginning the night of 27–28 March, the Japanese conducted several attacks on the Australian rear, all of which were repulsed. Then, from information obtained from a captured sergeant and the Japanese habit of cutting their opponent's communications wire before a major operation, it became known that a full-scale attack impended. The attack, beginning at 0700 on 30 March, focused on a single company in an advanced position to the south of Slater's Knoll. After repelling four assaults by screaming Japanese who charged with fixed bayonets and hurled grenades, the company, reduced to only sixteen unwounded men, retreated to link with a company immediately to its rear. The two companies were assailed that evening by heavy fire from three mortars that had been abandoned with considerable ammunition during the withdrawal and turned against the Australians.

Recognizing the seriousness of the situation, Bridgeford released his tanks that had so far been withheld. Through great effort by the engineers to bridge the intervening creeks and streams, three Matilda tanks made it from Toko to the 25th Battalion lines on 30 March. A composite infantry force was assembled the next day to accompany the tanks and relieve the two besieged companies.

Moving forward to the attack at 1600, the relief force went into action just minutes after the most determined Japanese attack of the day. With this first appearance of Australian tanks in the campaign, the Japanese fled and the weary defenders withdrew to the main defense line.

The next day, 1 April, two companies established a strong defensive line one thousand yards south of Slater's Knoll. A lull in the fighting ensued as Kanda and the new 6th Division commander, Akinage, planned a supreme effort. It began the night of 4–5 April with a heavy shelling of the Australian artillery battery and the usual cutting of communications wire. At 0500, about 1,000 Japanese from the 13th and 23rd regiments charged the knoll in waves from the north and southwest, and they paid dearly. For more than an hour, Bren and Vickers guns on Slater's Knoll and preregistered supporting artillery slaughtered the oncoming enemy. Separately, about 100 Japanese attacked the two companies entrenched to the south of Slater's Knoll and were driven away after a two-hour fight. At 1250 two Australian tanks advanced to the knoll and, together with infantry, flushed out and killed the survivors of the reckless attack. The nine-day battle cost the Japanese 620 killed and about 1,000 wounded out of approximately 2,400 engaged, while Australian killed and wounded amounted to 189.

The Japanese made the same mistakes as during the March attack against the American perimeter. Their practice of cutting communication lines before the attack clearly told that an attack was imminent. Also, their artillery fire was seriously inaccurate and repeated charges against well-fortified positions led to devastating losses without gain.

Kanda was highly critical of how Akinage fought the action. Instead of a frontal assault, Kanda later claimed he would have taken advantage of the Australian open right flank, severing their supply line to Toko and delaying their advance for months. Still, Kanda obtained a two-week respite while the Australians felled trees for corduroy trails and bridged streams to bring up supplies for the next forward movement. The Australians hoped the Japanese would meanwhile wear themselves down by further costly attacks, but Kanda did not oblige. He now carried out only small harassment actions to buy time while the final defense line was prepared in the Buin area.

For the renewed attack, Bridgeford brought in the highly experienced 15th Brigade to relieve the 7th Brigade. The 15th was led by colorful, aggressive, and aptly named Brigadier Heathcote "Tack" Hammer, a believer in using artillery and mortars to the fullest extent possible. He would have available four newly arrived 155-mm guns and increased support from the RNZAF on Bougainville, which had grown from two to four squadrons. The 29th Brigade would cover the 15th Brigade's line of communications.

The advance toward the Hongorai River resumed on 17 April with the 24th Battalion in the lead. Movement was soon interrupted by a series of Japanese counterattacks that were all defeated, after which the advance continued on 26

April. Preceded by intensive bombing and strafing by thirty-six RNZAF Corsairs and creeping artillery and mortar barrages, the 24th advanced almost three miles during the first two days against little opposition. As the Australians neared the river, the Japanese became more aggressive and more adept at targeting the tanks using concealed guns and mines. Also, their artillery was at last effectively employed using close-in observers, inflicting heavy casualties from shell bursts in the trees that showered fragments over a wide area. The Japanese will to resist was further demonstrated when an Australian broadcasting unit found no takers from its appeals to surrender.

In early May, a fresh Matilda tank squadron arrived to relieve the badly worn-down squadron that had been on Bougainville since December. On their part, to lessen vulnerability to tank attack, the Japanese no longer prepared defenses immediately across the track, but in positions inaccessible by tanks about a hundred yards away.

The most determined Japanese attempt to stop the advance occurred on 5–6 May. At the Buin Road, the action began when a concealed field gun fired on a disabled tank and was itself knocked out by a second tank. This was followed by a nighttime bombardment when about 160 shells fell on the 24th Battalion. The next morning, a fierce firefight was waged against about 100 Japanese who furiously attacked through the dense undergrowth and then withdrew, leaving 58 dead, their heaviest loss since Slater's Knoll.[4] That day, 6 May, the 57th/60th on the Commando Road crossed the Hongorai, followed across the next day by the 24th on the Buin Road. The three-week advance cost the 24th Battalion 25 killed and 95 wounded, against 169 Japanese dead.

For two weeks the Australians paused while supplies were drawn for the next leap forward, to the Hari River. Strong resistance was anticipated, as beyond the river lay an important garden area the loss of which would require drawing food from distant areas of the island. When Hammer was prepared to launch the offensive on 20 May, with much theatricality he proclaimed that the next weeks might see a major defeat of the Japanese in south Bougainville, adding, "Go to battle as you have done in the last month and no enemy can withstand you."[5] It sounded much like Hyakutake's exhortation in March 1944, but in this case Hammer's confidence was justified.

For eight days before the ground attack, RNZAF aircraft blasted the Buin and Commando roads. The main attack was then delivered on the Buin Road by the 24th Battalion, which advanced behind a creeping artillery and mortar barrage with tank support. The principal height in the area, dubbed Egan's Ridge, was heavily pummeled and abandoned by the Japanese.

Japanese defense west of the Hari had been broken. The brigade moved ahead rapidly against little opposition, slowed mostly by densely laid mines and booby traps. But as they neared the Hari River, it was evident the Japanese were prepared to put up strong resistance.

Australian major general Brigadier Heathcote H. Hammer, commanding 15th Infantry Brigade, explains his plan of attack to Lieutenant General Vernon A. H. Sturdee, Australian First Army commander. Behind is Major General William Bridgeford, commander of the Australian 3rd Division, with Lieutenant General Stanley G. Savige, commander of Australian II Corps at right, Bougainville, 12 May 1945. (By authorization of the Australian War Memorial: 091857)

On 9 June, Blamey visited the 15th Brigade. Under fire for his policies and rising casualties, he counseled his aggressive commander, "Take your time Hammer. There's no hurry."[6] But Hammer had a plan and was not to be restrained. To unseat the Japanese strongly entrenched on the high ground across the Hari, two companies from the 58th/59th Battalion with tanks crossed the Hari well upstream, then moved south to cut the Buin Road east of the river. While one company stayed in position at the Hari ford, another accompanying the flanking force attacked the enemy at the river from the rear. In addition, the 57th/60th Battalion executed an even larger flanking maneuver. Leaving the Commando Trail, the battalion advanced through trackless jungle accompanied by tanks, along with a bulldozer to clear a path, then swung south to meet the 58th/59th Battalion at the Buin Road on 16 June. With this highly successful operation the Australians were in position to advance to the next barrier, the Mivo River.

On the northern front, a lull in operations after late May provided little relief for the 26th Battalion, as their opponent, the 87th Naval Garrison Force, conducted an active defense. The Japanese commander ordered his men to harass the Australian supply lines and maintain ambushes on all main tracks while holding the line at the neck of the Bonis Peninsula from the Porton Plantation to

Tarbut. The fresh and eager sailors responded, striking far to the rear to disrupt the 11th Brigade's lengthy lines of communication.

The obvious solution was to break into the peninsula as was done at Soraken. The Australians planned to land a reinforced company at night on the western coast at Porton Plantation, well within range of their artillery. After establishing a perimeter that would be held by part of the attack force, the rest would drive east and meet troops advancing from the neck of the peninsula. While it was thought at first there were only about one hundred Japanese in the area, an aircraft observed pillboxes and much activity at Porton. The brigade commander, Stevenson, requested an air attack on the pillboxes but was refused by Savige's headquarters, which considered pillboxes unsuitable targets! As it unfolded, the operation would not resemble Soraken but rather the abortive Marine raid at Koiari, the attack force being deposited once again into a veritable hornet's nest.

On 8 June, at 0357, the first wave of the 190-man force debarked from three landing craft that grounded 50 yards offshore. The Australians waded ashore without opposition and, by 0430, formed a 100-yard wide perimeter extending 150 yards inland. The landing craft withdrew, after which the rest of the force arrived and debarked from three landing craft that grounded 75 yards offshore at 0435, their men then wading to the beach. Suddenly, the operation changed from an offensive movement to a struggle for survival.

Ten minutes after the second landing, the Japanese opened up with heavy machine-gun fire. One landing craft got away, but the other two remained stuck, the Japanese fire making it impossible to unload the heavy equipment, ammunition, and supplies. Artillery fire was called down on the enemy, silencing some of the machine guns and removing foliage that had concealed enemy pillboxes. With the coming of dawn, the Australians found themselves enclosed within a 400-yard arc of enemy trenches and pillboxes. During that day, the Japanese reinforced and pressed forward, later employing mortars that could not be answered by the Australians, who were still unable to retrieve their own mortars and ammunition. Toward evening, truck engines were heard and barges were observed crossing from Buka, ominously signaling the arrival of yet more Japanese.

That night, a supply and reinforcement convoy dispatched to the perimeter was unable to land and was forced to withdraw because of heavy enemy fire. Meanwhile, the Japanese attacked the perimeter through the night and were held at bay. In the morning they charged the Australian lines in waves, yelling phrases in English to confuse the defense, and were mowed down. But the Australians were forced back by the weight of the attack and dispatched a distress message at 1440 saying, "We are now near the beach and getting hell." Earlier in the day it was decided to withdraw the force at 2200 hours. Because of uncertainty that the perimeter could be held after dark, swifter evacuation became essential.

Three landing craft came in close off shore at 1630. Under intense fire, the wounded were loaded first and then everyone else. While one of the three craft carrying about fifty men managed to get away, the other two were weighed down too heavily and remained stranded. At 2240, one craft with twenty-four on board was lifted by the tide and made it away. There would be no immediate relief for company commander Captain Downs and sixty of his men who remained on board the other landing craft. The boat's means of defense, a twin Vickers gun, was lost when the gun was disabled and the gunner killed. A Japanese phosphorous grenade caused a wild scramble to avoid the flames, with many falling overboard including Downs, who disappeared, probably swept out to sea. Japanese swimmers who approached with grenades were fought off by small arms fire, and one was eliminated by a cooperative shark.

Reduced by dawn of the third day to thirty-eight living men, nearly out of food and with no drinking water, the besieged craft endured another day while successive attempts to relieve it failed. Another terror-filled night followed. At 0100 on the fourth day, a Japanese swimmer climbed to the stern and killed two and wounded others by machine-gun fire before he was shot. Soon after, fire from a Japanese antitank gun tore the stern off the craft. Rescue was finally effected that morning when, under cover of an intense barrage laid down by two Australian batteries at the neck of the peninsula, five boats dashed in to remove the survivors.

Porton cost the Australians 23 killed and 106 wounded, while Japanese casualties, as claimed by each side, differed too much to be even roughly estimated. What is certain is that Porton provided the Japanese an enormous morale boost and severe chastisement of the Australian command that had thrust troops into a death trap, Gallipoli in miniature. In the wake of this fiasco, the 23rd Brigade replaced the 11th Brigade, which departed to join the drive south.

The 23rd Brigade, since April responsible for the central front, now took on the added responsibility of covering the northern front. Spread thin to cover both areas, its forces on the Bonis Peninsula were insufficient to prevent infiltration, making them highly vulnerable to the same Japanese tactics that worked so well against the 11th Brigade. After a month in the line without any forward movement, the brigade's 27th Battalion lost ten killed and thirty-six wounded through patrol actions and ambushes, friendly mortar fire, and its own booby traps.

To Brigadier Potts, commander of the 23rd Brigade, a fresh attack was needed to break into the peninsula and destroy the Japanese. A naturally aggressive soldier with a deep-seated hatred of the Japanese, Potts had been relieved of command during the Kokoda Trail campaign on New Guinea, many claimed as a scapegoat for Blamey, and was eager to redeem his reputation. Knowing Potts' motivation full well and under pressure to minimize casualties, Savige denied permission for a renewed attack.

Unable to effectively contain the Japanese with the forces available, Potts was allowed on 22 July to withdraw his right flank and concentrate along a three-thousand-yard front. Thereafter, fighting was limited to patrols and other small actions that left the northern front essentially unchanged. The most notable of these final actions occurred on 24 July during an attack by two platoons from the 8th Battalion against a ridge position. Although wounded, Private Frank J. Partridge took over a Bren gun from a dead gunner. Maintaining fire against the enemy bunker, Partridge charged and destroyed it using a grenade, then leapt inside and killed the surviving occupant. Partridge was awarded the Victoria Cross, the second and last one awarded during the campaign, along with the honor of having the position cleverly renamed "Part Ridge."[7]

At mid-June, Australian forces on the southern front were only twenty-eight miles from Buin, but they were entering densely wooded and wet country where movement would be difficult. While the Japanese left flank along the sea lay open, Savige lacked the ships for a large-scale operation. Even a smaller amphibious operation was impractical. Formidable Japanese coast defense and anti-aircraft guns would have pounded landings near Buin, and suitable beaches could not be found between that zone and the Australian lines. Now led by the 29th Brigade, the advance toward the next target, the Mivo River, continued overland.

Fortuitously, torrential rains began, shutting down operations. Trails turned into seas of mud, and air supply became necessary to sustain the forward units. Raging watercourses washed out bridges and converted the terrain into scattered islands.[8] While conditions deteriorated, the advance was delayed repeatedly and finally deferred to late August. Patrolling went on, however, with the Japanese infiltrating and disrupting the Australian lines of communication as they had done so effectively on the northern front.

Meanwhile, Kanda took command of the 4th South Seas Garrison Unit and other naval units in southern Bougainville and prepared for the final battle. He planned to wait until the Australians reached the Silibai River, the last major water barrier before Buin, then launch his counterattack. Employing nine thousand fighters, some attacking from the river line while others attacked the Australian rear, Kanda hoped to force the Australians back to the Mivo. Aware that he lacked resources to push farther, he planned to withdraw those forces to a well-fortified inner defense zone where they would join eight thousand fighters waiting in the rear. Kanda exhorted his troops to fight to the last round of ammunition and then die for the emperor.

It can only be speculated how those final actions would have gone given the still numerous Japanese prepared to fight to the death and the Australian military committee's expectation that Blamey could achieve his objectives with only "light casualties." Mercifully, before the offensive could resume, the pointless conflict ended with the general Japanese surrender.

In the Australian phase on Bougainville, the Japanese lost 8,500 in battle and 9,800 through illness. Australian casualties amounted to 516 killed and 1,572 wounded, which might be considered "light casualties," but were substantial in relation to what little was gained.

CHAPTER 28

# "Japan Man 'E Cry Enough"

O n 26 November, the American XI Corps turned over the Aitape area to
Major General Jack E. S. Stevens' Australian 6th Division. Described
as "waspishly aggressive and persistent,"[1] Stevens had distinguished himself in
Syria in 1941. Like two of his three brigade commanders, he had never led forces
in combat on New Guinea. The division included many long-service troops,
some who had fought in North Africa, Greece, and the Middle East.

Because of a shortage of shipping, the division's transfer to New Guinea took
more than three months and was not completed until the end of 1944. While the
move was in progress, the Australians attempted to learn Japanese strength and
dispositions through patrolling and intelligence study. This was particularly necessary since the Americans had made few contacts since the Driniumor battle in
August. In mid-December, probes as far as forty miles east of Aitape and twenty
miles south in the Torricelli Mountains found no large Japanese concentrations.

Intelligence reports in October 1944 indicated that the Japanese 18th Army
numbered about 30,000, a fair approximation of the 35,000 there. Severely
under strength, Adachi's 20th, 41st, and 51st division infantry units were fleshed
out with technical personnel unneeded in their regular capacities. All except one
of the nine Japanese regiments had been badly depleted by their arduous retreat
from the Huon Peninsula and the Driniumor fighting. To regain their strength,
these forces were mostly dispersed well inland in food-growing areas, with outposts to oppose penetrations.

The 6th Division's mission, as laid down initially by Sturdee, was to defend
Aitape, prevent Adachi from moving westward, and seize any opportunity for
destruction of the enemy. On 10 February, after rejecting more ambitious plans
that would have required additional resources, Sturdee approved a limited
coastal advance. The attack initially would be directed toward the villages of But

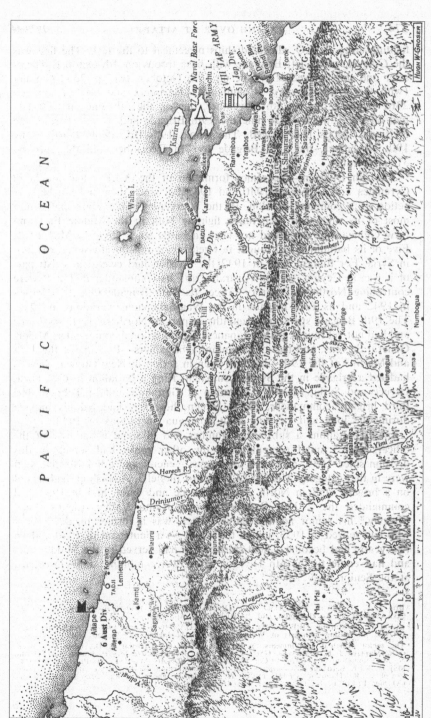

**Map 16. Wewak: The Australian Campaign** (Long, *Australia in the War of 1939–1945—The Final Campaigns*, 273 [under authorization of the Australian War Memorial])

and Dagua, continuing later to Wewak. As an unprotected anchorage, Aitape was a highly unreliable supply base, especially during the monsoon, and the road from there was poor. Hence Wewak and its harbor were much needed. Stevens' other principal target was the village of Maprik, across the Torricelli Range, in the central food-production area. An important goal in all the operations was "killing off the enemy."[2]

Distant from the gardening zones, and having lost most of its strategic value, the coastal belt was thinly occupied by the Japanese. Thus the Australian advance encountered only limited opposition. But it was seriously slowed by heavy rains that turned the poor coast road into a mire and washed out bridges, hampering supply. Unwilling to delay his attack, the commander of the 16th Brigade sent one company on a two-day dash to But. The coup de main on 16 March succeeded, and supports were rushed forward to hold the town and airstrip. Dagua and its airfield were taken soon after, bringing the Australians within twenty-one miles of Wewak. His ardor undimmed by these setbacks, Adachi proclaimed on 18 March: "It is not an impossibility for us, using our original all-out fighting tactics, to annihilate the 50,000 or 60,000 enemy troops with our present fighting strength."[3]

There was a danger that Japanese forces in the mountains might attack the exposed right flank and rear of the 16th Brigade during its coastal advance. Possibly caught off guard by the speed of the advance, the Japanese did not attack. But since the threat remained, the Australians conducted a sweep of the foothills. During one operation, Lieutenant Albert Chowne led his platoon in a wild bayonet charge with the Australians "yelling like stone age men."[4] Struck in the head by a bullet during the charge, Chowne was posthumously awarded the Victoria Cross.

Convinced by a presentation on 19 March about how increased naval resources could transform the situation, Blamey secured from MacArthur's headquarters ten additional LCTs for use in taking Wewak. Also, a sloop and other small gun craft were obtained, and air support was arranged for the attack. The 19th Brigade was brought forward for the operation, relieving the 16th Brigade, which had been continuously in the line for three months.

The attack plan approved by Blamey involved an overland march on Wewak by the 19th Brigade and severing the track leading south to prevent an enemy withdrawal in that direction. Meanwhile, a 623-man force built around the independent 2/6 Commando Regiment, dubbed Farida Force, would land east of Wewak to block Japanese retreat toward the Sepik River, where an Australian brigade held the east bank.

The attack along the coast began on 3 May and went forward rapidly, but four days later there was a serious friendly fire incident. A flight of American P-38 Lightnings, on a strafing mission to Wewak, inexplicably attacked the brigade headquarters, killing eleven and wounding twenty-one. Arriving at the outskirts of Wewak after a heavy artillery bombardment, two 19th Brigade companies went forward with tank supports on 10 May. The heaviest opposition came from caves, the entrances of which were systematically blown up, with the Japanese losing nearly two hundred while the Australians lost just two killed and seventeen wounded. Wewak's coveted harbor and its airfield fell on 11 May. During the next days, a unit operating south of Wewak to block the Japanese withdrawal was pinned down by enemy bunkers and incurred many casualties. Private Edward Kenna arose, drawing Japanese fire to himself, and engaged one bunker with his Bren gun. Switching to a rifle, he eliminated that position, then took up the Bren gun again to take out another machine-gun nest. For these actions, Kenna was awarded the Victoria Cross.[5]

On 11 May, Farida Force landed east of Wewak at Dove Bay. Late in the planning, cruisers HMAS *Hobart* and *Newfoundland* plus two destroyers from the British Pacific Fleet were assigned to the operation. Although coordination problems reduced the effectiveness of their gunfire, and in spite of the unavailability of American air support because of weather, the landings went smoothly. Troops and cargoes were all on shore by 1024 at the cost of just one Australian wounded. Farida Force then blocked the coast road until the 19th Brigade linked up with it on 22 May, placing the coastal plain fully in Australian hands.

Troops of the 6th Australian Division stream from their landing craft at Dove Bay during the amphibious assault on Wewak Peninsula, New Guinea, 11 May 1945. (By authorization of the Australian War Memorial: 018501)

The Japanese 18th Army was now confined to the mountains and jungles to the south, where a very different war had meanwhile been carried out in the bush and would continue until the end of the fighting. Bush warfare involved continuous patrolling and sweeps by companies and platoons to clear limited areas, and it disproportionately claimed the most experienced Australian fighting men. Having survived thus far, they particularly resented having to risk their lives in operations "not worth their blood and sweat."[6] When opportunity was eventually offered them to be discharged, few chose to stay.[7]

Much of the bush fighting took place in the Maprik sector, for which the 17th Brigade was responsible. Maprik was taken on 22 April, followed soon after by an area called Hayfield, eight miles away. An airstrip constructed at Hayfield and ready for the first DC-3 on 14 May would become the principal avenue for supply, reinforcement, and evacuation in that zone. With the delivery of heavy construction equipment, roads were built to connect the advancing troops with their supply base.

During the last months of the campaign, heavy patrolling was required at the coastal belt against specially trained Japanese raiders operating from the Torricelli Mountains. Also, the 19th Brigade was heavily engaged to win key mountains southwest of Wewak. By late July the 19th Brigade was badly in need of rest and was relieved by the 16th Brigade.

After many plan changes, Adachi established a last stand area south of Wewak, where he expected to fight as long as ammunition and food held out. A separate 2,800-man force in the Sepik River Valley was to fight on using "ambush warfare." With about 13,000 troops remaining, retreat impossible, and a fighter like Adachi at their head, the Japanese would almost certainly have sold their lives dearly had the Japanese government not surrendered in time.

The campaign cost the Australians 442 killed and 1,141 wounded, to which must be added more than 16,000 cases of sickness. More than 9,000 Japanese died in the fighting, and 14,000 are thought to have starved or died of illness. Only 269 surrendered. Both sides performed magnificently in their very different circumstances. The Australians never wavered in their duty, risking their lives in a meaningless war as though it counted. The 18th Army, worn out from earlier campaigns, starving and cut off from all aid, fought back and fell in their own devotion to duty. By way of an unprecedented commendation, the commander of the Southern Army recognized the performance of the 18th Army and its tenacious leader.

A very different war had meanwhile been conducted on New Britain. After the Cape Gloucester campaign, the Japanese withdrew to the Gazelle Peninsula at the northeastern end of the island, establishing scattered footholds on both coasts. While the American 40th Division troops were positioned well away from them and had few contacts with the Japanese, New Guinea native forces under Australian command patrolled the area immediately south of the Gazelle Peninsula, making occasional deep penetrations to learn enemy dispositions.

As the Japanese chose to commit only a small part of their forces at the neck of the Gazelle Peninsula, no sense was obtained of the sheer numbers of Japanese remaining on New Britain. While it had been supposed during the Australian takeover in November 1944 that the Japanese numbered about 35,000, there were in fact about 93,000 combatants and civilian workers. Even with the considerable underestimate, Blamey recognized that annihilating the Japanese would be more difficult than conquering the Japanese-held areas on Bougainville and New Guinea. One important difference was that unlike the starving and undersupplied forces in the other areas, the Rabaul garrison had ample food and supplies safely stored in hillside tunnels.

The 5th Australian Division that took over from the Americans was led by Major General Alan H. Ramsay, whose North African service included El Alamein, where his artillery expertise significantly contributed to the Allied victory. While Ramsay's principal officers were experienced as well, the rank and file of this militia division had no combat experience.

First of the units to arrive was the 6th Brigade, which landed on 4 November at Jacquinot Bay, about fifty miles southwest of Rabaul. Jacquinot Bay would become the site of the principal Australian base on New Britain and of an airfield that would be used by RNZAF squadrons in the campaign. By then, guerrilla forces had cleared the Japanese from the coast below Henry Reid Bay at the eastern end of the Gazelle Peninsula. These New Guinea native troops "achieved remarkable results in gaining information . . . and driving the enemy outposts out of about one-quarter of the island."[8] Only two natives were lost in these operations.

Initially, Ramsay was ordered only to relieve the Americans and protect the western part of the island. Later, in instructions that more closely mirrored Blamey's outlook, Sturdee asked Ramsay to conduct patrols and minor raids "to obtain the required information [for further action], to maintain the offensive spirit in our troops, to harass the enemy and retain moral superiority over him."[9] The most serious fighting flowing from this order occurred from 5 March to mid-April. During that period, the 13th Brigade relieved the 6th and a solid defense line was established at the neck of the Gazelle Peninsula that would remain essentially unchanged for the rest of the campaign.

In mid-June, Major General Horace C. Robertson, who earlier had replaced Ramsay, was authorized by Sturdee to undertake "minor offensive operations," ostensibly to maintain morale and fighting efficiency. Now under pressure for his policies, though, Blamey recoiled and ordered that Sturdee and he first approve all such operations. They were never requested.

In May, the New Guinea native troops resumed their deep penetrations into the Gazelle Peninsula. But problems emerged that were reflected in increasing cases of insubordination. Resentment had arisen about their treatment in comparison with the white soldiers, and there was discontent about having to fight away from their native soil. Like the Australian troops, they asked themselves, "Is it worth while?"[10] Further, rather than being used together in long-range patrols, their natural forte, they were often parceled out to perform lowly security duties for Australian troops. In addition, the native troops were unhappy about pay differences with the Australians, a highly explosive issue that Blamey addressed by obtaining speedy government approval for pay increases.

Shortly before the Japanese surrender, the division command changed yet again, with Robertson going to New Guinea to take over the 6th Division at Wewak, replaced by Major General Kenneth W. Eather, a veteran of the North African, New Guinea, and Borneo campaigns.[11] On 15 August, the Japanese surrender was announced. It included a separate announcement to the New Guinea native troops and workers, who were told, "Japan man 'e cry enough."[12]

The Australian phase of the New Britain campaign was fought at remarkably low cost to both sides. Australian losses were 53 killed and 140 wounded, plus 21 noncombat deaths, while just 206 Japanese were known to have been killed through the end of significant fighting in May. The most remarkable aspects of the campaign was the Japanese disinclination to commit more than a relative handful of troops to the front lines, and a refusal to take the offensive. A full-scale attack by the well-supplied and still fresh army and navy troops might well have broken the Australian front and created a crisis that would have drawn away Allied resources from distant campaigns. Fortunately for the Allies, Imamura was made of different stuff than Adachi and Kanda.

CHAPTER 29

# "Once It Was Over It Was Over"

O n 11 August, two days after the atomic bombing of Nagasaki, Sturdee signaled his commanders to suspend offensive action in anticipation of Japan's surrender. That came on 15 August, announced in a broadcast by Emperor Hirohito and speedily communicated to the armed forces and printed on thousands of leaflets showered by aircraft over many Japanese-held areas.

But the surrender process would not be easy given the multiple lines of authority and the remoteness of many units. On Bougainville, Kanda refused to act until he received authorization from his superior Imamura at Rabaul, and Imamura would take no action while awaiting instructions from Tokyo. Similarly, Samejima refused to allow Australian warships to enter the waters around Buin until he received authorization from Kusaka at Rabaul. Meanwhile, Japanese commanders attempted to get their forces to lay down their arms. A week after Hirohito's broadcast, however, Sturdee was informed that "in Bougainville on account of the dense jungle it has not been possible yet to deliver the order to . . . those units which have penetrated deep into your lines."[1]

Instead of giving first priority to the urgently needed liberation of prisoners, MacArthur forbade the signing of local surrender agreements until the general surrender was concluded. At ceremonies on board USS *Missouri* on 2 September, MacArthur signed the instrument of surrender for the Allied powers, followed by representatives of the Allied nations, including Nimitz for the United States, Blamey for Australia, and Air Vice Marshal Leonard M. Isitt for New Zealand.

Blamey delegated responsibility for accepting the surrender of Japanese forces on New Guinea, New Britain, and the Solomons to Sturdee as commander of the First Army. On 6 September, on board British carrier HMS *Glory*, anchored between New Britain and New Ireland, Sturdee met with a Japanese delegation headed by Imamura.

General Hitoshi Imamura surrenders his forces on New Guinea, New Britain, and the Solomon Islands to Lieutenant General Vernon A. H. Sturdee on board HMS *Glory*, 6 September 1945. (Govt. of Great Britain)

The ceremony was briefly interrupted when Imamura, described as "short and stubby, hard faced, with heavy lips and generous girth,"[2] protested that he did not have the authority to surrender the naval forces as specified in the instrument of surrender. The situation was quickly resolved by making Kusaka a cosignatory. It was only then discovered that instead of 50,000 army and 5,000 navy troops thought remaining in the Rabaul area, they in fact numbered 97,400 including civilian workers.[3] With such numbers and ample supplies, Imamura might have created serious problems for the Allies had he possessed a more aggressive spirit. The Japanese captured on New Britain would be joined in camps outside Rabaul by more than 12,000 troops from New Ireland, which had been wisely bypassed by Halsey.

At Bougainville on 8 September, Kanda and Samejima were taken on board a frigate and disembarked at Torokina, where they were led to Savige's headquarters. Present at the ceremony and doubtless feeling particular satisfaction was Lieutenant Colonel John P. Coursey (USMC), who had survived the sinking of USS *Arizona* the day it all began. Savige outlined the surrender terms, adding that he would not abide "delay, equivocation or neglect." In an extraordinary finale, Kanda and Samejima with two interpreters formed ranks, removed their headgear, and performed a one-minute silent bowing ceremony honoring the American and Australian dead.

As happened at Rabaul, there was great surprise in discovering how many Japanese remained on Bougainville. Rather than 13,000 as had been estimated, there were more than 23,000. The official Australian war history observed that "in August they were still so strong that the reduction of Buin would undoubtedly have involved longer and costlier operations than those already endured."

Lieutenant General Masatane Kanda (at left), commanding the Japanese 17th Army on Bougainville, surrenders at Australian II Corps Headquarters, Torokina. Seated opposite him is Vice Admiral Tomoshige Samejima, commander of the Japanese 8th Fleet, with Lieutenant General Stanley G. Savige, II Corps commander, presiding. American Marine Lieutenant Colonel John P. Coursey, survivor of the Pearl Harbor attack on USS *Arizona*, stands second from right, 8 September 1945. (By authorization of the Australian War Memorial: P00001.229)

Even so, Bougainville had been a terrible killing ground for the Japanese. Beginning with an estimated 65,000 troops at the American invasion, more than 41,000 perished, making it one of the war's costliest land campaigns for the Japanese, with losses far exceeding Saipan (30,000) and Guadalcanal (23,000). Of the more than 41,000 Japanese deaths, about 16,000 occurred in action, divided roughly equally between the American and Australian phases. About 25,000 died off the battlefield, firmly refuting Blamey's contention that the Japanese were not "withering on the vine."

The terms of surrender involved the removal of most of the Japanese from Bougainville to nearby Fauro Island, with the remainder concentrated at Torokina. Among those who surrendered was Hyakutake, paralyzed seven months earlier, who could not be evacuated until then.

The last of the South Pacific surrenders was on New Guinea. On 13 September, Adachi and his staff officers were flown from Hayfield to Wewak, where Adachi handed over his sword.

Lieutenant General Hatazo Adachi surrenders the Japanese 18th Army on New Guinea to Major General Horace C. H. Robertson, successor to Major General Stevens in command of the Australian 6th Division, Wom Airstrip, 13 September 1945. (By authorization of the Australian War Memorial: 019296)

The surrender might have occurred sooner, but Adachi insisted on a direct order from his superior. Unlike the Japanese at Rabaul, the 13,300 survivors of the 18th Army were in poor condition, many starving. Thus it is not surprising that on the march to Muschu Island, and on the island itself where they were gathered, about 1,000 may have died. It would later be charged that the prisoners were not provided with sufficient food, especially important given their weakened condition.[4] Only a small remnant had survived of the 140,000-man army that had fiercely contested eastern New Guinea.

The Allies were not finished with Imamura, Kanda, and Adachi. After evidence emerged of the execution of prisoners, Imamura was tried for war crimes and imprisoned for seven years until paroled in 1954. Although Kanda was not with the 6th Division during its rampage at the Rape of Nanking, he was called to account for other war crimes, serving four years of a fourteen-year sentence before being released in 1952. Adachi, who received a sentence of life imprisonment for the mistreatment and execution of prisoners by forces under his command, chose suicide instead after his 1947 sentencing. This most tenacious of Japanese commanders left a note declaring himself worthy of death, not for the actions for which he was tried, but for not achieving victory.[5]

Two months after Blamey represented Australia at the *Missouri* surrender, his enemies finally obtained his ouster and replacement by Sturdee. In retirement, Blamey continued his lifelong war against the political left through association with a militantly anticommunist group. After the return to office of his long-time supporter Sir Robert G. Menzies, Blamey was raised to the rank of field marshal in 1950, the only Australian-born soldier to attain that pinnacle.

Acknowledging Blamey's military gifts, the Australian army historian observed, "On his head descended perhaps the strongest vituperation to which any military leader in the war was subjected by people on his own side, and at the end the Government terminated his appointment in a summary fashion."[6] The causes cited there included a lack of tact, the persistence of the charges from his days with the police, and inability to compromise.

Blamey possessed great capacity for work and abilities that earned high praise from two eminent leaders, Australia's great citizen-soldier General Sir John Monash during World War I and General Archibald P. Wavell in World War II. At the same time, as with MacArthur, Blamey's self-centeredness easily led him to believe that his personal objectives and the best interests of the nation were one and the same.

The price borne by the fighting men was summed up by the historian of the 29th Brigade's 42nd Battalion that fought on Bougainville, but the same applied to Blamey's troops elsewhere in the South Pacific during the last months of war. He wrote,

> In the first place the campaign was futile and unnecessary. At Salamaua (i.e., during 1943) men went after the Jap because every inch of ground won meant so much less distance to Tokyo. But what did an inch of ground—or a mile—mean on Bougainville? Nothing! Whether Bougainville could be taken in a week or a year would make no difference to the war in general. Every man knew this. The Bougainville campaign was a politician's

war and served no other purpose than to keep men in the fight. . . . Men fought because there was no alternative. None wanted to lose his life on Bougainville.[7]

Compounding the bitterness felt by the fighting men was the almost complete lack of interest in their operations by the Australian press, which also recognized that the outcome had no bearing on the war. And yet the Australian troops fought as if it did matter, many risking everything. Hammer would observe, "they ignored the Australian papers, their relatives' letters advising caution, and got on with the job in hand, fighting and dying as if it was the battle for final victory."[8]

With the coming of peace in the South Pacific, each man needed to find peace on his own terms. Blamey left no question about his feelings when he presided over the capitulation of the Japanese Second Army in the Netherlands East Indies after the *Missouri* general surrender. He told the Japanese: "In receiving your surrender, I do not recognize you as an honourable and gallant foe, but you will be treated with due but severe courtesy in all matters."[9] He then recited the story of Japanese treachery in going to war and the atrocities committed by their forces.

But others felt differently. None of the Australian brigadiers was more fiercely anti-Japanese than Potts, who needed to be leashed in by Blamey in the final months of war. Placed in charge of Bougainville and its prisoners, Potts ordered a full dress inspection that included seventeen Japanese generals and fifteen admirals. It was wondered how he would react. To everyone's surprise, at the conclusion of the proceedings, Potts exclaimed "Good show" and shook hands with the conquered. He would explain, "Many dreadful things have been done during the course of the war—by both sides. There should not be recriminations after the event. Once it was over it was over."[10]

---

# NOTES

## Chapter 1. "The Hottest Potato"

1. J. Norman Lodge, "Halsey Predicts Victory This Year," *New York Times*, 3 January 1943. Halsey addresses this matter at length in William F. Halsey and J. Bryan III, *Admiral Halsey's Story* (New York: McGraw-Hill, 1947), 142–45. Unconvincingly, a note there says that "he made this bold assertive statement both to mislead the Japs and to cheer up our force."

2. Halsey and Bryan, *Halsey's Story*, 109.

3. The hasty planning and slight resources available caused some to call it Operation Shoestring.

4. Historians have come down hard on Fletcher for excessive caution. They include Samuel E. Morison, *History of United States Naval Operations in World War II: Volume V, The Struggle for Guadalcanal* (Boston: Little, Brown and Company, 1949), 28. Morison acidly comments: "Fletcher had no evidence of having been 'snooped'; his force could have remained in the area with no more severe consequences than sunburn."

5. Richard B. Frank, *Guadalcanal: The Definitive Account of the Landmark Battle* (New York: Random House, 1990), 36.

6. Both sides erred greatly in estimating the size of their opponent. Frank, *Guadalcanal*, 50, notes that it was expected before the landing that the Marines would face about 7,000 Japanese, whereas there were then just 2,571 Japanese on Guadalcanal and 886 on Tulagi and nearby islets.

7. Special Naval Landing Forces were battalion-sized units composed of sailors trained in assault, beach defense, and amphibious and infantry tactics. Commanded by naval officers, these elite units enjoyed reputations as especially fierce fighters.

8. Fletcher's performance is summed up in Frank, *Guadalcanal*, 205: "It is easy to caricature his penchant for fueling rather than fighting . . . the record of Fletcher from Savo Island to the Eastern Solomons shows he drifted from prudence into paralysis." For an alternative, positive assessment of Fletcher, see John B. Lundstrom's *Black Shoe Carrier Admiral* (Annapolis, Md.: Naval Institute Press, 2013).

9. Frank, *Guadalcanal*, 335. Frank writes, "[Halsey] was not so impulsive as the nickname 'Bull' . . . suggested, but he always displayed a certain indifference to detail that looked like carelessness." Critics of Halsey's performance late in the war would be less understanding about these qualities.

10. Halsey and Bryan, *Halsey's Story*, 117.

11. Ibid., 121.

12. E. B. Potter, *Bull Halsey* (Annapolis, Md.: Naval Institute Press, 1985), 175.

13. Japanese "long lance" torpedoes were remarkable for many attributes including their weight of nearly three tons, 1,100-pound warhead, and ability to travel 20 miles at 38 knots while leaving almost no wake.

14. Morison, *Guadalcanal*, 313.

15. Ibid., 314.

16. Jeter A. Isely and Philip A. Crowl, *The U.S. Marines and Amphibious War* (Princeton, N.J.: Princeton University Press, 1951), 164. The authors observe, with obvious reference to Halsey's conduct during the 1944 Battle of Leyte Gulf, "Halsey, not for the last time, jumped for the decoy and missed the real target."

17. Morison, *Guadalcanal*, 371.

18. Halsey and Bryan, *Halsey's Story*, 148.

19. John Miller Jr., *United States Army in World War II—The War in the Pacific: Guadalcanal: The First Offensive* (Washington, D.C.: Office of the Chief of Military History, 1948), 350.

20. Morison, *Guadalcanal*, 372.

21. Frank, *Guadalcanal*, 422–23.

22. Paul S. Dull, *A Battle History of the Imperial Japanese Navy 1941–1945* (Annapolis, Md.: Naval Institute Press, 1978), 340.

23. Isely and Crowl, *Marines and Amphibious War*, 164–65. The authors also cite the following statement by a former deputy chief of the Japanese Army's General Staff: "As for the turning point (of the war) when the positive action ceased or even became negative, it was, I feel, at Guadalcanal."

**Chapter 2. "I Want You to Take Buna, or Not Come Back Alive"**

1. D. Clayton James, *The Years of MacArthur, Volume II 1941–1945* (Boston, Mass.: Houghton Mifflin Company, 1975), 109.

2. Ronald H. Spector, *Eagle Against the Sun* (New York: Free Press, 1985), 107–10.

3. Louis Morton, *The United States Army in World War II—The War in the Pacific: Strategy and Command: The First Two Years* (Washington, D.C.: Center of Military History United States Army, 2000), 249.

4. Ibid., 255.

5. Ibid.

6. Ibid., 295.

7. Robert L. Eichelberger, *Our Jungle Road to Tokyo* (New York: The Viking Press, 1950), 33.

8. Thomas E. Griffith Jr., *MacArthur's Airman: General George C. Kenney and the War in the Southwest Pacific* (Lawrence: University Press of Kansas, 1998), 51–53.

9. George C. Kenney, *General Kenney Reports* (New York: Duell, Sloan, and Pearce, 1949), 52–53.

10. Dudley McCarthy, *Australia in the War of 1939–1945, Series I (Army), Volume V, South-West Pacific Area—First Year: Kokoda to Wau* (Canberra: Australian War Memorial, 1959), 176.

11. James, *MacArthur*, 208–10.

12. Harry A. Gailey, *MacArthur Strikes Back: Decision at Buna, New Guinea 1942–1943* (Novato, Calif.: Presidio Press, Inc., 2000), 80.

13. McCarthy, *Kokoda to Wau*, 240.

14. Ibid., 307.

15. Bruce Gamble, *Fortress Rabaul: The Battle for the Southwest Pacific, January 1942–April 1943* (Minneapolis, Minn.: Zenith Press, 2010), 277.

16. Matome Ugaki, *Fading Victory: The Diary of Admiral Matome Ugaki 1941–1945* (Pittsburgh, Pa.: University of Pittsburgh Press, 1991), 277.

17. Samuel Milner, *The United States Army in World War II—The War in the Pacific: Victory in Papua* (Washington, D.C.: Office of the Chief of Military History, 1957), 137.

18. James, *MacArthur*, 242.

19. Eichelberger, *Jungle Road*, 21.

20. Jay Luvaas, ed., *Dear Miss Em: General Eichelberger's War in the Pacific, 1942–1945* (Westport, Conn.: Greenwood Press, Inc., 1972), 63.

21. Eichelberger, *Jungle Road,* 50.

22. Milner, *Victory in Papua*, 329.

23. Wesley Frank Craven and James Lea Cate, eds., *The Army Air Forces in World War II, Volume Four, The Pacific: Guadalcanal to Saipan, August 1942 to July 1944* (Chicago: University of Chicago Press, 1950), 127.

24. Eichelberger, *Jungle Road*, 35.

25. James, *MacArthur*, 271.

26. Luvaas, *Dear Miss Em*, 63; Milner, *Victory in Papua*, 369 note 1.

27. Eichelberger, *Jungle Road*, 51.

28. Ibid., 18.

29. McCarthy, *Kokoda to Wau*, 532–33.

30. Luvaas, *Dear Miss Em*, 65; Eichelberger, *Jungle Road*, 99, mentions a photo taken in Australia in a jeep with MacArthur captioned in the newspapers as "General MacArthur and General Eichelberger at the New Guinea Front."

31. James, *MacArthur*, 278.

32. Luvaas, *Dear Miss Em*, 71.

33. Gailey, *MacArthur Strikes Back*, 233. As will be seen, MacArthur would forget his vow during the Battle of the Driniumor River.

34. Eric M. Bergerud, *Fire in the Sky: The Air War in the South Pacific* (Boulder, Colo.: Westview Press, 2000), 662.

35. Gailey, *MacArthur Strikes Back*, 84–85.

**Chapter 3. "There Was Indeed Only One Yamamoto"**

1. Morton, *Strategy*, 380–86.

2. Ibid., 390–92.

3. Ibid., 388.

4. Halsey and Bryan, *Halsey's Story*, 155. Privately, however, Halsey is known to have said, "I can work for Doug MacArthur, but he sure as hell could never work for me."

5. Dull, *Imperial Japanese Navy*, 268–69.

6. Edward J. Drea, *MacArthur's Ultra: Codebreaking and the War Against Japan, 1942–1945* (Lawrence: University Press of Kansas, 1992), 68–70.

7. There is disagreement about the numbers of aircraft available to Kenney for the battle. Morison, *Bismarcks*, 56 (full ref. below) claims 207 bombers and 129 fighters. This is disputed by Bergerud in *Fire in the Sky*, 590, who claims that only some 150 aircraft, half of them P-38 escorts, participated in the attack.

8. Samuel Eliot Morison, *History of United States Naval Operations in World War II: Volume VI, Breaking the Bismarcks Barrier* (Boston: Little, Brown and Company, 1950), 54–63.

9. James, *MacArthur*, 294–96.

10. Craven and Cate, *Guadalcanal to Saipan*, 146.

11. Bergerud, *Fire in the Sky*, 592.

12. James, *MacArthur*, 296–304.

13. Ibid., 296.

14. Morton, *Strategy*, 411–12.

15. Ibid., 412–13.

16. Robert Sherrod, *History of Marine Corps Aviation in World War II* (Washington, D.C.: Combat Forces Press, 1952), 138.

17. Morton, *Strategy*, 401–2.

18. E. B. Potter, *Nimitz* (Annapolis, Md.: Naval Institute Press, 1976), 233.

19. Craven and Cate, *Guadalcanal to Saipan*, 213–14.

20. Edwin T. Layton, *And I Was There: Pearl Harbor and Midway—Breaking the Secrets* (New York: William Morrow, 1985), 475. A different view was given by Dull in *Imperial Japanese Navy*, 341–42, who wrote, "It is difficult to see how Yamamoto can be called a great admiral, for his only great contribution was in planning the raid on Pearl Harbor. Even though the Japanese won most of their battles up to 1943, most of these battles were not fought under the direct command of Admiral Yamamoto, and when he did bring his Combined Fleet out . . . his tactics led to disaster." Dull concludes that "better than anyone, [Yamamoto] knew time was against him and that he could not afford the attrition he was allowing the Navy to suffer."

**Chapter 4. "The Most Unintelligently Waged Land Campaign"**

1. Morison, *Bismarcks*, 100.
2. Ibid., 177.
3. Craven and Cate, *Guadalcanal to Saipan*, 221.
4. Gordon L. Rottman, *U.S. Special Warfare Units in the Pacific Theater 1941–45: Scouts, Raiders, Rangers and Reconnaissance Units* (Oxford, UK: Osprey Publishing Ltd., 2005), 68.
5. Morison, *Bismarcks*, 153.
6. Ibid., 149.
7. John Miller Jr., *The United States Army in World War II—The War in the Pacific: Cartwheel: The Reduction of Rabaul* (Washington, D.C.: Office of Chief of Military History, 1959), 90–91.
8. Ibid., 91; Bergerud, *Fire in the Sky*, 566–67.
9. Andrieu D'Albas, *Death of a Navy: Japanese Naval Action in World War II* (New York: The Devin-Adair Company, 1957), 256.
10. Morison, *Bismarcks*, 163, calls this Japanese success on the Fourth of July "mud in Halsey's eye."
11. Walter Karig and Eric Purdon, *Battle Report, Pacific War: Middle Phase* (New York: Rinehart and Company, Inc. 1947), 215.
12. Dull, *Imperial Japanese Navy*, 276.
13. S. E. Smith, ed., *The United States Navy in World War II* (New York: William Morrow & Company, 1966), 450–60.
14. Online Resource: http: militarytimes.com/citations-medals-awards/.
15. Dull, *Imperial Japanese Navy*, 277.
16. Morton, *Strategy*, 510.

**Chapter 5. "A Custody Receipt for Munda . . . Keep 'Em Dying"**

1. Morton, *Strategy*, 510.
2. Joseph H. Alexander, *Edson's Raiders: The 1st Marine Raider Battalion in World War II* (Annapolis, Md.: Naval Institute Press, 2001), 289.
3. D. C. Horton, *New Georgia, Pattern for Victory* (New York: Ballantine Books Inc., 1971), 109.
4. Ibid., 84.
5. Ibid., 87–88.
6. John Kennedy Ohl, *Minuteman: The Military Career of General Robert S. Beightler* (Boulder, Colo.: Lynne Rienner Publishers, 2001), 109.
7. Craven and Cate, *Guadalcanal to Saipan*, 234.
8. Texts of Petrarca's and Scott's award citations, and of Young's (next below) are at www.history.army.mil/html/moh/index.html.
9. Ohl, *Minuteman*, 117. Young's sacrifice earned recognition throughout America in 1945 after composer Frank Loesser composed the *Ballad of Rodger Young*.
10. Halsey and Bryan, *Halsey's Story*, 164–65.

11. Collins' nickname was not based on the speed of his operations but from his headquarters code name "Lightning," obtained during Guadalcanal.

12. J. Lawton Collins, *J. Lawton Collins Papers* (Carlisle, Pa.: U. S. Army Military History Institute, 2010), Folder 5.

13. Moosbrugger rejected a suggestion by his other destroyer division commander that the Japanese in the water be killed using depth charges.

14. Dull, *Imperial Japanese Navy*, 278–79.

15. While Halsey credits his staff for the idea, others credit Nimitz and Wilkinson.

16. Morison, *Bismarcks*, 226–27.

17. Miller, *Cartwheel*, 180.

18. Sherrod, *Marine Aviation*, 156–57.

19. A New Zealand brigade group was roughly equivalent to an American regimental combat team.

20. While Morison, *Bismarcks*, 247, states that Walker struck the first blow, Dull, *Imperial Japanese Navy*, 284, says that "both sides opened up at 2256."

21. Dull, *Imperial Japanese Navy*, 286.

22. Morison, *Bismarcks*, 252, correctly concluded that "Ijuin had won the Battle of Vella Lavella"; Karig and Purdon, *Middle Phase*, 243, relying on overoptimistic American reports available at the time, claimed with equal assurance: "Yet [the Americans] had won the battle!"

23. Eric Bergerud, *Touched with Fire: The Land War in the South Pacific* (New York: Penguin Books, 1996), 230.

24. Morison, *Bismarcks*, 177.

25. Bergerud, *Touched with Fire*, 230.

26. Isely and Crowl, *Marines and Amphibious War*, 172.

27. Morton, *Strategy*, 512.

28. Halsey and Bryan, *Halsey's Story*, 161.

29. Miller, *Cartwheel*, 187.

30. Spector, *Eagle*, 237.

31. Ohl, *Minuteman*, 120.

32. Morton, *Strategy*, 510.

33. Bergerud, *Fire in the Sky*, 635.

34. Halsey and Bryan, *Halsey's Story*, 139.

35. Isely and Crowl, *Marines and Amphibious War*, 177.

## Chapter 6. "Lae and Salamaua Must Be Defended to the Death"

1. Craven and Cate, *Guadalcanal to Saipan*, 136.

2. Harry A. Gailey, *The War in the Pacific: From Pearl Harbor to Tokyo Bay* (Novato, Calif.: Presidio Press, 1995), 223.

3. David Dexter, *Australia in the War of 1939–1945, Series I (Army), Vol VI, The New Guinea Offensives* (Canberra: Australian War Memorial, 1961), 21.

4. Mark M. Boatner III, *The Biographical Dictionary of World War II* (Novato, Calif.: Presidio Press, 1996), 294–95.

5. Walter Krueger, *From Down Under to Nippon: The Story of the Sixth Army in World War II* (Washington, D.C.: Zenger Publishing Co., 1979), 10.

6. Dexter, *New Guinea Offensives*, 221–22.

7. Ibid., 222.

8. D. M. Horner, *Blamey: The Commander in Chief* (St. Leonards, N.S.W.: Allen and Unwin, 1998), 413.

9. Morison, *Bismarcks*, 134.

10. Dexter, *New Guinea Offensives*, 56.

11. Ibid.

12. Kenney, *Kenney Reports*, 256–57.

13. Dexter, *New Guinea Offensives*, 78–82.

14. Spector, *Eagle*, 233.

15. Miller, *Cartwheel*, 66.

16. Dexter, *New Guinea Offensives*, 103–4.

17. Harry A. Gailey, *MacArthur's Victory: The War in New Guinea 1943–1944* (New York: Presidio Press, 2004), 52.

18. Amalgamated Australian battalions retained their old designations in this way.

19. Dexter, *New Guinea Offensives*, 139.

20. Ibid., 182, note 8.

21. Ibid., 140.

22. Ibid., 161.

23. Craven and Cate, *Guadalcanal to Saipan*, 167.

24. Drea, *MacArthur's Ultra*, 81.

25. Kenney, *Kenney Reports*, 276–78. Parafrags were relatively small bombs dropped by parachute to permit aircraft to get away before detonation. Designed to saturate the ground with bomb fragments, they were particularly effective in destroying parked enemy aircraft.

26. Ibid., 278–79.

27. Craven and Cate, *Guadalcanal to Saipan*, 181.

28. Dexter, *New Guinea Offensives*, 136.

Chapter 7. "Prevent Your Troops Engaging My Troops"

1. A detailed table of organization of Australian forces is at Dexter, *New Guinea Offensives*, 280.

2. Kenney, *Kenney Reports*, 273–74.

3. James, *MacArthur*, 477.

4. Griffith, *MacArthur's Airman*, 133–34, 242–43. Griffith sees Kenney's attitude as probably fueled by the Navy's unwillingness to share the proximity fuse with him.

5. Dexter, *New Guinea Offensives*, 273.

6. Eichelberger, *Jungle Road*, 75–76. Eichelberger quotes Wootten, who said, "Not for one hour has my advance on Lae been held up by the failure of the [EBSR] to deliver troops, supplies, or ammunition."

7. Drea, *MacArthur's Ultra*, 85.

8. Dexter, *New Guinea Offensives*, 390.

9. Ibid., 391.

10. Bergerud, *Touched with Fire*, 505.

11. James, *MacArthur*, 328. Drea, *MacArthur's Ultra*, 85, says that Japanese losses were higher, claiming "Two thousand of the marchers never came out. Most of them simply starved to death."

12. Dexter, *New Guinea Offensives*, 392.

**Chapter 8. "The Weakness of Trying to Fight Battles from a Distance"**

1. Dexter, *New Guinea Offensives*, 444.

2. James, *MacArthur*, 329.

3. Morison, *Bismarcks*, 270.

4. Griffith, *MacArthur's Airman*, 137.

5. Dexter, *New Guinea Offensives*, 454.

6. Griffith, *MacArthur's Airman*, 137.

7. Dexter, *New Guinea Offensives*, 488.

8. Modeled on the British army commandos, independent companies were specially trained for raiding, sabotage, reconnaissance, and other irregular warfare activities.

9. Kenney, *Kenney Reports*, 301.

10. Dougherty replaced Potts as commander of the 21st Brigade in October 1942 (see chapter 2).

11. Dexter, *New Guinea Offensives*, 426.

12. Ibid., 433.

13. Griffith, *MacArthur's Airman*, 139.

14. Dexter, *New Guinea Offensives*, 507. This would be the end of Herring's military service in the war, as he would next become chief justice of the Victoria Supreme Court. "Ming the Merciless" was the villain in the popular *Buck Rogers* comic strips.

15. Gailey, *MacArthur's Victory*, 87–88.

16. Dexter, *New Guinea Offensives*, 551.

17. Ibid.

18. James, *MacArthur*, 336.

Chapter 9. "It's Torokina. Now Get on Your Horses!"

1. Morton, *Strategy*, 401–2.
2. Miller, *Cartwheel*, 226–27.
3. Ibid.; also, Morton, *Strategy*, 534.
4. Harry A. Gailey, *Bougainville 1943–1945: The Forgotten Campaign* (Lexington, Ky.: University Press of Kentucky, 1991), 34–35.
5. Halsey and Bryan, *Halsey's Story*, 174.
6. Morison, *Bismarcks*, 408–9.
7. John N. Rentz, *Bougainville and the Northern Solomons* (Washington, D.C.: Historical Branch, U.S. Marine Corps, 1948), 12.
8. The components of the attack force are given in detail in Miller, *Cartwheel*, 235.
9. Morton, *Strategy*, 546–47.
10. Bergerud, *Fire in the Sky*, 626.
11. Miller, *Cartwheel*, 235.

Chapter 10. "Halsey Knows the Straight Story"

This chapter is largely derived from an article by the author in the August 2008 issue of *Naval History* magazine titled "Halsey Knows the Straight Story." The article was based principally on letters found among the unpublished papers of General Thomas Holcomb in the Archives and Special Collections of the Library of the Marine Corps, Quantico, Virginia. The letters cited below are given as to or from Holcomb with the name of the sender or recipient and the date of the letter, the year in all cases understood as 1943.

1. The renaming recognized that Corps troops might include Army as well as Marine forces.
2. Holcomb to Nimitz, 4 June. In addition to Vandegrift, they included Major Generals Holland "Howling Mad" Smith, who would be at the forefront of Marine campaigns in the Central Pacific, and Charles D. Barrett, who is discussed at length here.
3. Ibid.
4. Vandegrift to Holcomb, 23 April.
5. Peck to Holcomb, 26 April. Peck specifically requested that "you would destroy [the letter] as soon as you have read it," certainly inserted at the request of Halsey.
6. Holcomb to Nimitz, 4 June. The following excerpts from Holcomb's letter are especially of interest: "There is no worthy job to which Vogel could be promoted in the States, and to relieve him would end his career . . . it seemed to me so unlike Halsey, as I know him, to act in this way. I have always regarded him as a courageous frank type who would himself send for Vogel and say that he was going to ask to have him relieved if he felt that necessary . . . of course Halsey had the power to act on his own responsibility if he wished." Holcomb

considered a possible replacement: "We have in the Marine Corps at least four general officers thoroughly competent for such command—Vogel, Holland Smith, Vandegrift, and Barrett. If Vogel has slipped he should be immediately replaced, and Vandegrift is the logical one to get it. As between Vandegrift and Barrett, Vandegrift is preferable in one respect—that is that through his successful operations on Guadalcanal he enjoys the confidence of the Admirals and would probably be permitted to carry out his job without interference; in all other respects Barrett would make a better Corps commander." This commendation of Barrett is noteworthy in light of later events.

7. Nimitz to Holcomb, 19 June. Nimitz mentioned in his letter that during his three days at Noumea, Vogel was away from IMAC's headquarters and was not available to hear his side of the story. In fact, the problem was that Vogel was afraid to fly and found himself in New Zealand for almost two months, much of the time only waiting for a ship.

8. Isely and Crowl, *Marines and Amphibious War*, 168, describes the Marines' situation then. The 1st and 2nd divisions were undergoing rehabilitation after Guadalcanal, while the 3rd Division still required six months of intensive training.

9. Holcomb to Vandegrift, 29 June.

10. A. A. Vandegrift, *Once a Marine: The Memoirs of General A. A. Vandegrift* (New York: W. W. Norton, 1964), 218. Vandegrift dealt with this situation in a single, unrevealing half-sentence: "the Commandant in a change of slate on July 1 brought Barney Vogel back to the States and gave me command of the I Corps in Noumea."

11. Vandegrift to Holcomb, 16 July. Vandegrift's referring to "enemies in uniform" apparently relates to ongoing complaints by Holcomb about those on the American side who attempted to diminish the Marine forces and their mission. In November 1942, Holcomb wrote to Holland Smith on his return from a trip to the Pacific: "The climate in the South Pacific is pleasanter and all your enemies are distinguished by wearing a special uniform."

12. Halsey and Bryan, *Halsey's Story*, 139.

13. Vandegrift to Holcomb, 19 June. Vandegrift passed along a conversation that he had with Halsey, during which Halsey said that "he would want me to come over if only for a month or two [to lead IMAC] and that when I left he would like to have Barrett, then Price [Marine commander of rear South Pacific bases] in the order named. Told him that as far as I was concerned Price would not be available as I thought him too old for an active combat job with the Force."

14. Allan R. Millett and Jack Shulimson, *Commandants of the Marine Corps* (Annapolis, Md.: Naval Institute Press, 2004), 295.

15. Merrill B. Twining, *No Bended Knee: The Battle for Guadalcanal* (Novato, Calif.: Presidio Press, 1996).

16. Holcomb to Barrett, 28 July. Informing Barrett that he would be taking over IMAC when Vandegrift departed, Holcomb wrote, "You are the unanimous choice of Nimitz, Halsey, Vandegrift, and myself to succeed to the command of the Corps in the South Pacific. I was most anxious that you should have an opportunity to command your Division in action before taking over the Corps; but it begins to look as if that might not happen."

17. Tom FitzPatrick, *A Character That Inspired: Major General Charles D. Barrett, USMC* (Fairfax, Va.: Signature Book Printing, 2003), 40. Fitzpatrick lists distinguished traits in Barrett's family. Feeling obligated to meet such high standards may well have caused Barrett to act as he did when faced with failure.

18. See note 6.

19. Holcomb to Vandegrift, 6 August.

20. Vandegrift to Holcomb, 14 October. This letter included details about Barrett's performance during the month before his death. "When he took over this job, and after I left, he immediately began to find reasons why the mission should be changed. . . . Halsey was greatly worried by his attitude and actions and told me that he was going to request his relief. . . . [Barrett] said on more than one occasion that he thought that he had more influence than he had and he wondered what he could do to impress the higher echelons; that he did not approve, that he thought if he shot himself that might do the work."

21. Twining, *No Bended Knee*, 185.

22. Ibid., 185–89.

23. Ibid., 189.

24. FitzPatrick, *A Character That Inspired*, 542.

25. Brewster to Holcomb, 10 October. This is the single source from which it is known that upon arriving in Noumea the evening of 7 October, "[Barrett] went straight to the office of ComSoPac [Halsey] for a conference which lasted until quite late." It was almost certainly then that Halsey told Barrett he would be relieved. The letter concludes: "While the records of the Board of Investigation which I convened that night will show that he died of a cerebral hemorrhage, there is no question that after leaving the urinal he started into his room and 'cracked' at that moment. He made for the window on the porch and stepped from a chair to the windowsill and plunged to the street below."

26. Vandegrift to Holcomb, 10 October.

27. FitzPatrick, *A Character That Inspired*, 512–43, presents a full transcript of the proceedings, which is particularly interesting in light of present knowledge. One of the many elements that should be noted is the absence of photographs of the porch area, which would have shown that the windows were too high for someone to fall accidentally.

28. Holcomb to Vandegrift, 21 October.

29. Halsey and Bryan, *Halsey's Story*, 174.

30. Vandegrift to Holcomb, 10 October.

31. Holcomb to Vandegrift, 21 October. "I was glad that Halsey asked for Geiger. He was my choice, as I know he was yours. I was afraid Halsey would pick Price, but probably what you said changed his original idea" (see note 13 above).

32. Holcomb to Vandegrift, 22 October.

## Chapter 11. "Make Sure They Think the Invasion Has Commenced"

1. Kenney, *Kenney Reports*, 313.

2. Ibid., 313–14.

3. Ibid., 319.

4. Craven and Cate, *Guadalcanal to Saipan*, 325–26.

5. Ibid., 326.

6. Morison, *Bismarcks*, 288. Referring to Kenney's repeated exaggerations, Morison wrote that "the Japanese out-Kenneyed Kenney by claiming 22 B-25s and 79 P-38s as 'sure kills.'"

7. Kenney, *Kenney Reports*, 320–21.

8. Craven and Cate, *Guadalcanal to Saipan*, 250.

9. Griffith, *MacArthur's Airman*, 142.

10. A detailed table in Sherrod, *Marine Aviation*, 175–79, gives targets on or near Bougainville struck during the second half of October, together with the forces employed and results.

11. Morison, *Bismarcks*, 292.

12. Henry I. Shaw and Dwight T. Kane, *History of U.S. Marine Corps Operations in World War II, vol. 2, Isolation of Rabaul* (Washington, D.C.: Historical Branch, U.S. Marine Corps, 1963), 189.

13. Ibid., 191.

14. John C. Chapin, *Marines in World War II Commemorative Series: Top of the Ladder: Marine Operations in the Northern Solomons* (Washington, D.C.: Marine Corps Historical Center, 1997), 8.

15. Oliver Gillespie, *Official History of New Zealand in the Second World War 1939–45: The Pacific* (Wellington, N.Z.: Historical Publications Branch, 1952), 143–59.

16. Morison, *Bismarcks*, 295.

17. Stephen R. Taaffe, *MacArthur's Jungle War* (Lawrence: University Press of Kansas, 1998), 52.

18. Sherrod, *Marine Aviation*, 181.

19. James F. Christ, *Mission Raise Hell: The U.S. Marines on Choiseul, October–November 1943* (Annapolis, Md.: Naval Institute Press, 2006), xiv.

20. Chapin, *Top of the Ladder*, 9.

21. Christ, *Mission Raise Hell*, 8.

22. Shaw and Kane, *Isolation of Rabaul*, 204 notes, "There is little indication that enemy forces in Bougainville were drawn off balance . . . enemy records attach little significance to the Choiseul attack."

23. Krulak's courage extended to giving President Lyndon Johnson his candid opinion about the Vietnam War, which likely cost him appointment as commandant of the Marine Corps.

24. Morison, *Bismarcks*, 292–93.

### Chapter 12. "Guadalcanal—Minus Most of the Errors"

1. Robert A. Aurthur and Kenneth Cohlmia, *The Third Marine Division* (Washington, D.C.: Infantry Journal Press, 1948), 56.

2. Isely and Crowl, *Marines and Amphibious War*, 178.

3. Francis D. Cronin, *Under the Southern Cross: The Saga of the Americal Division* (Washington, D.C.: Combat Forces Press, 1951), 120.

4. Morison, *Bismarcks*, 282.

5. Isely and Crowl, *Marines and Amphibious War*, 175–76.

6. Morison, *Bismarcks*, 289, 297.

7. Vandegrift, *Once a Marine*, 227–28.

8. William L. McGee, *Amphibious Operations in the South Pacific in World War II, Volume II, The Solomons Campaign 1942–1943, from Guadalcanal to Bougainville, Pacific War Turning Point* (Santa Barbara, Calif.: BMC Publications, 2002), 494.

9. Rail loading involved embarking troops on landing craft suspended from ship davits. The procedure eliminated the need for a lengthy descent by the troops into landing craft on cargo nets.

10. J. M. S. Ross, *The Official History of New Zealand in the Second World War: Royal New Zealand Air Force* (Wellington, N.Z.: Historical Publications Branch, 1955), 206.

11. Aurthur and Cohlmia, *Third Marine Division*, 63.

12. Gailey, *Bougainville*, 73.

13. Richard Wheeler, *A Special Valor: The U.S. Marines and the Pacific War* (New York: New American Library, 1983), 146.

14. Henry Berry, *Semper Fi, Mac: Living Memories of the U.S. Marines in World War II* (New York: Arbor House, 1982), 126, describes McCaffery's death as seen by Major Richard Washburn, who then assumed command: "The first thing that happened as we hit the beach was the killing of our battalion commander, Lieutenant Colonel McCaffery. . . . Poor guy, he never got started with the 2nd Battalion. Sometimes it happened like that. You could go through some extremely hot action and never get touched and then, bang! One sniper's bullet could kill you right off the top of the barrel."

15. Miller, *Cartwheel*, 246.

16. Aurthur and Cohlmia, *Third Marine Division*, 64.

17. Isely and Crowl, *Marines and Amphibious War*, 179.

18. Ross, *RNZAF*, 208.

19. Miller, *Cartwheel*, 248, differing from Gailey, gives Japanese losses based on their records as 19 lost and 10 damaged.

20. McGee, *Guadalcanal to Bougainville*, 507.

21. Vandegrift, *Once a Marine*, 229.

**Chapter 13. "The Final Outcome . . . Was Never in Doubt"**

1. Burke's nickname was acquired in an earlier operation after he signaled that he was slowing to a speed of 31 knots because of a power plant problem. What began as an inside joke was picked up by the press and interpreted as meaning a hard-driving destroyer leader, which was certainly true.

2. Karig and Purdon, *Middle Phase*, 247, quotes Burke: "Everybody tried to get more capacity out of the barge fuel pumps than was in them. It was a battle for fuel."

3. Dull, *Imperial Japanese Navy*, 288. Dull worked from the Japanese naval records, which often differ from Morison.

4. Morison, *Bismarcks*, 310. While Dull, *Imperial Japanese Navy*, 288, indicates that Omori "had no radar," that apparently was not literally the case. Gailey, *Bougainville*, 82, quotes Omori: "we had some modified radar sets in action but they were unreliable. I do not know whether the sets or operators were poor, but I did not have confidence in them."

5. Morison, *Bismarcks*, 309.

6. Ibid., 311–12. Dull, *Imperial Japanese Navy*, 289, indicates that the collision occurred before *Sendai* was hit, caused when *Samidare* tried to avoid the cruiser as it executed a wide turn.

7. Ibid., 321.

8. Ibid., 315, note 8. Until he met with Morison in 1950, Omori believed he faced seven heavy cruisers and a dozen destroyers.

9. Omori's fleet would get back to Rabaul just in time to get caught in Kenney's attack on 2 November.

10. Little Beaver, an Indian boy in the popular Red Ryder comic strip, was used as the squadron's logo.

11. Dull, *Imperial Japanese Navy*, 290.

12. D'Albas, *Death of a Navy*, 264. Considering the treatment of Omori a "heavy penalty," D'Albas adds: "To fight blindfolded [i.e., without radar] against an enemy who can see you is a mad enterprise, even for the strongest will."

13. Morison, *Bismarcks*, 322.

## Chapter 14. "The Most Desperate Emergency"

1. Halsey and Bryan, *Halsey's Story*, 180–81.

2. James H. Belote and William M. Belote, *Titans of the Seas: The Development and Operations of Japanese and American Carrier Task Forces During World War II* (New York: Harper & Row, 1975), 191.

3. Clark G. Reynolds, *The Fast Carriers: The Forging of an Air Navy* (New York: McGraw-Hill Book Company, 1968), 97–98.

4. Halsey and Bryan, *Halsey's Story*, 181.

5. Morison, *Bismarcks*, 325–26.

6. Dull, *Imperial Japanese Navy*, 292.

7. Morison, *Bismarcks*, 327.

8. Ibid., 328. Belote and Belote, *Titans of the Seas*, 194, writes that the bomb went down *Maya's* stack, but Dull, *Imperial Japanese Navy*, 292, claims the hit was on the catapult plane deck.

9. Dull, *Imperial Japanese Navy*, 292, writes that light cruisers *Agano* and *Noshiro* "received no damage," but D'Albas, *Death of a Navy*, 265, claims they were "struck and were no longer battleworthy."

10. Griffith, *MacArthur's Airman*, 204, describes Kenney's attitude throughout the war: "Kenney had little use for the complaints or suggestions of naval officers . . . there were few, if any, attempts to define what targets had the highest priority or to combine the efforts of the two services."
11. Halsey and Bryan, *Halsey's Story*, 183.
12. Dull, *Imperial Japanese Navy*, 183.
13. Reynolds, *The Fast Carriers*, 99, quoting from Frederick Sherman's diary.
14. Morison, *Bismarcks*, 329–30.
15. Dull, *Imperial Japanese Navy*, 293, does not show heavy cruiser *Chokai* there, but Morison and Belote place her there.
16. Reynolds, *The Fast Carriers*, 100.
17. United States Strategic Bombing Survey, *Interrogations of Japanese Officials —Vice Admiral Fukudome, Shigeru, IJN*, Online Resource: www.ibiblio.org/hyperwar/AAF/USSBS/IJO/, 516.
18. Morison, *Bismarcks*, 353.
19. Ibid., 358. Austin reported a fuel leak that would prevent his continued pursuit, to which Burke responded: "Unless we can get fuel in Rabaul." Austin countered, "O.K., but we might have trouble with the fuel hose connections!"
20. Ibid.
21. Dull, *Imperial Japanese Navy*, 295.
22. Ibid., 341.

### Chapter 15. "The Closest Thing to a Living Hell"
1. Bergerud, *Touched with Fire*, 66.
2. Wheeler, *Marines and the Pacific War*, 150.
3. Chapin, *Top of the Ladder*, 12.
4. Wheeler, *Marines and the Pacific War*, 152.
5. Rentz, *Bougainville and the Northern Solomons*, 43.
6. Gailey, *Bougainville*, 97–98.
7. Chapin, *Top of the Ladder*, 16, quotes a Marine who liked best that no Japanese could slip through the lines with a dog on duty, providing the rare chance to sleep in peace.
8. Aurthur and Cohlmia, *Third Marine Division*, 368.
9. Chapin, *Top of the Ladder*, 16.
10. Wheeler, *Marines and the Pacific War*, 155.
11. Ibid., 163.

### Chapter 16. "A Shop in the Japs' Front Yard"
1. Shaw and Kane, *Isolation of Rabaul*, 256.
2. S. E. Smith, ed., *The United States Marine Corps in World War II* (New York: Random House, 1969), 461.
3. Ibid., 472.

4. Shaw and Kane, *Isolation of Rabaul*, 262.
5. Ibid., 264.
6. Aurthur and Cohlmia, *Third Marine Division*, 78.
7. Miller, *Cartwheel*, 265.
8. Shaw and Kane, *Isolation of Rabaul*, 281.
9. Patrick K. O'Donnell, *Into the Rising Sun* (New York: Free Press, 2002), 88, includes the recollections of a raider at the disbanding formation, at which the general who made the announcement concluded by saying, "Welcome back to the *real* Marine Corps."
10. Morison, *Bismarcks*, 365.
11. Chapin, *Top of the Ladder*, 30.

## Chapter 17. "More Nerve-Racking Than . . . Tobruk or El Alamein"

1. Dexter, *New Guinea Offensives*, 652.
2. Ibid., 650.
3. Morison, *Bismarcks*, 391. Miller, *Cartwheel*, 303, says that Adachi went overland.
4. Dexter, *New Guinea Offensives*, 736.
5. James, *MacArthur*, 347.
6. Miller, *Cartwheel*, 304.
7. Japanese records indicate there were 787 men on 2 January. Adachi claimed after the war that there were only about 400 during the battle, which appears highly unlikely.
8. Dexter, *New Guinea Offensives*, 817.

## Chapter 18. "Nature Proved to Be a Worse Enemy Than the Japanese"

1. Morison, *Bismarcks*, 370–71, provides several reasons why Cape Gloucester was "superfluous" including the observation that the English Channel and Straits of Gibraltar were effectively controlled without securing both shores.
2. The abortive attack, in fictionalized form, appears in Norman Mailer's *The Naked and the Dead*. The author heard about it while serving with the 112th Cavalry in the Philippines.
3. Craven and Cate, *Guadalcanal to Saipan*, 336.
4. Miller, *Cartwheel*, 289. Japanese losses were fewer, amounting to 116 killed and 117 wounded.
5. Frank O. Hough and John A. Crown, *The Campaign on New Britain* (Washington, D.C.: Historical Branch, Headquarters, U.S. Marine Corps, 1952), 36.
6. Craven and Cate, *Guadalcanal to Saipan*, 345.
7. Morison, *Bismarcks*, 386.
8. Hough and Crown, *New Britain*, 61, notes that Japanese records show more modest losses of thirteen bombers and four fighters.

9. Craven and Cate, *Guadalcanal to Saipan*, 341. Through December, an estimated 163 Japanese aircraft were lost over Cape Gloucester and Arawe, with 22 more probable.

10. Morison, *Bismarcks*, 388.

11. Hough and Crown, *New Britain*, 95.

12. Ibid., 99.

13. Casualties for the Aogiri Ridge battle were never tabulated.

14. Hough and Crown, *New Britain*, 113.

15. Ibid., 183.

16. Gailey, *MacArthur's Victory*, 132.

**Chapter 19. "Keep Rabaul Burning!"**

1. Morison, *Bismarcks*, 395.

2. Bergerud, *Fire in the Sky*, 652.

3. Ibid., 647–48.

4. Sherrod, *Marine Aviation*, 194.

5. Ibid., 195.

6. Craven and Cate, *Guadalcanal to Saipan*, 351.

7. Morison, *Bismarcks*, 397.

8. Ibid., 398.

9. Sherrod, *Marine Aviation*, 197. Sherrod here cites the U.S. Strategic Bombing Survey.

10. Ibid. Boyington scored two victories on the day he was shot down that were not known about until his release, giving him a final score of twenty-eight.

11. Sherrod, *Marine Aviation*, 198.

12. Morison, *Bismarcks*, 400.

13. Reynolds, *The Fast Carriers*, 137–39.

14. Morison, *Bismarcks*, 403.

15. Bergerud, *Fire in the Sky*, 655.

16. Morison, *Bismarcks*, 407.

17. Ibid., 416. Morison wrote, "[Wilkinson] himself regarded this as the neatest landing that III 'Phib ever pulled off."

18. Gillespie, *New Zealand*, 178. The historian wrote, "In accordance with American procedures, the orders of subordinate commanders were incorporated in detail in those of the higher command, a system which hampers to some degree any last-minute changes dictated by tactical necessity."

**Chapter 20. "The Worst-Kept Secret of the War in the South Pacific"**

1. Stanley A. Frankel, *The 37th Infantry Division in World War II* (Washington, D.C.: Infantry Journal Press, 1948), 142–43. The lengthy message concluded: "Our cry of victory at Torokina Bay will be shouted resoundingly to our native land. We are invincible! Always attack! Security is the greatest enemy. Always be alert. Execute silently."

2. Gailey, *Bougainville*, 147. Kanda's poem began: "To avenge our mortification since Guadalcanal, will be our duty true and supreme. Strike, strike, then strike again, until our enemy is humbled forevermore!"

3. Ibid., 140.

4. Miller, *Cartwheel*, 351.

5. Bergerud, *Touched with Fire*, 511.

6. Ibid. While postwar interrogations and examination of records indicate 15,400 army troops, Kanda recalled in 1949 that there were 19,000 soldiers and 2,000 sailors available.

7. Gailey, *Bougainville*, 140.

8. Ohl, *Minuteman*, 131.

9. Cronin, *Under the Southern Cross*, 133.

10. Ibid., 135–38.

11. Gailey, *Bougainville*, 144–45.

12. Cronin, *Under the Southern Cross*, 142.

13. Bergerud, *Touched with Fire*, 511.

14. Frankel, *37th Division*, 143.

**Chapter 21. "But for the Stern Resistance . . . of the XIV Corps"**

1. Frankel, *37th Division*, 144, quotes a prisoner who lamented, "Each time we fire one round, you send back a hundred in return. No Good."

2. Cronin, *Under the Southern Cross*, 147. Cronin notes that "the Bougainville-based missions [were] among the shortest missions flown in the Pacific."

3. Frankel, *37th Division*, 145.

4. Ibid., 146. When the men's bodies were recovered, twelve dead Japanese were found with them in the pillbox, and other Japanese found dead nearby were probably eliminated by them as well.

5. Cronin, *Under the Southern Cross*, 166.

6. Miller, *Cartwheel*, 369.

7. Ohl, *Minuteman*, 135.

8. Ibid., 136–37.

9. Ibid., 138. As an intelligence officer described it, "General Beightler contacted General Griswold . . . and walked out with fifteen thousand rounds of artillery shells figuratively in his pocket."

10. Miller, *Cartwheel*, 377.

11. Ibid., 357.

12. Ohl, *Minuteman*, 138–39. Beightler would say that he preferred to have "machines fight for us before committing a single American life."

13. Miller, *Cartwheel*, 365.

14. Frankel, *37th Division*, 154.

15. Gailey, *Bougainville*, 168.

16. Morison, *Bismarcks*, 431.

## Chapter 22. "They Wanted to Fight"

1. Gailey, *Bougainville*, 169.
2. Ulysses Lee, *United States Army in World War II, Special Studies: The Employment of Negro Troops* (Washington, D.C.: Center of Military History, 1963), 498.
3. "U.S. Negro Troops Crack Bougainville Foe," *New York Times*, 17 March 1944.
4. Lee, *Employment of Negro Troops*, 499.
5. Ibid., 495–96.
6. Ibid., 499.
7. Cronin, *Under the Southern Cross*, 170.
8. Lee, *Employment of Negro Troops*, 506–9. First Lieutenant Oscar Davenport, the weapons platoon leader, was posthumously awarded the Bronze Star for his actions. Remaining behind while his platoon withdrew, Davenport went to the aid of a wounded soldier from another platoon, and although wounded reached the man and administered first aid until he was shot and killed.
9. Ibid., 505–6.
10. Ibid., 508.
11. Ibid., 512.
12. Ibid., 516–17.
13. Ibid., 517.
14. Ibid., 533–35.
15. Ibid., 511, provides excerpts from a report by the 93rd Division psychiatrist describing attitudes of the African American troops. Many saw themselves "as fighting to maintain gains that Negroes had made in the past seventy years." But 25 percent consisted of "uneducated rural men who viewed their mission with apathy and better educated urban men who considered the war little of their affair."
16. Ibid., 704–5.

## Chapter 23. "The South Pacific Campaign Was Finished"

1. Morton, *Strategy and Command*, 535.
2. Kenney, *Kenney Reports*, 359.
3. Ibid., 360.
4. Drea, *MacArthur's Ultra*, 102.
5. William C. Frierson, *The Admiralties: Operations of the 1st Cavalry Division, 29 February–18 May 1944* (Washington, D.C.: United States Army Center of Military History, 1990), 17.
6. Taaffe, *MacArthur's Jungle War*, 61.
7. Ibid., 64.
8. Eric Larrabee, *Commander in Chief: Franklin Delano Roosevelt, His Lieutenants, and Their War* (New York: Simon & Schuster, 1987), 340. Larrabee considered MacArthur at his best during the campaign: bold, resourceful, effective.

9. Taaffe, *MacArthur's Jungle War*, 66.

10. Frierson, *The Admiralties*, 148.

11. Potter, *Bull Halsey*, 294.

12. Miller, *Cartwheel*, 379.

13. Ibid., 381.

14. Bergerud, *Fire in the Sky*, 656.

15. Ibid., 659.

16. Halsey and Bryan, *Halsey's Story*, 191.

## Chapter 24. "Kicking Around a Corpse"

1. Samuel Eliot Morison, *History of United States Naval Operations in World War II: Volume VIII, New Guinea and the Marianas, March 1944–August 1944* (Boston, Mass.: Little, Brown and Company, 1953), 161.

2. Newton left Nimitz's staff for a position of such limited consequence that neither his appointment nor any subsequent activities in South Pacific waters are mentioned in Morison's history of naval operations.

3. Reynolds, *The Fast Carriers*, includes many specific complaints by Halsey's air commanders.

4. Samuel Eliot Morison, *History of United States Naval Operations in World War II: Volume XII, Leyte* (Boston, Mass.: Little, Brown and Company, 1958), 33. Morison observed: "Admiral Halsey . . . proposed on 13 September to bypass the Palaus, but Admiral Nimitz did not accept this suggestion. . . . From hindsight it appears probable that [the operation order] should have been countermanded. [Peleliu] was useful, but hardly worth the expenditure of 1950 American lives."

5. Potter, *Nimitz*, 40.

6. Bergerud, *Fire in the Sky*, 377.

7. Craven and Cate, *Guadalcanal to Saipan*, 647.

8. Halsey and Bryan, *Halsey's Story*, 231.

9. Sherrod, *Marine Aviation*, 290. Sherrod continues, "The lessons learned on the paddy fields of Luzon paid off five and six years later on the paddy fields of Korea."

10. Ibid., 213.

## Chapter 25. "The Japanese Could Die Where They Were or Die Advancing"

1. Cronin, *Under the Southern Cross*, 201–9.

2. Robert Ross Smith, *United States Army in World War II—The War in the Pacific: The Approach to the Philippines* (Washington, D.C.: Center of Military History, 1984), 129.

3. Edward J. Drea, *Leavenworth Papers, Defending the Driniumor: Covering Force Operations in New Guinea, 1944* (Fort Leavenworth, Kan.: Combat Studies Institute, 1984).

4. Charles Willoughby, *Reports of General MacArthur: Japanese Operations in the Southwest Pacific, volume 2, part 1* (Washington, D.C.: Government Printing Office, 1966), 299.

5. Taaffe, *MacArthur's Jungle War*, 192.

6. Stephen R. Taaffe, *Marshall and His Generals: U. S. Army Commanders in World War II* (Lawrence: University Press of Kansas, 2011), 145, characterizes Gill as "efficient and overbearing."

7. Drea, *Leavenworth Papers*.

8. Taaffe, *Marshall and His Generals*, 146.

9. Taaffe, *MacArthur's Jungle War*, 192.

10. Ibid., 194.

11. H. W. Blakeley, *The 32d Infantry Division in World War II* (Madison, Wisc.: History Commission, 1945), 160.

12. Taaffe, *Marshall and His Generals*, 147, quotes Gill, who would write in later years that the XI Corps was "untrained in this thing from the top down. They had never been in any combat like that and they didn't know anything about jungle fighting."

13. Smith, *Approach to the Philippines*, 137.

14. Taaffe, *MacArthur's Jungle War*, 200.

15. Smith, *Approach to the Philippines*, 138.

16. Gailey, *MacArthur's Victory*, 236.

17. Smith, *Approach to the Philippines*, 154.

18. Blakeley, *32d Infantry Division*, 161.

19. Morison, *New Guinea*, 74.

20. Smith, *Approach to the Philippines*, 162.

21. Taaffe, *MacArthur's Jungle War*, 207.

22. Ibid.

23. Craven and Cate, *Guadalcanal to Saipan*, 614.

24. Taaffe, *MacArthur's Jungle War*, 208.

25. Bergerud, *Touched with Fire*, 509.

**Chapter 26. "Doubtful That He Checked with the Ordinary Foot Soldier"**

1. Gavin Long, *Australia in the War of 1939–1945, Series 1 (Army), Volume VII, The Final Campaigns* (Canberra: Australian War Memorial, 1963), 20.

2. Ibid., 19.

3. Ibid., 22.

4. Taaffe, *Marshall and His Generals*, 229–30.

5. Ohl, *Minuteman*, 141.

6. Ibid., 244–45. That Beightler's attitude has some validity was confirmed by remarks by Krueger, who, acknowledging Beightler as one of his best division commanders, added, "Beightler's trouble was that he was a damn National Guardsman."

7. Taaffe, *Marshall and His Generals*, 223.
8. Ibid.
9. Taaffe, *MacArthur's Jungle War*, 208.
10. Gailey, *Bougainville*, 191.
11. Australian National University, *Australian Dictionary of Biography*, National Center of Biography (Canberra: AUST Online Resource: http: adb.anu.edu.au).
12. Ibid.
13. Gailey, *Bougainville*, 192.
14. Alex Danchev and Daniel Todman, eds., *War Diaries 1939–1945: Field Marshall Lord Alanbrooke* (Berkley: University of California Press, 2001), 546.
15. *Australian Dictionary of Biography*.
16. Long, *Final Campaigns*, 60.
17. Ibid., 65.
18. Ibid., 25.
19. Ibid., 25–26.
20. Ibid., 23.
21. Gailey, *Bougainville*, 193.

## Chapter 27. "No Enemy Can Withstand You"

1. Long, *Final Campaigns*, 114.
2. Ibid., 126. A Japanese officer marveled that the Australians could take such punishment and persist in their attacks.
3. Ibid., 133–34.
4. Ibid., 184.
5. Ibid., 189.
6. Ibid., 193.
7. Ibid., 236–37.
8. Ibid., 223. Even carrier pigeons refused to deliver messages in such weather, causing their crusty handler to growl, "The — won't fly. Ceiling too low. . . . Bloody sorry I didn't eat them the other night when they were making so much din."

## Chapter 28. "Japan Man 'E Cry Enough"

1. *Australian Dictionary of Biography*.
2. Long, *Final Campaigns*, 306.
3. Ibid., 319.
4. Ibid., 322.
5. Ibid., 351. After Kenna was seriously wounded, he married his nurse, and before his death was the last surviving Australian Victoria Cross holder from World War II.
6. Ibid., 327.

7. Ibid., 367.
8. Ibid., 248.
9. Ibid., 250–1.
10. Ibid., 263.
11. A harsh disciplinarian nicknamed "28 days" for the period of confinement to barracks he favored as punishment for infractions, Eather was the last surviving Australian World War II general at his death in 1993.
12. Ibid., 265.

**Chapter 29. "Once It Was Over It Was Over"**

1. Long, *Final Campaigns*, 555.
2. Ibid., 556.
3. Ibid., 555, which gives head counts for all the South Pacific surrenders.
4. Ibid., 559.
5. The lengthy note included the following: "the hoped for end was not attained because of my inability. Thus, I paved the way for my country to be drawn into the present predicament. The crime deserves death. During the past three years of operations more than 100,000 youthful and promising officers and men were lost and most of them died of malnutrition. When I think of this, I know not what apologies to make to His Majesty the Emperor and I feel that I myself am overwhelmed with shame." Australia-Japan Research Project, http://ajrp.awm .gov.au/ajrp/remember.nsf.
6. Long, *Final Campaigns*, 586.
7. Ibid., 235.
8. Ibid., 239–40.
9. Ibid., 556.
10. Bill Edgar, *Warrior of Kokoda: A Biography of Brigadier Arnold Potts* (St. Leonards, N.S.W.: Allen & Unwin, 1999), 278.

# BIBLIOGRAPHY

## Books

### Official Histories

The U.S. Army, Army Air Forces, Marine Corps, and Australian Army histories listed below are available online, including complete charts and campaign maps.

Chapin, John C. *Marines in World War II Commemorative Series: Top of the Ladder: Marine Operations in the Northern Solomons*. Washington, D.C.: Marine Corps Historical Center, 1997.

Craven, Wesley Frank, and James Lea Cate, eds. *The Army Air Forces in World War II, Volume Four, The Pacific: Guadalcanal to Saipan August 1942 to July 1944*. Chicago: University of Chicago Press, 1950.

Dexter, David. *Australia in the War of 1939–1945, Series I (Army), Vol VI, The New Guinea Offensives*. Canberra: Australian War Memorial, 1961.

Frierson, William C. *The Admiralties: Operations of the 1st Cavalry Division, 29 February–18 May 1944*. Washington, D.C.: United States Army Center of Military History, 1990.

Gillespie, Oliver. *Official History of New Zealand in the Second World War 1939–45: The Pacific*. Wellington, N.Z.: Historical Publications Branch, 1952.

Hoffman, Jon T. *Marines in World War II Commemorative Series, from Makin to Bougainville: Marine Raiders in the Pacific War*. Washington, D.C.: Marine Corps Historical Center, 1995.

Hough, Frank O., and John A. Crown. *The Campaign on New Britain*. Washington, D.C.: Historical Branch, Headquarters, U.S. Marine Corps, 1952.

Hough, Frank O., Verle E. Ludwig, and Henry I. Shaw, Jr. *History of U.S. Marine Corps Operations in World War II, volume 1: Pearl Harbor to Guadalcanal*. Washington, D.C.: Historical Branch, U.S. Marine Corps, 1958.

Karig, Walter, and Eric Purdon. *Battle Report, Pacific War: Middle Phase*. New York: Rinehart and Company, Inc., 1947.

Long, Gavin. *Australia in the War of 1939–1945, Series 1 (Army),Volume VII, The Final Campaigns*. Canberra: Australian War Memorial, 1963.

McCarthy, Dudley. *Australia in the War of 1939–1945, Series I (Army), Volume V, South-West Pacific Area—First Year: Kokoda to Wau*. Canberra: Australian War Memorial, 1959.

Melson, Charles D. *Marines in World War II Commemorative Series: Up the Slot: Marines in the Central Solomons*. Washington, D.C.: Marine Corps Historical Center, 1993.

Miller, John, Jr. *The United States Army in World War II—The War in the Pacific: Cartwheel: The Reduction of Rabaul*. Washington, D.C.: Office of the Chief of Military History, 1959.

———. *The United States Army in World War II—The War in the Pacific: Guadalcanal: The First Offensive*. Washington, D.C.: Office of the Chief of Military History, 1948.

Milner, Samuel. *The United States Army in World War II—The War in the Pacific: Victory in Papua*. Washington, D.C.: Office of the Chief of Military History, 1957.

Morison, Samuel Eliot. *History of United States Naval Operations in World War II: Volume V, The Struggle for Guadalcanal*. Boston, Mass.: Little, Brown and Company, 1949.

———. *History of United States Naval Operations in World War II: Volume VI, Breaking the Bismarcks Barrier*. Boston, Mass.: Little, Brown and Company, 1950.

———. *History of United States Naval Operations in World War II: Volume VIII, New Guinea and the Marianas*. Boston, Mass.: Little, Brown and Company, 1953.

———. *History of United States Naval Operations in World War II: Volume XII, Leyte*. Boston, Mass.: Little, Brown and Company, 1958.

Morton, Louis. *The United States Army in World War II—The War in the Pacific: Strategy and Command: The First Two Years*. Washington, D.C.: Center of Military History United States Army, 2000.

Nalty, Bernard C. *Marines in World War II Commemorative Series: Cape Gloucester: The Green Inferno*. Washington, D.C.: Marine Corps Historical Center, 1994.

Rentz, John N. *Bougainville and the Northern Solomons*. Washington, D.C.: Historical Branch, U.S. Marine Corps, 1948.

Ross, J. M. S. *The Official History of New Zealand in the Second World War: Royal New Zealand Air Force*. Wellington, N.Z.: Historical Publications Branch, 1955.

Shaw, Henry I., Jr. *Marines in World War II Commemorative Series: First Offensive: The Marine Campaign for Guadalcanal*. Washington, D.C.: Marine Corps Historical Center, 1992.

Shaw, Henry I., Jr., and Douglas T. Kane. *History of U.S. Marine Corps Operations in World War II*, vol. 2: *Isolation of Rabaul*. Washington, D.C.: Historical Branch, U.S. Marine Corps, 1963.

Smith, Robert Ross. *United States Army in World War II—The War in the Pacific: The Approach to the Philippines*. Washington, D.C.: Center of Military History, 1984.

Willoughby, Charles. *Reports of General MacArthur: The Campaigns of MacArthur in the Pacific. volume 1*. Washington, D.C.: Government Printing Office, 1966.

————. *Reports of General MacArthur: Japanese Operations in the Southwest Pacific, volume 2, part 1*. Washington, D.C.: Government Printing Office, 1966.

## Unit Histories

Aurthur, Robert A., and Kenneth Cohlmia. *The Third Marine Division*. Washington, D.C.: Infantry Journal Press, 1948.

Blakeley, H. W. *The 32d Infantry Division in World War II*. Madison, Wisc.: History Commission, 1945.

Cronin, Francis D. *Under the Southern Cross: The Saga of the Americal Division*. Washington, D.C.: Combat Forces Press, 1951.

Frankel, Stanley A. *The 37th Infantry Division in World War II*. Washington, D.C.: Infantry Journal Press, 1948.

Wright, Bertram C. *The 1st Cavalry Division in World War II*. Tokyo: Toppan Printing Company, 1947.

## Other Books

Alexander, Joseph H. *Edson's Raiders: The 1st Marine Raider Battalion in World War II*. Annapolis, Md.: Naval Institute Press, 2001.

Belote, James H. and William M. Belote. *Titans of the Seas: The Development and Operations of Japanese and American Carrier Task Forces During World War II*. New York: Harper & Row, 1975.

Bergerud, Eric M. *Fire in the Sky: The Air War in the South Pacific*, Boulder, Colo.: Westview Press, 2000.

————. *Touched with Fire: The Land War in the South Pacific*. New York: Penguin Books USA Inc., 1966.

Berry, Henry. *Semper Fi, Mac: Living Memories of the U.S. Marines in World War II*. New York: Arbor House, 1982.

Boatner, Mark M., III. *The Biographical Dictionary of World War II*. Novato, Calif.: Presidio Press, 1996.

Christ, James F. *Mission Raise Hell: The U.S. Marines on Choiseul, October–November 1943*. Annapolis, Md.: Naval Institute Press, 2006.

D'Albas, Andrieu. *Death of a Navy: Japanese Naval Action in World War II*. New York: The Devin-Adair Company, 1957.

Danchev, Alex, and Daniel Todman, eds. *War Diaries 1939–1945: Field Marshall Lord Alanbrooke*. Berkeley: University of California Press, 2001.

Drea, Edward J. *Leavenworth Papers, Defending the Driniumor: Covering Force Operations in New Guinea, 1944*. Fort Leavenworth, Kan.: Combat Studies Institute, 1984.

————. *MacArthur's Ultra: Codebreaking and the War Against Japan, 1942–1945*. Lawrence: University Press of Kansas, 1992.

Dull, Paul S. *A Battle History of the Imperial Japanese Navy 1941–1945*. Annapolis, Md.: Naval Institute Press, 1978.

Edgar, Bill. *Warrior of Kokoda: A Biography of Brigadier Arnold Potts*. St. Leonards, N.S.W.: Allen and Unwin, 1999.

Eichelberger, Robert L. *Our Jungle Road to Tokyo*. New York: The Viking Press, 1950.

FitzPatrick, Tom. *A Character That Inspired: Major General Charles D. Barrett, USMC*. Fairfax, Va.: Signature Book Printing, 2003.

Frank, Richard B. *Guadalcanal: The Definitive Account of the Landmark Battle*. New York: Random House, 1990.

Gailey, Harry A. *Bougainville 1943–1945: The Forgotten Campaign*. Lexington: University Press of Kentucky, 1991.

———. *MacArthur Strikes Back: Decision at Buna, New Guinea 1942–1943*. Novato, Calif.: Presidio Press, Inc., 2000.

———. *MacArthur's Victory: The War in New Guinea 1943–1944*. New York: Presidio Press, 2004.

———. *The War in the Pacific: From Pearl Harbor to Tokyo Bay*, Novato, Calif.: Presidio Press, 1995.

Gamble, Bruce. *Fortress Rabaul: The Battle for the Southwest Pacific*. Minneapolis, Minn.: Zenith Press, 2010.

Griess, Thomas E., ed. *West Point Military History Series: The Second World War, Asia and the Pacific*. Wayne, N.J.: Avery Publishing Group Inc., 1984.

Griffith, Thomas E. Jr. *MacArthur's Airman: General George C. Kenney and the War in the Southwest Pacific*. Lawrence: University Press of Kansas, 1998.

Halsey, William F., and J. Bryan III. *Admiral Halsey's Story*. New York: McGraw-Hill, 1947.

Horner, D. M. *Blamey: The Commander in Chief*. St. Leonards, N.S.W.: Allen and Unwin, 1998.

Horton, D. C. *New Georgia: Pattern for Victory*. New York: Ballantine Books Inc., 1971.

Isely, Jeter A., and Philip A. Crowl. *The U.S. Marines and Amphibious War*. Princeton, N.J.: Princeton University Press, 1951.

James, D. Clayton. *The Years of MacArthur, Volume II 1941–1945*. Boston: Houghton Mifflin Company, 1975.

Kenney, George C. *General Kenney Reports*. New York: Duell, Sloan, and Pearce, 1949.

Krueger, Walter. *From Down Under to Nippon: The Story of the Sixth Army in World War II*. Washington, D.C.: Zenger Publishing Co., 1979.

Larrabee, Eric. *Commander in Chief: Franklin Delano Roosevelt, His Lieutenants, and Their War*. New York: Simon & Schuster, 1987.

Layton, Edwin T. *And I Was There: Pearl Harbor and Midway—Breaking the Secrets*. New York: William Morrow, 1985.

Lee, Ulysses. *United States Army in World War II, Special Studies: The Employment of Negro Troops*. Washington, D.C.: Center of Military History, 1963.

Lundstrom, John B. *Black Shoe Carrier Admiral*. Annapolis, Md.: Naval Institute Press, 2013.

Luvaas, Jay, ed. *Dear Miss Em: General Eichelberger's War in the Pacific, 1942–1945.* Westport, Conn.: Greenwood Press, Inc., 1972.

McGee, William L. *Amphibious Operations in the South Pacific in World War II, Volume II, The Solomons Campaigns 1942–1943, from Guadalcanal to Bougainville, Pacific War Turning Point.* Santa Barbara, Calif.: BMC Publications, 2002.

Millett, Allan R., and Jack Shulimson. *Commandants of the Marine Corps.* Annapolis, Md.: Naval Institute Press, 2004.

O'Donnell, Patrick K. *Into the Rising Sun.* New York: Free Press, 2002.

Ohl, John Kennedy. *Minuteman: The Military Career of General Robert S. Beightler.* Boulder, Colo.: Lynne Rienner Publishers, 2001.

Potter, E. B. *Bull Halsey.* Annapolis, Md.: Naval Institute Press, 1985.

———. *Nimitz.* Annapolis, Md.: Naval Institute Press, 1976.

Reynolds, Clark G. *The Fast Carriers: The Forging of an Air Navy.* New York: McGraw-Hill Book Company, 1968.

Rottman, Gordon L. *Japanese Army in World War II: The South Pacific and New Guinea, 1942–43.* Oxford, UK: Osprey Publishing Ltd., 2005.

———. *U.S. Special Warfare Units in the Pacific Theater 1941–45: Scouts, Raiders, Rangers and Reconnaissance Units.* Oxford, UK: Osprey Publishing Ltd., 2005.

Sherman, Frederick C. *Combat Command: The American Aircraft Carriers in the Pacific War.* New York: E. P. Dutton & Company, Inc, 1950.

Sherrod, Robert. *History of Marine Corps Aviation in World War II.* Washington: Combat Forces Press, 1952.

Smith, S. E., ed. *The United States Marine Corps in World War II.* New York: Random House, 1969.

———. *The United States Navy in World War II.* New York: William Morrow & Company, Inc., 1966.

Spector, Ronald H. *Eagle Against the Sun.* New York: The Free Press, 1985.

Stanton, Shelby L. *World War II Order of Battle.* Novato, Calif.: Presidio Press, 1984.

Taaffe, Stephen R. *MacArthur's Jungle War.* Lawrence: University Press of Kansas, 1998.

———. *Marshall and His Generals: U.S. Army Commanders in World War II.* Lawrence: University Press of Kansas, 2011.

Twining, Merrill B. *No Bended Knee: The Battle for Guadalcanal.* Novato, Calif.: Presidio Press, 1996.

Ugaki, Matome. *Fading Victory: The Diary of Admiral Matome Ugaki 1941–1945.* Pittsburgh, Pa.: University of Pittsburgh Press, 1991.

Vandegrift, A. A. *Once a Marine: The Memoirs of General A. A. Vandegrift.* New York: W. W. Norton & Company, Inc., 1964.

Wheeler, Richard. *A Special Valor: The U.S. Marines and the Pacific War.* New York: New American Library, 1983.

## Online Resources

Australian National University. *Australian Dictionary of Biography.* Canberra: National Center of Biography. http:adb.anu.edu.au (07/13).

Medals of Honor. www.history.army.mil/html/moh/index.html (07/13).

Military Awards. http:militarytimes.com/citations-medals-awards/ (07/13).

United States Strategic Bombing Survey. *Interrogations of Japanese Officials—Vice Admiral Fukudome, Shigeru, IJN.* www.ibiblio.org/hyperwar/AAF/USSBS/IJO/ (07/13).


## Periodicals

Guenther, John C. "Artillery in the Bougainville Campaign." *Field Artillery Journal* (June 1945).

Lodge, J. Norman. "Halsey Predicts Victory This Year." *New York Times,* 3 January 1943.

Rems, Alan P. "Halsey Knows the Straight Story." *Naval History* 22, no. 4 (August 2008).

"U.S. Negro Troops Crack Bougainville Foe." *New York Times,* 17 March 1944.


## Archival Resources

Holcomb, Thomas. Unpublished Papers. Quantico, Va.: Library of the Marine Corps, 2007.

Collins, J. Lawton. *J. Lawton Collins Papers.* Carlisle, Pa.: U.S. Army Military History Institute, 2010.

# INDEX

Australia: Advisory War Council, 215–
16; Brisbane submarine base, 36, 85;
defense, 13, 28; MacArthur in, 12, 21;
Parliament, 214–15
Australian air force. *See* Royal Australian
Air Force
Australian Army: 3rd Division, 57–58,
61, 62–64, 218, 234; 5th Division, 64,
71, 235; 6th Division, 150, 216, 230,
236; 7th Division, 14, 16, 17–18, 20,
31, 61, 66, 70, 71, 77–78, 148–49; 9th
Division, 61, 66–69, 71, 72–74, 76,
78, 79–80, 147; amphibious landings,
66–68, 72–75, 227–28, 232, 233;
on Bougainville, 212, 213, 214–17,
218–29, 241–42; decorations, 70–71,
147, 223, 229, 232, 233; Farida Force,
232, 233; intelligence, 218, 230;
Kanga Force, 57, 58; leaders, 23; under
MacArthur's command, 13, 22, 23,
58, 148, 212, 214–16; on New Britain,
212, 213, 214, 216–17, 234–36;
offensive operations (1945), 214–17,
218–29, 241–42; relations with
Americans, 62–63, 68, 212; replacing
Americans, 212, 213, 218, 230, 235.
*See also* Blamey, Thomas W.; Papua
New Guinea, Australian Army

Barbey, Daniel E.: Admiralty Islands
invasion, 190, 192; amphibious
landings, 58–59, 68, 74–75, 148,
154–55; Cartwheel plan and, 58–59,
151; Kenney and, 68, 74
Barrett, Charles D., 84, 89–92, 93, 102–
3, 144, 200
Barrowclough, Harold E., 164–65
Basilone, John, 8
Beightler, Robert S.: on Bougainville,
170, 174, 175, 176–77, 178–79, 180;
as National Guard officer, 213; on
New Georgia, 45, 47, 55; personal
role in battle, 177; in Philippines, 213;
roads built, 169
Bergerud, Eric M., 86, 198, 211
Berkey, Russell S., 192
Berryman, Frank H., 68
Bigger, Warner, 100
Bismarck Sea, 26–28, 57, 151

black troops. *See* African American
troops
Blamey, Thomas W.: in Australia, 21;
career, 213–14, 241; command
style, 23; as commander in chief,
13; commanders, 78–79; criticism
of, 23, 241; Finschhafen attack and,
76; Lae campaign, 61, 66–68, 71;
MacArthur and, 19, 20, 212, 214,
215; New Guinea Force, 58, 66–68,
78, 150; New Guinea native troops
and, 236; offensive operations (1945),
214–17, 218, 226, 232, 235, 241–42;
reputation, 213–14; Rowell and, 16–
17; surrender ceremonies, 237, 242; on
Trobriand operation, 59
Bong, Richard, 122
Bonis Peninsula, New Guinea, 86, 101,
220, 221–22, 226–27, 228
Bougainville: aerial battles, 52; air
support, 143; Allied airfields, 134,
143, 144–45, 162, 173; Allied attacks,
36, 101; Allied forces in 1944, 203;
Australian forces, 212, 213, 214–17,
241–42; Australian offensive (1945),
214–17, 218–29; battles (1943),
129–35, 137–43, 144; battles (1944),
181–87; Cape Torokina, 82–84, 103,
104–7, 109–10, 128; Cartwheel plan,
31, 81–85, 91, 101, 102; casualties,
105, 108, 109, 133, 135, 140, 141,
142, 144; Cibik's Ridge, 137–39, 140,
141; earthquake, 142; East-West Trail,
82, 133, 134, 135, 137, 140, 141,
142, 187; Halsey on, 133; Halsey's
leadership of campaign, 56, 81–85,
118–19; Hellzapoppin Ridge, 142–43,
144; Hill 260, 170, 172, 175–78,
179, 180, 184; Hill 600A, 142, 143;
Hill 700, 169, 170, 172, 174–75,
176–77; jungles, 128, 222, 226, 229,
237; Kahili airfield, 31, 32–33, 81,
96, 103; Koiari raid, 141–42, 190,
227; Koromokina River, 129–31,
134, 136; Marines, 109, 118, 128–36,
137–44; minefields, 100, 103; natives,
222; naval battle, 110, 111–17; naval
defense, 118–21; Numa Numa Trail,
82, 132, 133, 134, 135, 136, 137, 177,

# ABOUT THE AUTHOR

Retired CPA **Alan Rems** has been a regular contributor to *Naval History* since his first attempt earned him the U.S. Naval Institute's 2008 Author of the Year award. Responding to veteran complaints in the literature that the war in the South Pacific is little known, Rems has written the first complete history of World War II there. He and his wife, Janet, a retired newspaper editor, live in Centreville, Virginia.